The Ethics of Stakeholding

*Also by Keith Dowding*

RATIONAL CHOICE AND POLITICAL POWER (1991)

THE CIVIL SERVICE (1995)

POWER (1996)

PREFERENCES, INSTITUTIONS AND RATIONAL CHOICE (*co-editor with Desmond King*, 1995)

CHALLENGES TO DEMOCRACY (*co-editor with James Hughes and Helen Margetts*, 2001)


*Also by Stuart White*

NEW LABOUR: The Progressive Future? (2001)

THE CIVIC MINIMUM: On the Rights and Obligations of Economic Citizenship (2003)

# The Ethics of Stakeholding

160401

Edited by

## Keith Dowding
*Professor of Political Science*
*London School of Economics and Political Science, UK*

## Jurgen De Wispelaere
*London School of Economics and Political Science, UK*

and

## Stuart White
*Tutorial Fellow in Politics*
*Jesus College, University of Oxford, UK*

First published 2003 by
PALGRAVE MACMILLAN
Houndmills, Basingstoke, Hampshire RG21 6XS and
175 Fifth Avenue, New York, N.Y. 10010
Companies and representatives throughout the world

PALGRAVE MACMILLAN is the global academic imprint of the Palgrave
Macmillan division of St. Martin's Press, LLC and of Palgrave Macmillan Ltd.
Macmillan® is a registered trademark in the United States, United Kingdom
and other countries. Palgrave is a registered trademark in the European
Union and other countries.

ISBN 1–4039–05800

This book is printed on paper suitable for recycling and made from fully
managed and sustained forest sources.

A catalogue record for this book is available from the British Library.

Library of Congress Cataloging-in-Publication Data
    The ethics of stakeholding/edited by Keith Dowding, Jurgen De
Wispelaere, and Stuart White.
        p. cm.
    Includes bibliographical references and index.
    ISBN 1–4039–0580–0 (cloth)
    1. Income distribution. 2. Distributive justice. 3. Equality. 4. Economic
policy—Moral and ethical aspects. 5. Economics—Social aspects.
    I. Dowding, Keith M. II. Wispelaere, Jurgen De, 1970– III. White, Stuart
Gordon, 1966–

HB523.E89   2003
174—dc21                                                    2003050910

10  9  8  7  6  5  4  3  2  1
12  11  10  09  08  07  06  05  04  03

Printed and bound in Great Britain by
Antony Rowe Ltd, Chippenham and Eastbourne

# Contents

# Preface

Stakeholding is a term that captures the imagination. The idea that all of us as citizens have a stake in our society – and through it in our own future – is a powerful image. It conveys the idea that each citizen is by right a beneficiary of the social goods that are passed on through society. Such an inheritance represents a major asset in social and economic life. But the idea of holding a stake in society also suggests that one needs to actively take charge of one's stake, using it wisely and diligently to bring about whatever sort of life we wish to lead. Of course, between these two parameters – one 'socialist', the other 'liberal' if you will – lies an immense area in which many policies compete to bring about the radical idea of a stakeholder society.

The aim of this collection of essays is to further explore this idea of a stakeholder society, and to systematically compare those policies that best capture the ideal of stakeholding from an ethical perspective. Familiar examples of stakeholder policies are a basic income (in its unconditional and participation variants), basic capital or stakeholder grant, and various forms of individual ownership accounts. It is fair to say that the past two decades have witnessed a massive increase in scholarly attention on this topic. Perhaps even more important, scholarly attention is mirrored in social policy – witness the genuine, if sometimes surprising, interest of politicians and policy-makers in both the developed and developing world for stakeholding proposals. What was considered a somewhat daft idea only a few years ago is slowly turning into an agenda-setter in the fields of employment regulation, social security and welfare policy. Two prominent examples of stakeholder ideas actually influencing welfare policy are the British Government's plans to institute a *Child Trust Fund*, first announced just before the 2001 general election but only now ready to go ahead, and the publication of the *Green Paper on Basic Income* by the Irish Government in October 2002.

The editors were keen to deliver a book that was comparative in outlook. First we insisted on a collection of essays that would compare various proposals, teasing out many intricate aspects – similarities as well as tensions within and across diverse policies – that often remain hidden when only looking at one's preferred policy. In our view, in a world in which complex background conditions often dictate a mixture of policies to achieve a single ethical ideal, a comparative focus becomes invaluable. The collection is also intended to be comparative in a quite different sense: it outlines a variety of ethical perspectives that engage with the stakeholder ideal. After a decade or so of intense debate, the time has come to offer a novel systematic evaluation of the arguments on offer, giving ample room for the many competing ethical perspectives to develop arguments in favour or against. Bringing both comparative aspects together offers important insights that we hope will not only further the debate in political theory and social policy, but in time will actually help to improve the living conditions of those who are often left unable to properly 'stake' their legitimate claims in contemporary society.

The book has taken some time to come to fruition. The idea and project were formulated in 1998, but the busy agendas of the editors and contributors (we insisted on 'grabbing' some of the best contributors currently working in the field) made it a little more drawn-out than originally envisaged. With hindsight this delay has turned out to be quite beneficial. Important insights in the stakeholder debate have appeared only in the past two or three years; we are now able to capture these. The result, we hope, is a key text for the years to come. About half of the contributions to this book were originally presented at the 50th Annual Meeting of the British Political Studies Association, London, 11–13 April 2000. The others were specifically written for this collection with the exception of David Nissan and Julian Le Grand's chapter, an earlier version of which appeared as a Fabian Paper.

All editor royalties of this volume will be donated to the UK Citizen's Income Trust (CIT), a charity organization that promotes Citizen's Income and related policy measures in Britain. For more information, visit the CIT website at www.citizensincome.org

# List of Contributors

**Bruce Ackerman**, Sterling Professor of Law and Political Science, Yale Law School, Yale University

**Jurgen De Wispelaere**, Fund for Scientific Research Flanders (FWO) and PhD Student Political Theory, Government Department, LSE

**Keith Dowding**, Professor of Political Science, Government Department, LSE

**Cécile Fabre**, Lecturer in Political Theory, Government Department, LSE

**Andrew Gamble**, Professor in Political Science, Department of Politics, and Director, Political Economy Research Centre (PERC), University of Sheffield

**Robert Goodin**, Professor of Philosophy, Research School of Social Sciences, Australian National University

**Gavin Kelly**, Senior Researcher, Institute for Public Policy Research (IPPR), UK

**Julian Le Grand**, Richard Titmuss Professor of Health Policy, Department of Social Policy, LSE and Co-Director, Center for the Analysis of Social Exclusion (CASE), STICERD

**David Nissan**, was Research Fellow, Commission on Taxation and Citizenship, Fabian Society. Before that he worked in journalism; as Acting News Editor for the *Financial Times*, and editor of *The Money Programme*, BBC

**Carole Pateman**, Professor of Political Theory, Department of Political Science, University of California, Los Angeles

**Will Paxton**, Institute for Public Policy Research (IPPR), UK

**Robert van der Veen**, Professor, Amsterdam School of Social Science Research, University of Amsterdam

**Gijs van Donselaar**, Post-doctoral Research Fellow Dutch Research Foundation (NWO), Faculty of Humanities (Ethics Section), University of Amsterdam

**Stuart White**, Lecturer in Politics, Department of Politics and International Relations, and Tutorial Fellow of Jesus College, University of Oxford

# 1
# Stakeholding – a New Paradigm in Social Policy

*Keith Dowding, Jurgen De Wispelaere and Stuart White*[1]

## 1 Welfare policy in turmoil?

In recent years welfare policy has been through turmoil. Because of large shifts in a number of key trends – demographic, socio-economic, political – immense pressure has been put on the traditional pillars of the modern welfare state, causing them to 'crumble' (Goodin, 2000). The outcome can today be viewed in terms of widespread inequality, poverty, unemployment, social exclusion and, perhaps most importantly, a widespread sense of insecurity in many aspects of social life, notably the labour market (Standing, 1999, 2002). In addition, there is a general feeling that traditional responses to these problems may not be up to the job. Market-based strategies have largely failed to deliver the goods: in many cases they have exacerbated the situation. At the same time the traditional Socialist solutions of corporatist and statist interventionism are often thought to be discredited (Ackerman, this volume), leaving the Left in search of new answers to old, but ever pressing questions.

In an influential book, the French sociologist Pierre Rosanvallon (2000) suggests that the (in)famous 'crisis of the welfare state' went through three stages – each progressively weakening the welfare state. The first two, respectively 'financial' and 'ideological' are well-known and their impact has been analysed in political science, economics and political economy (for a recent discussion of these issues, see Pierson, 2001). It is the third stage, however, that according to Rosanvallon gives rise to the *new social question*. In the third stage of crisis, it is the *philosophical underpinnings* of the welfare state that are affected: the very ideas of social solidarity and social justice that underlie the modern concept of the welfare state (Baldwin, 1990) are retreating, giving way to a situation that is perhaps best described with Durkheim's notion of anomie. The challenge for the coming decades is not merely to give an answer to questions of financial and political stability in the area of welfare reform (though they are of crucial importance); what is needed is nothing less than the emergence of a *new social paradigm*, a radical perspective in social and political thought that has the capacity to merge the efficient coordination of markets with the equality and social inclusion of state-directed intervention. Responding to this need, a number of writers have begun to lay out and explore what may be termed a 'stakeholding' paradigm, and it is this paradigm with which we are concerned in this volume.

The core of the stakeholding paradigm can be elaborated in a number of ways. To decide between alternative forms of stakeholding, we need to first clarify the basic values that motivate the stakeholder agenda, and we need then to consider what kind (or kinds) of policy best serves these values. In this introductory essay we provide an overview of the main strategic choices facing those who favour the idea of stakeholding, and of the main values that we think inform these choices. In the chapters that follow, the contributors will develop their own, differing positions on which values are most important, and on what given values imply, and thus, in turn, on what form of stakeholding is most desirable. Our hope is that by reflecting on the debate provided by these contributors, the reader will be able to make a more informed assessment of the relative merits of different forms of stakeholding – and, indeed, of the core idea of stakeholding itself.

## 2   The idea of the stakeholder society

Stakeholding is a fashionable word but it is currently used to mean a number of different things and not all of them are the concern of this volume of essays (see Kelly and Gamble, 1997 for a sample). In one familiar sense of the term, stakeholding refers to a theory of how business (and, indeed, other) enterprises should be organized and managed. Firms are seen as sites in which the interests of various 'stakeholders' are implicated: those who advance the firm's capital; those who provide it with labour; those who buy its products; perhaps even the environment or the wider society. The stakeholder theory of enterprise, developed by economists such as John Kay (Hutton, 1994; Kay, 1996), argues that the economy flourishes when decision-making processes within firm give formal rights of representation to all the firm's various stakeholders. This model of the corporate stakeholder firm is contrasted with the orthodox capital shareholder model of the firm in which decision-making power resides wholly with the firm's owners. There is a lively debate within economics about the respective strengths and weaknesses of these two models of business organization (Prabhakar, 2003).

This book will not review or make any contribution (at least directly and intentionally) to that debate. We are concerned with stakeholding in a much broader sense (Leadbeater and Mulgan, 1996). We are concerned in this book with what might be called individualized stakeholding (Prabhakar, 2003) which refers to a particular paradigm within social policy that looks to empower individuals by granting them or helping them to acquire assets or a near equivalent guaranteed future stream of income. These assets or income streams are, metaphorically, 'stakes' in the economic system, enabling individuals to participate in the economy and enjoy its rewards on a more secure and equitable basis than they otherwise would. We will say more about possible forms of stakeholding below, but for immediate illustrative purposes, stakes might take the form of a basic capital grant, received by all citizens on maturity, or they might be a periodic income paid to each citizen as of right without any test of means or willingness to work (a basic income or citizen's income).

It is also suggested that traditional welfare policies are ameliorative, rather than preventative: they take the background distribution of assets and economic opportunities as a given, and they then seek to mitigate the worst effects of this on the final distribution of income. Stakeholding proposals, by contrast, tend to be more preventive in orientation, being targeted directly at changing the background distribution of assets and opportunities so as to make it less likely that the economy will produce unacceptable distributions of income (Perri 6, 1999; Nissan and Le Grand, this volume). Asset values have appreciated considerably in recent years, widening the gap between those with and those without assets. So why not attack asset inequality directly, rather than just mitigating the symptoms of this through conventional welfare policies? There is, moreover, growing evidence of how low wealth diminishes life-chances and quality of life independently of low income, the more usual concern of policy (Bynner and Paxton, 2001). This has led policy thinkers and political theorists to think more about the importance of assets and the potential of stakeholder policies to promote egalitarian ends through a more inclusive distribution of these assets.

The basic idea is not new. Simplifying a little, the modern Left emerged as a protest against what one might call the proletarian condition: the condition of surviving precariously through the sale of labour-power to an employer, an employer typically situated so as to drive a hard bargain and to dominate one's life within the workplace. One proposal for abolishing the proletarian condition is state socialism: to do away with the market and private ownership of the means of production, putting common ownership and planned coordination in its place. But state socialist ideas emerged in competition with other currents of Left thinking that proposed alternative, stakeholder-style remedies to the ills of the proletarian condition. These ideas have only recently re-emerged into mainstream philosophical and policy writings.

Particularly important here is the social republican current of Left thinking which can be traced back at least as far as the late eighteenth century, to the economic writings of Jean-Jacques Rousseau (1755) and to the theory of citizens' social rights developed by Thomas Paine (1797). In his *Agrarian Justice*, Paine argued that all citizens should receive a capital grant on maturity of some £15, financed from a tax on 'ground rents' and other forms of wealth. Paine (1987: 483) argues: 'When a young couple begin the world, the difference is exceedingly great whether they begin with nothing or with fifteen pounds apiece. With this aid they could buy a cow, and implements to cultivate a few acres of land; and instead of becoming burdens upon society (...) would be put in the way of becoming useful and profitable citizens.'

This current of social republican thinking developed and continued to exert influence well into the nineteenth century, interacting, in the British case, with movements such as Cooperativism and Chartism. Intellectuals and activists such as John Stuart Mill, Giuseppe Mazzini, and the artisan William James Linton, were all influenced by this movement of ideas and, especially in Mill's case, contributed to the development of this intellectual tradition. Outside of Britain, social republican ideas found expression in the 'Mutualism' of Pierre-Joseph Proudhon in France, and in the philosophy of workers' movements such as Terence Powderly's Knights of Labor in the USA. The social republic is, unlike state socialism, a society in which the market and private ownership of the means of production are central institutions. But the vision is emphatically not of a society divided into bourgeois and proletarian, but of a commercial society in which a system of generous stakeholder property rights works to lessen and prevent the emergence of such a division, of a dynamic economy made up of independent citizen-farmers or citizen-artisans (White, 2000b). An alternative both to laissez-faire liberalism and communism, social republican platforms, such as the Chartist platform of 1851, combined demands for political democratization with demands for greater economic independence and equality of opportunity for producers within a reformed private ownership market economy. Specific commitments included land reform (usually some form of land-nationalization), low-interest 'national credit', and other measures to encourage cooperative retail and production.

Contemporary stakeholder thinking is one major expression of an ongoing rediscovery, or perhaps reinvention, of this social republican ideal. This ideal does not involve a repudiation of the welfare state. But it points social democracy beyond the welfare state and the prevention of poverty, expanding and renewing the Left's ambition to build a society in which both economic and political power are more widely dispersed. As John Rawls puts it in the preface to the revised edition of *A Theory of Justice*, '[t]he idea is not simply to assist those who lose out through accident or misfortune (although this must be done), but instead to put all citizens in a position to manage their own affairs and to take part in social cooperation on a footing of mutual respect under appropriately equal conditions' (Rawls, 1999: xiv–xv).

Economies, like the polities in which they are embedded, have constitutions, even if these are implicit and unwritten. In the British context, for example, it is part of the nation's unwritten economic constitution that the economy be oriented towards private ownership and to a market-determined allocation of resources. But certain basic 'social rights' (Marshall, 1963 (1949)) are also a key part of the nation's unwritten economic constitution: centrally, the right to a decent primary and secondary education and the right to health-care. Stakeholder policies offer the prospect of revising the unwritten economic constitution in a more inclusive egalitarian direction, adding a new social right, the right of social inheritance to a decent minimum of capital (or to a near equivalent guaranteed income stream). As such, they connect with a long tradition of egalitarian thinking that has sought to promote the values of freedom and equal opportunity in a way that is compatible with a market economy, rather than through the substitution of bureaucratic coordination for market processes.

## 3. Stakeholder policies: a simple typology

The idea of the stakeholder society represents a broad ideal, encompassing a host of 'stakeholder policies'. In order to clarify the focus of our investigation further, we take a brief look at the various forms of stakeholding that feature in the contemporary debate. Simplifying for convenience, we may distinguish at least four different general types of stakeholder policy: universal basic income, universal basic capital, targeted asset-building and universal asset-building. Of course, the state can influence the distribution of assets and opportunities in many ways other than by policies of these four general kinds. Universal education and health-care systems, for example, represent a major contribution to creating and sustaining a degree of asset equality amongst citizens (Fogel, 2000). Taxes on wealth transfers, such as the oft-proposed accessions tax[2] (Meade, 1989), might also promote a wider sharing of wealth. However, we will not discuss all of these policies directly here.

### 3.1   Universal basic income

Universal basic income is the proposal that all citizens receive a uniform income grant as a right without a means test or a requirement to work (Van Parijs, 1992a, 1995). It makes sense to distinguish between the radical or 'pure' form of basic income and more modest versions that relax one or more of these dimensions. For instance, the radical form of basic income can be relaxed to differentiate the level of the grant between children, adults or the elderly (basic pension), or allowing for grants that remain sensitive to household composition or geographical location.[3] The most important dimension, however, is the unconditionality requirement: many scholars, for ethical or political reasons, subscribe to Tony Atkinson's (1972, 1996) *participation income*, which demands that recipients undertake some broad notion of civic activity (care work in the family, volunteering, education, for example) in return for the grant (see White, 2002 for discussion).

The idea of a universal basic income has a long history. Historical pedigrees include proposals by the sixteenth-century Humanists Thomas More and Johannes Ludovicus Vives, seventeenth-century Republicans Condorcet and Paine, and the eighteenth-century Utopian Socialists Fourier and Mill, as well as a host of influential thinkers in the nineteenth century.[4] In political philosophy the proposal has re-emerged largely because of the work of one man – Philippe Van Parijs. In a number of publications – notably his book *Real Freedom for All* (1995) – he has mounted a sophisticated defence of what he often calls a 'disarmingly simple idea' (Van Parijs, 1992a).[5] As can be appraised from the contributions to this volume, Van Parijs's idea has spurred an intense academic debate, resulting in many books, edited collections, as well as special journal issues devoted to the analysis of basic income and cognate proposals. Advocates include many prominent academics, including Nobel Prize winners such as James Meade, Herbert Simon and

James Tobin, but many controversies remain and are taken up in the contributions below. In addition and perhaps more importantly, universal basic income has started to influence policy-making in various countries,[6] made a marked entrance in the political arena in countries like Brazil and South Africa, and has shaped an increasing number of national organizations and international networks devoted to its advocacy.[7]

### 3.2 Universal basic capital

The main 'competitor' within the stakeholding family of universal basic income is the idea of universal basic capital. Essentially, universal capital grants aim to provide all citizens with a uniform capital grant on maturity. In some versions the proposal is for what might be called a development account or grant: use of the funds is restricted, in this case, to a range of specific purposes that are linked to approved personal development goals (Haveman, 1988; White, 1991; Unger and West, 1998; Nissan and Le Grand, 2000; Kelly and Lissauer, 2000; Regan, 2001b; Paxton, 2001; Halstead and Lind, 2001). These approved purposes might include education and training, setting up a small business, or a house purchase. In other versions, the proposal is for what might be called a life account or grant: in this case, account holders are free to use the funds as they like (Ackerman and Alstott, 1999; Regan, 2001a). Hybrids can be readily imagined.

Julian Le Grand and David Nissan (this volume, Nissan and Le Grand, 2000) and Ackerman and Alstott (1999, 2003; also Ackerman, this volume) lay out the basic principles of the universal basic capital form of stakeholding, and the normative ideas or intuitions underlying it. Universal basic capital is the form of 'stakeholding' that is usually referred to when the stakeholder society is discussed in the academic literature (outside of the business literature mentioned above). The most immediately ascertainable distinction between basic income and basic capital forms of stakeholding is that the former is concerned with guaranteeing 'streams', whereas the latter provides citizens with a capital stake in society. However, whether this distinction is as clear-cut as might seem is heavily disputed since under certain conditions 'streams' can be transformed into 'stocks', and vice versa (van der Veen, this volume; also Van Parijs, 2001). Leaving technicalities aside, there are nevertheless ethical arguments that may arise favouring one over the other. These arguments are discussed in the contributions below.

One particular advantage of basic capital over basic income, Ackerman (this volume) argues, is that it coincides better with 'ordinary morality' – commonly held views about what is morally required in order to 'deserve' publicly funded grants. This has immediate implications for the political feasibility of 'capital' as opposed to 'income' forms of stakeholding (Goodin, this volume). In line with this argument the Labour government in Britain has recently floated a modest proposal of this kind (HM Treasury, 2001a,b). In its initial consultation paper, the government set out the plan for a *Child Trust Fund* – what journalists have called 'baby bonds' – in which, at birth, 'every baby would receive an endowment' that would grow over time so that on maturity each citizen would have at least a modest amount of financial assets (HM Treasury, 2001a: 17).[8] The government initially declared its sympathy for restricting the uses to which these funds could be put. But it also frankly acknowledged the 'regulatory and implementation issues' (HM Treasury, 2001a: 18) raised by restricting the way citizens might use these funds, and restriction as to use was not a feature of its final proposal (2001b).

### 3.3  Targeted asset-building

Targeted asset-building proposals imply that some citizens, generally those judged to fall below some specified level of income or wealth, should receive subsidies to enable them to accumulate assets. Many diverse policies fall under this heading. One possibility is to offer tax relief on savings to low- or moderate-income households to encourage them to save more. However, traditional tax relief methods do not seem to reach down to the poorest, most asset-deprived households. Another possibility, which many think more promising in this respect, is exemplified by the *Individual Development Accounts* (IDAs) recently pioneered in the USA (Friedman and Sherraden, 2001; Beeferman and Venner, 2001; Gamble, Kelly and Paxton, this volume).

IDA schemes have the following structure: eligible individuals (those with incomes at or below some proportion of the poverty line) agree to save for specified purposes (for example, a training course) and for every dollar they save the government provides a matching contribution in the ratio of 1 : 1 or higher. The schemes are administered by local organizations, based in low-income communities, and offer savers training in financial literacy: indeed, participation in programmes designed to build financial literacy may be a requirement of receiving the government's matching contribution. Underpinning the IDA schemes is a so-called 'institutional' theory of non-saving – that the poor fail to save less because of low income than because they lack the relevant kind of knowledge and access to saving institutions. In this volume, IDAs in the specific form of '*Individual Ownership Accounts*' that have provided a model for the *Savings Gateway* recently proposed by the British government (HM Treasury, 2001a) are discussed below by Andrew Gamble, Gavin Kelly and Will Paxton. They consider various practical proposals for introducing such accounts and consider numerous problems and solutions, while Cécile Fabre offers a critical review of some of the scheme's ethical assumptions.

### 3.4  Universal asset-building

Under proposals of this kind, the state establishes a regulatory framework that encourages or even requires *all* citizens to accumulate at least a minimum quantity of specific assets. This idea has clear application, for example, in the realm of pensions policy (Field, 1996). Specific proposals of course allow for significant variation: for instance, the state can opt to make such schemes more or less redistributive, and thus more or less egalitarian in their net effects, depending on how far it subsidizes the contributions of the low paid or unpaid with contributions it extracts from the better off. In what follows this type of stakeholder policy is not discussed; instead contributors focus primarily on basic income, basic capital and targeted asset-building policies.

## 4  Normative arguments in the stakeholder debate

This volume focuses primarily on one particular aspect of the stakeholder debate: the normative principles and ethical values underpinning various proposals. Competing ethical rationales in favour of or against stakeholder policies, or even the stakeholder paradigm itself, will be systematically discussed in the remaining chapters. In this section we will briefly outline the main normative arguments in the stakeholder debate.

### 4.1  Entitlement

One kind of argument for stakeholding centres on the claim that each individual has a right to an equal (tradable) share of certain scarce external assets, which can be understood as some sort of entitlement. Liberal-egalitarian political theorists often regard entitlement theories with a measure of suspicion. But stakeholder theory appears to provide arguments that allow for an entitlement theory which satisfies strong egalitarian intuitions (for a critique, see Fabre, this volume).[9]

The argument runs as follows. In order to respect individuals' entitlements or rights to an equal (tradable) share of scarce external assets, the state should appropriate the current market value of these assets, through taxation, and return the funds to individual citizens as a uniform income or capital grant (Steiner, 1994; Van Parijs, 1995). What sort of external assets should we be concerned with? First, most versions of this type of argument include *natural resources* as assets which should enter the pool for financing the stake (Robertson, 1996). But, for a number of reasons, distributing the value of natural assets may not prove sufficient to alleviate the social problems discussed above, and an additional source of funding may be required.[10] Moreover, it may be hard, conceptually and normatively, to distinguish typical natural resources such as land or solid fuels from other types of external assets; if this is the case then surely one would have to consider those resources as part of the funding base for a stakeholder society. Thus, Hillel Steiner (1994) has argued that the *estates of dead persons* should contribute towards raising the stakes of every citizen.[11] Van Parijs (1995), in turn, suggests that what he calls 'job assets' in fact constitute by far the largest source of external assets. According to Van Parijs (1995: 129), jobs 'can be viewed as taps fitted on to a pool of external assets to which all have an equal claim'. Now, if individuals have entitlements to an equal tradable share of job assets, they also have a right to an equal share of the 'employment rents' attached to these assets. Once these employment rents are included in the funding base for the stakeholder society, the value of citizens' stakes increases significantly.

Typically, these arguments (which contain a strong echo of arguments voiced in the nineteenth century by 'left libertarians' such as Herbert Spencer and Henry George) make reference to one or more values such as freedom, equality and so forth. The arguments typically start from the claim that there is, as it were, a right to equal (or 'maximin') freedom or opportunity from which is derived the right to equal (or maximin) shares of certain, freedom-endowing resources (Van Parijs, 1995; Ackerman and Alstott, 1999). But, unlike arguments that are directly rooted in theories of freedom or equality that tend to leave unanswered the question of how policies are most appropriately financed, entitlement arguments of this kind tie the proposed stakeholder policies to specific tax bases. Stakes and taxes are two sides of the same social justice coin, both being essential to implementing the claimed underlying resource entitlement. Arguments of this sort typically come with very definite implications as to how stakeholder proposals ought to be funded.

There are two further implications of the entitlement argument for the stakeholder society worth spelling out. First, entitlement arguments of the sort described above are clearly universalistic in character: they affirm that each and every citizen has a right to an equal (or at least maximin) share of specific external resources. The ideal policy would thus seem to be the radically universalistic one of taxing all holdings of the relevant resources at 100 per cent and to include everyone in a uniform share-out of the resulting funds. But some scholars have suggested that a more selective policy approach is consistent with the underlying philosophy: in principle, one could achieve the same outcome by taxing only those with holdings above a per capita level and then distributing the funds raised only to those with holdings below this level. The issue of justice and taxation is of course a complicated matter,[12] and is taken up further by Cécile Fabre and Robert van der Veen (this volume).

Second, it is often suggested that entitlement-based arguments defend a policy of unconditionality in the use of stakes: the stake is, according to this view, a monetization of a right each citizen has to equal/maximin tradable shares of specific resources. Thus, in the same way that it would not be proper for the state to tell individuals what they should do with resources that they have a tradable right to, it would not be proper for the state to direct citizens as to how they may or may not use their stakes. But this raises the question of whether all individuals can in fact plausibly be said to have such strong entitlements to equal or maximin tradable shares of specific resources. Gijs van Donselaar (1997, this volume) in particular opposes this view, grounding his argument in a concern about stakes having the capacity to increase social 'parasitism'. Briefly, van Donselaar denies that individuals all have uniform stakes in society's assets; instead, he argues that a just distribution of external resources depends on the 'independent interest' that people have in making use of these resources (that is, their interest in using the resources independently of the use that others wish to make of them). To distribute a given asset to all equally, regardless of the pattern of independent interests, will allow those who end up with more resources than they have an independent interest in using to extract exploitative rents from those who have an independent interest in using more than an equal share (van Donselaar, 1997, this volume; see also Ackerman, this volume). Entitlement to the value of 'stakes' should be distributed in a way that discriminates between those who do and those who do not have independent interests in using the resource in question. In particular, the funds raised by taxing 'job assets' should be distributed only amongst those interested in getting a job, and not to 'surfers' who prefer leisure to taking available work.[13]

## 4.2   Individual freedom

A concern for individual freedom also looms large in the rhetoric and philosophy of stakeholder theorists. The essential insight, elaborated and refined by different authors in different ways, is simply that personal freedom depends on reasonable access to a minimally decent share of resources and that stakeholding policies are necessary to provide access to this minimum. If freedom is understood as the ability to do as one wishes without being subject or vulnerable to interference by others (Pettit, 1997; Skinner, 1998) then asset poverty reduces freedom directly by reducing the range of actions that it is possible for the asset-poor individual to perform without the permission of others (Waldron, 1993c; Cohen, 1997b). Moreover, in the effort to escape poverty, poor individuals may agree to trades that compromise their independence, for example, to labour contracts giving others considerable power of arbitrary interference in their lives. All too easily, the poor find themselves living at the mercy of those on whom they depend for a living, and so constrained to act in ways that those on whom they are dependent find acceptable.[14] Stakeholding then represents an emancipatory strategy that promises to end this state of unfreedom and domination by giving each citizen the material independence necessary to have effective freedom from actual interference by others and from the dependency that makes one all too vulnerable to arbitrary interference. Arguments along these lines can be found in Walter (1989), Van Parijs (1992, 1995), Ackerman and Alstott (1999), Fitzpatrick (1999).

But if freedom is the primary value for stakeholding, what implications does this have for the form of stakeholder policy? First, it might be argued that a concern for freedom supports the adoption of the more permissive forms of stakeholder policy, in particular that of giving all citizens a lump-sum endowment on maturity that each is then free to use as they wish.[15] However, this conclusion is by no means as obvious as at first sight it might appear. Those who support conditionality in the use of stakes, for example, might argue that material independence is of such importance that it should not be too easily alienable. In the same way that people's interest in personal freedom is protected by prohibiting voluntary enslavement (Mill, 1985), it might be argued that restrictions on how stakes can be used are justified as a way of protecting individuals from the vulnerability and dependency that would come from a reckless blowing of their stakes. Much depends on how we flesh out the value of individual freedom – as the absence of constraints on choice and options, or as the absence of arbitrary interference and domination.[16] Depending on which view one takes, freedom arguments generate different conclusions and this precludes a speedy conclusion as to the appropriate form of stakeholding even amongst those who agree that freedom is the primary value underpinning the stakeholder society. Moreover, freedom is by no means the only social value. Our freedom is quite properly limited in all sorts of ways that seem necessary to secure justice. One cannot rule out a priori that some restrictions on use of (or eligibility for) stakes may be justified on grounds of justice, even if this is at the expense of some freedom (White, this volume).

But there appears to be a second complication in the freedom-based justification of the stakeholder society. Fabre (this volume) points out a tension between equality of opportunity and the related concept of autonomy, arguing that stakeholding concentrates more on the former. The educative aspects of stakeholder arguments may however, also be thought to enhance autonomy. The issue concerns the importance of *personal character* to the success of stakeholder policies. Many advocates of stakeholder policies will find a focus on individual character invidiously moralistic. But it might be argued that the success of stakeholder initiatives depends in part on the capacity of stakeholders to plan ahead, to think about the future and to prioritize longer-term interests over short-term advantage – counteracting David Hume's 'narrowness of the soul'. Without those capacities, individuals will make poor use of their stakes, and their material independence will be precariously held and frequently lost (compare Goodin, this volume; van der Veen, this volume).

Accordingly, it might be argued that part of the aim of any stakeholder policy must be not only to spread assets to all citizens, but to educate them in the effective management of their asset holdings and encourage the development of the virtues of forward planning and self-discipline. Considerations of this sort surely underlie Ackerman's and Alstott's (1999) insistence that eligibility for capital grants be restricted to those who lack a criminal record and who successfully complete High School: such restrictions give individuals an incentive to stay on the right side of the law and to finish school and this, in turn, will nurture dispositions towards forward thinking and personal responsibility. At the same time, it can be argued that stakeholder policies, precisely by ensuring that every citizen has some minimum endowment of wealth on maturity, make it that much easier to inculcate these virtues.[17] But failure associated with personal character, bad education or socialization is only part of the 'stakeblower' story. In reality, structural and institutional elements regularly interact with personal actions (or inactions), rendering it hard to pinpoint the exact location of 'stakeholder failure'. This raises the further issue of what is to be done when one gambles and loses (Goodin, this volume). Because of design features, basic capital forms of stakeholding are more troubled by this prospect than those forms that take the form of a regular income stream or allow for 'second starts' (van der Veen, this volume). One of the key arguments of stakeholding against traditional welfare policies is that it does not undermine market processes, indeed strengthens them, but this renders them hostage to the spirit of entrepreneurial behaviour and the associated notion of risk-taking. One might then question the egalitarian credentials of forms of stakeholding that deliver equality of opportunity – but *only once* at the point when you get your initial stake (Fabre, this volume). Advocates of stakeholding have not yet given full consideration to these important matters of equality and responsibility (for discussion of some complex related philosophical issues, see Ripstein, 1999; Lake, 2001).

### 4.3   Equality of opportunity

Stakeholding proposals are frequently defended in terms of their contribution to equality of opportunity (Haveman, 1988; Le Grand, 1989; Unger and West, 1998; Ackerman and Alstott, 1999; Freeman, 1999). Equality of opportunity is a hotly contested concept. Some theorists understand the concept in essentially meritocratic terms: equal opportunity obtains when people from different social backgrounds have the same opportunity to develop their natural abilities and to reap the market-determined rewards of exercising these abilities (Miller, 2000). Others understand the concept in more radical terms, as requiring that the rules of economic cooperation control for a wide range of 'brute luck' inequalities, including inequalities in natural ability (Dworkin, 1981; Cohen, 1989). Understood in either way, stakeholding proposals promise to promote equal opportunity to some extent. Universal capital grants, for example, can be expected to help equalize access to further and higher education, and to overcome the wealth constraints that prevent many people from ever being in a position to start their own business. Whilst governments in Europe already subsidize those going into higher education, young people who do not go into higher education do not get any equivalent helpful 'hand-up' at the start of their working life. A policy of universal capital grants would redress this inequality.

Most advocates of stakeholding take the meritocratic stance on equality of opportunity, with only a sidelong glance at other issues concerning opportunities. Where governments promote stakeholding, meritocracy rules. In its recent consultation paper, *Saving and Assets for All*, the British government sounds a resoundingly meritocratic note when it explains that one of the main motivations for its *Child Trust Fund* proposal is to promote 'inter-generational mobility – extending to the children of low-income families the opportunities that might be taken for granted higher up the income ladder' (HM Treasury, 2001: 1).

The appeal to equal opportunity in defence of stakeholding raises a number of questions. One question is how far a given stakeholder policy, taken by itself, will realize a given conception of equal opportunity (Fabre, this volume; Ackerman, this volume). And even if a given policy goes a long way towards realizing one conception of equal opportunity, a critic might argue that it does not suffice to meet the specific kind of equal opportunity that social justice really demands, for example because it does little or nothing to redress inequalities in income and wealth attributable to brute luck differences in natural ability. In addition, greater equality of opportunity is in principle compatible with considerable inequality of outcome (whether measured in terms of income, wealth, or some conception of welfare). Stakeholding is an approach to social policy that, while egalitarian in its essential thrust, is essentially individualistic: it gives people opportunity, but leaves them responsible for what they make of their opportunity (Pateman, this volume). What does society owe to those who make poor use of the opportunities that stakeholding affords? Is there a residual obligation to assist those who end up badly off?[18] How much account of 'irresponsibility' should be factored into these considerations?

These questions are all relevant in considering how far stakeholder policies should be seen as alternatives to more traditional social policies and how far they should be seen as complements. On one view, associated with 'left-libertarian' thinkers such as Hillel Steiner, stakeholder policies exhaust the demands of social justice, rightly understood (Steiner, 1994; Vallentyne and Steiner, 2000). It would be a violation of citizens' rights for the state to offer assistance or to try to equalize opportunities beyond provision of the basic, uniform stake to all. On another view, stakeholder policies are properly seen as one element – albeit a vitally important, and perhaps neglected, one – in a broad package of policies aimed at realizing the (often competing) demands of social justice. In this vein, for example, Will Paxton describes 'asset-based welfare' as a 'third pillar' of welfare policy, complementing public service provision and cash transfers (Paxton, 2001).

## 4.4   Democratic participation

Yet another value that frequently appears in arguments for stakeholder proposals is that of democratic participation (Pateman, this volume). Democracy (or at least, a healthy democracy) is said to require widespread and active political participation (Almond and Verba, 1963), and stakeholding is regarded by some as a key instrument in boosting democratic participation across society. It seems there are at least two mechanisms in play.

First, stakeholder policies are seen as securing the *material basis for effective political participation*. Political participation in modern polities requires time and money. Many stakeholder policies would allow citizens interested in devoting time to political activities – from running for candidate, over working in party offices to canvassing the streets on behalf of political candidates – to do so while granting them a means of income support. This is of course true in all unconditional versions of stakeholder policies, but also applies to most conditional proposals (for example, participation income). Most stakeholder advocates would readily admit that being engaged in political activities renders one eligible for this type of support. In addition, in some electoral environments, a stake might even provide additional capital for running a particular political agenda. While stakeholder proposals can hardly be expected to generate the amount of funds regularly spent on top-level electoral campaigns, they may go some way in providing a coalition of citizens to promote their favourite cause. In fact, one could even take it a step further and propose to earmark part of society's stake for purely political purposes – a type of voucher scheme only to be spent on supporting political candidates or parties.[19] The key challenge facing those who advocate stakeholder initiatives on these particular democratic grounds, however, remains to show how stakeholding proposals *in particular* are necessary to make democratic citizenship rights effective. Why aren't conventional public services and welfare policies sufficient in this respect? Other questions include: Are all forms of stakeholding equally effective in enabling democratic participation? Or does this consideration point clearly towards some types of stakeholding rather than others?

A second mechanism comes into its own in stakeholder proposals that have conditions attached to them. The recent literature on political participation is very concerned about the low levels of participation in politics – not merely voting turnout, since democratic participation can mean much more than simply voting. One of the challenges in effect is to somehow 'induce' citizens to become more actively engaged in various aspects of the political process. By attaching some notion of 'civic duties' to stakeholder proposals, the latter could effectively become a tool for improving democratic politics. Different design questions emerge immediately. What expectations of citizen behaviour can the state engender with stakeholder policies? What forms of participation can be expected? Should we require citizens to participate directly in the political process in return for a publicly funded stake, or should we be content with the broad sort of participation requirements proposed by, for instance, Tony Atkinson (1996)? And will such participation in itself be sufficient to engender the sort of broad involvement that democratic theorists are keen to see emerge? These and many related questions are not the subject of this book, but it is worth pointing out how stakeholding may have broader implications that have yet to be fully explored.

## 4.5 Efficiency

The emerging literature on 'asset-based egalitarianism' is replete with arguments that stakeholding initiatives will promote equality in a way that does not compromise, or even increases, economic efficiency. Bowles and Gintis (1998) discuss how 'asset-based redistribution' can result in efficiency gains. When asset users are distinct from asset holders the holders may not be able to make incentive-compatible contracts for efficient use of the assets. When assets are put into the hands of users (for example, productive capital is given to workers, houses are given to those who live in them), incentives to make efficient use of the assets improve. Other writers stress the way in which stakeholding proposals may release untapped entrepreneurial talent; or how they may help increase the supply of skilled workers with desirable knock-on effects on the equilibrium rate of unemployment or rate of economic growth. In the case of the basic income proposal in particular, there is a long tradition of what might be called 'humane neo-liberalism' which argues that with a substantial basic income in place, markets can be more thoroughly deregulated, resulting in efficiency gains (Brittan, 1983; Van Parijs, 1992a).

Such arguments can be very important in making the *political case* for stakeholding (van der Veen and Groot, 2000). Egalitarian politics is often perceived – and always portrayed by its opponents – as a zero-sum endeavour that will make some worse off in order to make others better off.[20] And this is thought to make it difficult to articulate an egalitarian project that can command widespread support. But if egalitarian objectives can be advanced in an efficiency-promoting way, then, in principle, everybody can benefit from the adoption of such policies: in principle, the 'winners' from such policies could fully compensate the 'losers' and still have some left over to be better off than they were before. Egalitarians make their advances when they can find ways to pursue their objectives in this positive-sum manner (Van Parijs, 1992b; Rogers and Streeck, 1994; Bowles and Gintis, 1998). Does stakeholding promise such a 'marriage of justice and efficiency' (Van Parijs, 1992b)? One might of course question whether the alleged efficiency gains will ever materialize: the impact of how a given stakeholding policy is financed could, after all, produce inefficiencies that outweigh those that result from the policy. Moreover, even if there is a net efficiency gain, it may not be feasible in practice to fully compensate those who stand most immediately to lose from stakeholder policies – the asset-rich who might well bear the brunt of financing ambitious stakeholder policies. Moreover, even if we could compensate these 'losers', would it be desirable to do so? Could this not compromise the egalitarian objectives that animate stakeholder proposals? These and many related questions are taken up in subsequent chapters.

## 5   Critical reflections

Having briefly discussed the main ethical arguments that play in the advocacy of stakeholding, there are still a number of issues that remain unresolved in the stakeholding debate. The purpose of this section is to chart some of the key issues; they are more fully discussed in the remainder of this volume.

### 5.1   Conditional or unconditional?

Let us imagine that all citizens are endowed with a capital grant on maturity. For example, imagine that we have adopted the proposal outlined by Bruce Ackerman and Anne Alstott to give each citizen on maturity a lump-sum grant equivalent to $80,000 financed from a tax on inheritance and wealth.[21] Should citizens have a right to use the funds so granted to them in any way they wish? Or, should they be free to use the funds only in a range of approved ways – for example, to help finance higher education or to set up a new business? Should the grant be effectively conditional on its responsible use?

Conditionality can also be built into the circumstances of initial eligibility for the capital grant, rather than into the terms of its use.[22] For example, it might be proposed that the level of the grant should vary according to whether individuals participate in national service schemes: those who undertake some form of national service might be thought to have thereby earned the right to a higher capital grant. Or eligibility might be made conditional, as Ackerman and Alstott propose, on a minimum level of educational achievement and on the lack of a criminal record. Much of the discussion in this volume explores the vexing question of conditionality.

A case for a degree of conditionality in use of stakeholder grants can be made in at least two ways. The first is a *paternalist* argument that holds that conditionality is justified by the need to prevent account-holders using their capital grants in ways that would not well serve their own long-term interests. The second argument appeals to *considerations of distributive justice.* According to proponents of this argument, there is something unfair about a citizen inheriting a substantial capital grant and then using it to live a self-indulgent life that gives nothing back to the community in return (White, 1997, 2002, this volume; van Donselaar, 1997, this volume). Perhaps some degree of conditionality in how grants are used will encourage citizens not to make unfair use of their stakes in this way. Alternatively, conditions on initial eligibility for the grant might reduce the risk of (alleged) unfairness.

## 5.2 Income or assets?

We have imagined that each citizen receives a uniform capital grant on maturity. But should citizens receive their stake as a lump-sum on maturity or should they rather receive it as a guaranteed periodic income, that is, as a basic income – 'stock' or 'stream' (van der Veen, this volume)?[23]

Some argue that the lump-sum option is more equitable as everyone receives the same amount of money whereas the citizen's income gives those who live longer a larger life-time endowment. Of course, they also have more life on which to spend that endowment. Another way of looking at the same question is that those who die young have much more to spend on each year of life from the initial endowment than those who live long. This is especially pertinent when we recognize that the aged need a great deal of health and social care. Outside of a specific thesis of human identity – and what should be equalized on the basis of that identity – there is no obvious argument based on either way of counting the egalitarian metric.

Others have suggested that basic income proposals are paternalistic in that it is a sum paid by the state on a regular basis as opposed to a one-off grant that individuals could invest or spend as they choose from the beginning. According to Carole Pateman (this volume; also Pateman, 2003) unconditional basic income is not paternalistic in any sense. There are many ways of losing a lump sum, not all of which require 'childish' behaviour. One egalitarian argument for providing basic income rather than a lump-sum capital grant is for reasons of social insurance. The lump sum could be lost if invested in an enterprise which was designed to secure the future income of the asset-holder but is lost due to the vagaries of the market. Over half of new businesses go under in the first two years of operation so any investment involves a risk. Basic income insures against one risking one's entire stake and ensures a steady stream of income. Risks must be taken from income or borrowing over-and-above that provided by the state. Some see such arguments as paternalistic. Certainly Ackerman and Alstott (1999) discuss this issue in terms of the whole stake being 'blown' by reckless adolescent squandering. Because of this, Ackerman and Alstott argue for a paternalistic intervention. They argue for a two-tiered stake consisting of a large grant on maturity *plus* a citizen's pension at state retirement age – an 'expanded stake' (van der Veen, this volume). Individuals are not allowed, in their proposal, to capitalize their future citizen's pension entitlements when young.[24] Others more explicitly see the social insurance aspect arguing that individuals' long-term interests are better served by providing the stake as a periodic guaranteed income (Van Parijs, 1995, 2001).

What are the wider implications of introducing paternalistic or social insurance considerations into the argument for stakeholding? One could argue that if proponents of basic income, for example, use social insurance or paternalistic arguments to defend their preferred form of stakeholding against an unconditional lump-sum capital grant, they cannot then dismiss other such arguments for more conditional forms of stakeholding on the grounds of individual freedom. But this argument in turn depends on whether we view these two cases as exhibiting the same amount of prudential paternalism – a matter of some contention. Cécile Fabre in Chapter 7 rightly suggests that proponents of both basic income and stakeholding often make claims on the basis of individual autonomy but ideas of social responsibility and the good of the community underlie much of their rhetoric. How well do these positions fit together?

## 5.3 Universalism

We have thus far assumed that each and every citizen receives exactly the same initial capital endowment or periodic income grant. But why should stakeholder policies take this indiscriminately uniform and universalistic shape? There are two ways in which stakeholder proposals can be modified. First, we may decide to target stakeholder policies towards the more asset-poor instead of handing them out to all citizens – an approach often referred to as 'selectivism'. Second, we may want to give some grants or accounts to all citizens, but vary the level of grants in accordance with how asset-poor recipients are. This approach – called 'progressive universalism' (HM Treasury, 2001a,b) – has obvious advantages in terms of securing political support across party families.

Stakeholder proponents hold different views about the question of whether strict universalism is a matter of principle for the stakeholder paradigm, or whether justice in fact permits – perhaps even requires – that policies should be more targeted towards those who need it. In the latter case there is also difference of opinion about the reasons – 'principled' versus 'pragmatic' (Barry, 1996) – why some measure of targeting might be justified.[25]

Fabre (this volume), following Arneson (1989, 1990) and Sen (1982), points out that equality of resources does not imply equality of welfare. To the extent that both basic income and lump-sum grants are about the former this may pose a moral problem: those who are, for whatever reason, badly situated in the labour market (or in the education market, or in the health market, and so on) may have to use up more of their stake to reach a level of welfare comparable to those who are more advantaged. Should we not therefore adjust the level of the grant in accordance with individuals' capacity to achieve welfare (even discounting certain 'tastes' and focusing on more objectively verifiable 'needs')? Carole Pateman (this volume) discusses a particularly salient version of this general objection: implicitly discounting power distribution within households implies that universalistic measures cannot resolve inequalities of welfare between the different partners within the household. She claims that advocates of 'individualistic' stakeholder proposals need to be made aware of this blind spot in their social outlook.

Next to these principled reasons for targeting stakeholders, forms of targeting often re-appear because of purely pragmatic considerations. Even the most radical defender of universalism may have to accept certain compromises lest she wants to render the debate entirely futile and vacuous. Once we look at the pragmatics of stakeholder proposals the devil is often in the detail (Goodin, this volume) – not merely the details of the proposals themselves, but perhaps more importantly also the precise social, economic and political environment in which the policies operate (see De Wispelaere and Stirton, 2003). A well-known example of a purely pragmatic argument restricting the universalism of stakeholding is to be found in Atkinson's justification of a *participation income* on grounds of political efficiency, but many more scenarios are currently being investigated (Atkinson, 1995, 1996; van der Veen and Groot, 2000).

### 5.4   Financial base?

Thus far we have said nothing about how citizens' stakes are to be financed. What sources of finance would be most appropriate? There is a clear divide here between stakeholder theorists who see the question of how to finance the stakeholder policy as one that is essentially independent of the policy itself, and those for whom the policy and its financing are interdependent issues, being two sides of the same basic requirement of justice. Ackerman and Alstott (1999), for example, fall into the first camp. They argue that their ambitious stakeholder proposal should be financed from a tax on inheritance and on wealth. But, while preferring this option, they explicitly state that they would accept a proposal that took the necessary funds from other sources, such as a sales tax. Philippe Van Parijs (1995), by contrast, falls into the latter camp. He argues that the state should seek to capture through taxation the market value of certain scarce 'external assets' and redistribute the revenue as a uniform income or capital grant. Note that both authors are not merely arguing for the legitimacy of a particular stakeholder policy, but for the legitimacy of specific taxes linked to a particular stakeholder policy.

Proponents of stakeholding do not necessarily look only to taxes to finance their proposals. Closely related to the growing interest in stakeholding is the proposal to establish a *Community Fund* under which the state obtains a portfolio of assets and uses the funds and their returns to finance public spending. Gerald Holtham, for example, has proposed a community fund invested in equities (Holtham, 1999; see also Meade, 1989; Crosland, 1956). 'A rate of return of 6% would allow 3 per cent per year to be devoted to health expenditure, some £1.5 bn annually, while the fund continued to grow at 3% per annum.' Holtham proposes hypothecating receipts from a reformed inheritance tax and capital gains tax, and allowing companies the option of paying taxes 'by issuance of scrip, which would dilute the holdings of existing share-holders but not affect cash flow'. He suggests that by using these measures a fund of £50 bn could be built up in about a decade. Robert Kuttner links the Community Fund idea explicitly to the idea of universal asset-building and universal capital grants (Kuttner, 1998). He proposes that the US federal government invest a proportion of the budget surplus it enjoyed until recently in shares, and allocate the fund to individual accounts that would be set up for all newborn children. The funds in the accounts would grow as the children mature, so that each would inherit a reasonable capital grant on maturity. Kelly and Lissauer (2000) explored a similar 'baby bond' idea in the British context, and one sees a clear echo of this idea in the British government's proposal for a *Child Trust Fund* (HM Treasury, 2001a,b; see Kelly, Gamble and Paxton, this volume, for a full discussion of these ideas).

## 6 Outline of the book

From the previous discussion it has clearly emerged that support for stakeholding as a general idea is compatible with disagreement over a number of basic ethical and design questions which arise in elaborating this idea. The answers that theorists and policy-makers give to these questions depend to a considerable extent on the arguments they use to defend stakeholding in the first place. This is the primary concern of this book. Before moving to an in-depth discussion of different stakeholder policies, and their underlying ethical ideals, we want to provide a brief route map to the remainder of this volume.

*The Ethics of Stakeholding* is in two main parts. The first part charts various stakeholder proposals and discusses the main arguments in favour of a particular stakeholder policy. In Chapter 2, Julian Le Grand and David Nissan present their proposal – previously published as a Fabian Society paper (2000) – to give each adult citizen in the UK a (conditional) capital grant of £10,000. This proposal has obvious similarities with the one advanced by Ackerman and Alstott (1999) in the US, but important differences are noted and elaborated upon.

Gavin Kelly, Andrew Gamble and Will Paxton in Chapter 3 focus on another main contender in the stakeholder debate – Individual Ownership Accounts. The authors provide a comprehensive overview of the different types of IOAs and relate the background in both the US and the UK that has led these proposals to feature prominently in recent policy debates. This chapter provides a welcome introduction into one of the fascinating recent developments in stakeholder policy and provides welcome insight into the similarities and differences of the UK and US cases.

Robert Goodin, in Chapter 4, discusses what he labels 'project capital', a basic capital grant which (in its basic version) includes *two* conditionality tests – a test to target these grants to those who are one-year unemployed and a test to sort out good from bad projects to spend public funds on. Goodin's contribution devotes special attention to pragmatic arguments about the political efficiency of stakeholding.

In the final contribution to the first part, Stuart White presents his preferred form of stakeholding. This consists of a stake which contains a time-limited unconditional citizen's income component plus a development grant, a capital grant linked to specified personal development purposes. White's chapter not only merges two practical proposals into a coherent policy, but in doing so also attempts to resolve the tension between the values of reciprocity and freedom.

The second part of the book then takes a critical look at the different stakeholder policies on offer and at the ideal of stakeholding. Contributors from various positions in the spectrum of political philosophy assess stakeholding from their favoured perspective. In Chapter 6 Gijs van Donselaar challenges stakeholder policies for becoming a recipe for exploitation. Van Donselaar's main concern is that, due to the unconditionality attached to most proposals, stakeholder recipients may enter into a parasitical relationship with those who are 'net contributors' to the scheme. The solution, for van Donselaar, is to restrict eligibility of stakeholder grants to those who want to make 'independent' use of them.

Where van Donselaar believes stakeholding fails because it is too egalitarian (strictly speaking), Cécile Fabre takes the opposite view. In Chapter 7 she investigates whether stakeholding is the egalitarian proposal it claims to be. Fabre shows how some stakeholder policies – her prime target is the Ackerman–Alstott version of basic capital – contain surprisingly inegalitarian aspects, not least in respect to the tax component associated with each proposal. Fabre believes these inegalitarian aspects are at least in part explained because stakeholder proponents are often more concerned with autonomy than equality as such.

Carole Pateman, in turn, believes that the focus on exploitation or equality is misguided. In fact, she argues, in Chapter 8, that proponents of the stakeholder paradigm have been going down the wrong track by focusing too narrowly on justice as the primary justification. Pateman then goes on to show how taking recourse to democratic arguments, as opposed to justice considerations, provides important insights in the nature and workings of the stakeholder society – in particular where it concerns questions related to the gender distribution of labour (and power) within households and society at large.

Robert van der Veen, in Chapter 9, aims to provide a comprehensive assessment of the two most important stakeholder competitors: Ackerman and Alstott's capital grant and Van Parijs's basic income. Van der Veen's contribution first makes the case that on a number of dimensions both proposals score similarly. Under certain conditions, basic income and basic capital can be transformed into one another, at first sight rendering the whole debate somewhat futile. But next van der Veen explains that there remains a substantial difference between the proposals with respect to their 'cultural content of freedom': basic capital envisages a culture of property ownership, whereas basic income is primarily concerned with establishing a culture of disposable time. Van der Veen provides not only a very systematic and in-depth account of two chief stakeholder policies, but also relates their key distinctiveness to the social and cultural background in which these ideas came about.

Finally, Bruce Ackerman, one of the authors of *The Stakeholder Society*, assesses various arguments and criticisms presented in this volume. Starting from the idea that liberalism needs radical rethinking, he engages with his critics and reiterates and defends the views that have led him to write *The Stakeholder Society*. Faced with a body of criticism that is often informed by distinctively European concerns – considerations that sometimes appear inimical to the particularly American aspects of *The Stakeholder Society* – Bruce Ackerman's contribution allows us to discern which parts of the stakeholder paradigm can be easily 'exported', and which aspects in contrast are too heavily rooted in the local idiosyncrasies of the particular welfare regime where it emerged.

## Notes

1. We would like to thank Malcolm Torry, Will Paxton and Guy Standing for their comments on this chapter.
2. Whereas a conventional inheritance (or estates) tax is levied on the estate of a dead person, the tax paid varying with the size of the estate, an accessions tax is a tax levied on the recipient of a gift, inheritance or bequest, the rate of tax varying with the amount of wealth that the recipient has already received in these ways. In most proposals, individuals are allowed a limited 'accessions quota', a sum of wealth that may be acquired through gift, inheritance or bequest, without incurring any tax liability; and tax is then paid, possibly at a progressive rate, on all wealth received above the quota.

3. Geographical location here mainly refers to the regional differences of living standards within a single polity. Living in London or New York is more expensive than living in rural UK or US, so some might think a uniform grant advantages those in rural areas (see Van Parijs, 1995 for an argument to the contrary).

4. A brief introduction to early and late modern thought on basic income and cognate proposals can be found at BIEN*Online* <www.basicincome.org>. For more sustained research, see in particular Cunliffe and Erreyghers (2003) and Cunliffe, Erreyghers and Van Trier (2002) and references therein.

5. Van Parijs's most important contributions to the basic income debate include Van Parijs (1991, 1992a,b, 1995, 2001) and van der Veen and Van Parijs (1986).

6. On 4 October 2002 the Irish Government launched a *Green Paper on Basic Income* <www.cori.ie/justice/basic_income/greenpaper/1660.pdf> as part of its *Partnership 2000 for Inclusion, Employment and Competitiveness* commitment. In its report the Steering Group on Basic Income advocated further debate on how to design and implement tax and welfare programmes to achieve the many positive effects associated with unconditional basic income schemes. For useful background discussion, see Clark and Healy (1997) and briefings by the CORI Justice Commission <www.cori.ie/justice/basic_income/index.htm>.

7. The most important organization is the Basic Income European Network (BIEN). BIEN bi-annually organizes an international conference, sends out a newsletter to over 900 individuals and organizations which contains a listing of recent events and publications on basic income, and maintains a website <www.basicincome.org>. BIEN also coordinates or assists in the working of a large number of national groups or associations committed to the promotion of basic income (see BIEN's web site for links and further information). Since 2000, the *US Basic Income Guarantee* (USBIG), an organization very similar to BIEN, has been focusing on promoting basic income in the US (for further information, see <www.usbig.net>). In the UK the relevant organization is the Citizen's Income Trust <www.citizensincome.org>.

8. It is not a *uniform* scheme, however: 'those with families on lower incomes would receive a larger sum' (HM Treasury, 2001: 17).

9. So-called Left-libertarians are the exception of course (Vallentyne and Steiner, 2000). Philippe Van Parijs's 'real-libertarianism' too has some key characteristics of entitlement theories (Vallentyne, 1997; de Wispelaere, 2000).

10. One reason may be that not all natural resources can be easily 'commodified'. On the stakeholder argument, the value of those natural resources that enter the production process must be distributed to all citizens, but what of those natural resources that do not enter the production process? This points to an interesting dilemma within the green argument in favour of stakeholding. Environmentalists often like basic income and cognate proposals because it is non-productivist and subsidizes alternative ways of life. But suppose, as some environmentalists argue, we were to make the funding of a basic income dependent on the use of natural resources by 'earmarking' a green tax? This would introduce an unfortunate double bind since the boosting of basic income revenue would depend on more natural resources being used, which is precisely the opposite of what environmentalists want.

11. More controversially, Steiner (1992) maintains the same applies to the value of a person's genetic make-up.
12. Murphy and Nagel (2002) provide a recent book-length treatment of the issue.
13. On the famous 'Feeding the Surfers' argument, see Van Parijs (1991, 1995: ch. 4) responding to a comment made by John Rawls (1974, 1993).
14. The same account of domination is used to explain how stakeholder grants may liberate those with few marketable skills from the stronghold of employers and high-skill workers, as well as how it frees women household workers from the stronghold of male earners in male breadwinner-type societies. In recent years the feminist angle is becoming increasingly important in the stakeholder debate (Pateman, this volume; also Alstott, 2001; Robeyns, 2000, 2001).
15. At first sight, an unconditional basic income too is compatible with this freedom requirement, but because basic income only hands out small grants on a regular basis (as opposed to a large one-off lifetime capital grant) it decreases the risks attached with 'gambling' with one's stake (Goodin, this volume). Some authors see this form of paternalism as a hidden constraint on freedom (see below, section 5.2).
16. Consider again the case of unconditional basic income: if we take the view that options should be as unrestricted as possible, regular basic income instalments appear to contradict our concern with personal freedom. But if non-domination is in fact our primary concern, mildly paternalistic in-built safety measures at the level of design do not violate personal freedom because while they strictly speaking restrict one's options, they do not imply any form of domination and help protect people against it. For a discussion of these two views of freedom see the debate between Van Parijs (1999) and Pettit (1999).
17. If, for example, financial literacy programmes are introduced in schools, children will probably be more eager to learn about financial management if they know that there is a 'stake' there, in their name, waiting for them on maturity. On the other hand, if children expect to inherit no stake on maturity, they may regard lessons in financial management as irrelevant to their life situation. The *educative* effects of different forms of stakeholding should be taken into account, therefore, in assessing their respective impact on individual freedom.
18. As is shown by Robert van der Veen's contribution in this volume, to the extent that basic capital forms of stakeholding propose an 'expanded' form of the stakeholder society, they would support such a residual obligation. Compare also Goodin (this volume) on the continuing need for social assistance.
19. In effect Bruce Ackerman and Ian Ayres (2002) suggest such a system of 'Patriot Dollars', radically redesigning the campaign finance in the US. Ackerman clearly views *The Stakeholder Society* as one part of an overall project to fundamentally reform social and political life in the US. For a discussion of these two components in Ackerman's just society, see Wigley (2002).
20. Or worse, in so-called 'leaky bucket' arguments egalitarian redistribution is considered to imply a dead-weight loss, amounting to a negative-sum game (Okun, 1975).
21. This is a simplification of what is, in fact, quite a nuanced proposal. More exactly, Ackerman and Alstott (1999) propose the following: (1) Grants: (i) All citizens will be eligible for an $80,000 grant (1996 prices) to be received in four

instalments up to age 21. Those entering college will be able to use the grant to meet college fees. Access to the principal will be frozen for those who fail to graduate from high school. The level of the grant may also be cut for those with a criminal record, though the lost grant may be restored if criminals become law-abiding. (ii) All citizens will receive a citizen's pension of $670 per month from age 65. (2) Taxes: (i) The basic grant will be paid for in the short-run by a 2 per cent tax on all individual wealth over $80,000. In the long term, the grant will be financed from taxes on estates and gifts (with modest exemptions), with a wealth tax being retained to cover any shortfall from estate/gift taxes. (ii) The citizen's pension will be paid for by a tax on 'childhood privilege'. An individual's degree of childhood privilege is to be defined by reference to the level and stability of parental income during his/her childhood years. High and stable parental income puts one in the 'high privilege' category and leads to a high privilege tax. Illustrative figures: High, $3800 pa; Medium, $2090 pa; Low, $380 pa. The introduction of the childhood privilege tax is to be accompanied by repeal of the payroll tax. Ackerman and Alstott envisage that this scheme will run along-side various forms of social insurance targeted at specific contingencies such as unemployment and ill health.

22. We can discern a third, 'hidden' or 'implied', form of conditionality attached to the level of the grant. Suppose we would have a fully unconditional basic income (in the two senses defined above) but we instal a measure that varies the *level* of the grant depending on how individuals behave overall. For instance, we could attach the level of the grant to a macro-economic performance indicator such as GDP or employment rates which would mean that the level of grant would decrease if more people were to opt out of formal employment, or if productivity were to decrease below a certain threshold indicator. This in turn would serve as a 'soft incentive' towards pushing people back into work, as it were. While such a scheme does not have any formal conditions attached to it, it is implied that, overall, individuals should contribute towards maintaining a certain level of production or employment, and so on.

23. Tangential to this dimension, but not entirely disconnected, is the question of whether stakes should be provided in cash or in kind. This dimension is relatively underexplored, but see Van Parijs (1995) for discussion.

24. Thus, it is not quite true to say that Ackerman and Alstott propose a uni-versal capital grant rather than a basic income. More exactly, they propose a universal capital grant for working-age adults combined with a basic income for those above a certain age. See in particular van der Veen (this volume) for a discussion of the different components of the Ackerman–Alstott proposal and their complex interaction.

25. See van der Veen (1997) for discussion of the principled-pragmatic distinction in relation to universal grants (originally due to Barry, 1996). Essentially, principled arguments in favour of targeting would include moral arguments about why it is wrong to divert resources to the rich when they could (and rightly should) be spent on the poor directly. Stakeholder propo-nents use pragmatic arguments, by contrast, when they believe that, in ideal circumstances, we should not compromise on the principle of universalism, but that compromising on universality is a second-best strategy in a con-strained policy environment to be preferred over not having any form of stakeholding at all.

# 2
# A Capital Idea: Helping the Young to Help Themselves[1]

*Julian Le Grand and David Nissan*

This chapter discusses the idea of a capital grant that has received widespread attention in recent years.[2] It suggests that each individual, on attaining the age of majority, should receive a grant of capital that he or she can use as a springboard to accumulate wealth. The grant would be financed by funds from a new tax on inheritance. In that way the accumulated wealth of one generation would fertilize the development of the next.

## 1  Curative versus preventive welfare states

When looking at different kinds of welfare states, or, more specifically, at policies aimed at promoting greater equality or social justice, it is helpful to borrow from health policy debates and distinguish between 'curative' and 'preventive' policies. Curative policies take the market-determined distribution of income and wealth as their starting point, allowing the market to interact with the initial distribution of resources between individuals to determine the initial pattern of wages, salaries and wealth holdings. Those policies then attempt to *re*-distribute that income and wealth in a direction determined by a balance between social justice and other considerations, such as economic efficiency.

Put another way, curative policies allow the 'disease' of poverty and inequality to take hold and then attempt to cure it. They wait until market forces have done their worst, massively enriching some individuals and families while impoverishing others through unemployment or low wages. Only then do they try to cure the illness or at least try to alleviate its symptoms. These are fiscal policies: they tax market winners, and use the proceeds (or the revenue from other forms of taxation) to pay cash benefits or provide various social services to the losers.

In contrast, preventive measures try to prevent inequality, poverty or social exclusion appearing in the first place. They intervene directly in the market-determined distribution of income and wealth, either through affecting the initial distribution of resources available to each individual or through affecting the prices that individuals get for their resources when they bring them to the market place. Examples of the first kind of preventive policy (those directed at the initial distribution) include education and training: policies directed at improving each individual's stock of human capital. An example of the second kind (directed at influencing the price of resources) is the minimum wage: an attempt to put a floor under the price of labour. Our proposal is for an additional preventive policy. It is designed to increase the stock of financial capital with which each individual begins their adult life, and to reduce the inequalities between individuals in their receipt of private windfalls of such capital, such as those that arise through inheritance or gifts. So it is intended to contribute to greater equality in the resources with which individuals come to the market place, and thereby reduce the risk of market outcomes that are grossly unequal.

As a preventive policy it goes with the grain of much current thinking about welfare reform. A welfare state based around curative policies has two fundamental limitations. First, though making the consequences of market or individual failure less painful, at best it does little to reduce the extent of those failures and at worst makes them more likely to occur. Although the perverse incentive effects of cash benefits can be exaggerated, even their most diehard defender would find it difficult to argue that they do much to encourage people to take positive steps to look after themselves (see Beveridge, 1942: 58, for a classic statement of this concern).

Second, curative welfare states are politically unpopular. People often suspect that those who contract the disease of poverty have done so because of their own fault or volition (for example, Mead, 1992, who argues that poverty in the US largely reflects a lack of appropriate economic ambition or 'competence' on the part of the poor). This is usually unfair; but the fact that the suspicion exists means that the help offered is often grudging and mean. In consequence they generally do not eliminate poverty (although they do reduce it); and they are vulnerable to populist political attacks that can reduce even their limited effectiveness yet further. Of course, curative policies have their place. If a 75 year old has an inadequate pension, no amount of training courses is going to improve her lot. A single parent with three hungry children under the age of five needs money more than relationship counselling or a lecture on sex education. But a 'preventive' welfare state that ensures that as few of these problems as possible arise in the first place is better still (compare Goodin, this volume).

However, preventive measures are not an easy alternative. Their pay-off is often a long time in the future, so their effectiveness is often difficult to evaluate. They are not cheap: to make sure that no one slips through the net, preventive programmes usually have to be applicable to everyone, and that can cost. Also, most such policies overlap the responsibilities of different government departments. The rhetoric of joined-up government has to be translated into reality. Moreover, many preventive measures have as bad a track record as some curative measures in terms of their effectiveness in curbing poverty and inequality. Government-sponsored training programmes for the low-skilled, for instance, are notorious for their lack of impact on trainees' job prospects (Gallie, 2002: 116–17; also Crouch, Finegold and Sako, 1999: 109–34). The effect of more general education is also controversial. Most forms of school or post-school education benefit the children of the better off more than the poor, arguably thereby contributing more to increasing eventual inequality in outcomes than reducing it (Le Grand, 1982; also Fogel, 2000: 157, for a contrary view about the effects of primary and secondary schooling in the US case).

However, we believe that the relative failure of existing measures, curative or preventive, to reverse or even prevent the growth of poverty and inequality comes not only from their own weaknesses but also from their failure to tackle a fundamental cause of inequality in our society: the unequal distribution of wealth, or, more specifically, the unequal distribution of receipts of wealth.

## 2   The distribution of wealth

Capital distribution matters more now than ever before. Changes in the British economy are enabling more people to accumulate wealth. In the last few decades owner-occupation, driven in part by council house sales, and the growth of occupational and personal pensions have massively expanded the numbers of wealth-holders. But the gains have not been spread evenly. The Inland Revenue estimates that the share of marketable wealth of the top 10 per cent increased from 49 per cent to 52 per cent between 1982 and 1996, while the share of the top 50 per cent rose from 91 per cent to 93 per cent. Alongside this the proportion of households with no wealth at all is also on the increase: a study by the

IFS estimates that twenty years ago only 5 per cent of households had no assets, whereas a decade later 10 per cent had none (Banks and Tanner, 1999). An already grossly inequitable distribution has become even more unequal.

Moreover, the trend is set to continue. In the years ahead equity-sharing schemes and share options, encouraged by government policy, will boost personal wealth further. But inevitably many will miss out on the bonanza. These will include not just the low-paid and the unemployed, but also workers in the public and voluntary sectors, where there are no profits to share or equity to hold. In addition, an increasing proportion of already wealthy owner-occupiers are now inheriting the houses of their parents. In a meritocracy some of this may have to be accepted. Wealth inequality is the product of many factors. Over a working lifetime assets are built up through saving, and then, at least partially, consumed in retirement. Thus the age profile of the population will be one determinant of the degree of wealth inequality. Other significant factors are income and educational achievement. The potential to accumulate wealth is as valid an incentive to performance as is the opportunity for higher pay. An equal distribution within a generation cannot, and should not, be the ideal for policy-makers.

But entrenching wider wealth inequality across the generations has consequences for the agenda of social inclusion, as it expands the class of those who, by accident of birth alone, have greater opportunities than the rest (Hills, Le Grand and Piachaud, 2002). While personal wealth in one generation may, for some at least, be the result of admirable qualities such as entrepreneurship, thrift, self-improvement and hard work, it is also, for the next generation, an important determinant of later success. Parental wealth is linked with children's educational attainment; and inheritance is an important determinant of later levels of entrepreneurship (Bynner and Paxton, 2001; Kelly, Gamble and Paxton, this volume). It is natural and welcome for parents to assist their children. But existing levels of inequality mean that already a sizeable proportion of children can expect no such leg-up, and many more very little help at all. One in five asset-less households are headed by people aged 20–34 (Banks and Tanner, 1999). The wealth problem is most acute for the age group where choices will have most effect on life chances. The aim of policy should not be to stop the wealth of one generation boosting the chances of the next, but to spread such opportunity more widely.

# 3 Why a capital grant?

The children of the wealthy can look forward to help throughout their adult lives: with university fees, housing deposits and start-up capital for business ventures. But others, especially those brought up in poverty, are significantly disadvantaged by their lack of access to capital. Without capital they cannot start a business, put a down payment on a house, or, sometimes, even go to university. Their parents have not got the wherewithal to supply them with that capital. Nor do they find it easy to borrow: banks and other financial institutions are reluctant to lend to poor families, and indeed even to the non-poor if they live in poor areas.

Few young adults have pension schemes or equity in owner-occupied housing. What counts for them are financial assets, which can readily be used for any number of worthwhile purposes. Huge numbers have no access to such capital. Banks and Tanner estimate that in 1997–98, of the wide age group 22–29, 45 per cent did not have a deposit account, and the median wealth of those that did was just £750. Fifteen per cent had National Savings, holders of these having median wealth of £1050. Holdings of other financial assets such as PEPs, TESSAs, privatization or other shares and unit trusts were practically negligible.[3] The few owners of these more sophisticated savings had average wealth of £3500 to £5000.

These reasons would be enough to justify a capital grant to the children of the poor, or at the least to the children of those who live in poor areas. However, we believe that there is a case for a universal grant: one going to the children of the poor and non-poor alike. This is partly because of the general case for universal benefits over ones targeted on the poor. Universal benefits contribute to the sense of national community, whereas targeted ones can be socially divisive. Also, targeted benefits require a cumbersome apparatus for determining eligibility: one that is expensive to administer and can be demeaning to the recipient (Titmuss, 2001: 121–2). In contrast, universal benefits require only the information necessary to determine that the individual concerned falls into the relevant category: in our case, simply their age.

In fact targeting a capital grant would pose far greater problems than are encountered with the array of means-tested benefits currently available. As its purpose is to distribute capital, the wealth of potential recipients would be the appropriate criteria. But if the grant were to be distributed to young adults, it is likely that almost all would have no capital, unless they had benefited from parental or grandparental gifts, or an inheritance. A means-test based on wealth would be far more likely to lead to the gifts being deferred until after any deadline for assessment than to the exclusion of a sizeable number of beneficiaries. Other assessments could be made on, say, parental wealth or even grandparental wealth. But then there would be difficult and expensive problems of assessment, and an implication in denying someone a grant that their parents should make capital available.

But there is an additional, more fundamental reason for a universal grant. Everyone born into a developed country benefits from a share in a common inheritance: a set of capital assets, including buildings and other physical infrastructure, transport links, capital equipment and agricultural land. The vast majority of these are the results of the labours and efforts of previous generations, the members of which have struggled together to produce what is in effect a gift of wealth to the next. It is largely because of this inheritance that the current inhabitants of any developed country are as wealthy as they are; without that enormous accumulation of capital over the centuries, no amount of effort by the current generation could generate the levels of current production that maintain our standards of living.

This idea, that the wealth of one generation is a common asset to the next, is important for it cuts across the argument that individuals who have created wealth should be free to give it all to their children. Ownership gives personal command of resources, but it is not easy to justify this persisting beyond the grave, especially when, as we have seen, the life chances for many are reduced by lack of access to start-up capital. How can one argue that people have as great a right to inherited wealth as to, for instance, the income or profits that result from their own efforts? It would seem fairer if the right to our national patrimony was more equally distributed – as would happen if our proposal for a universal capital grant were to be implemented.

A standard argument used against any universal benefit is what we might call the 'Prince William objection': should the benefit be paid to the better off who are unlikely really to need it, such as Prince William, as well as to the really needy? The answer is, in general, yes: for this is a price that has to be paid if the other advantages of universality are to be obtained and the problems of means-tested targeting avoided. Moreover, if, as we go on to discuss, the grant is financed through inheritance tax then, as parents pay the tax, so a significant portion of their wealth will now be going to pay for the start-up costs for thousands of other children, as well as their own. In the case of the young prince, an exception may be made as long as his family, uniquely, are exempt from inheritance tax.

It is also worth noting that the children of the better off in the UK already receive a form of grant through subsidies to higher education. Although with the introduction of tuition fees and student loans these subsidies are being reduced, they remain considerable. Most students come from middle-class backgrounds. Hence our proposal can be viewed as simply a means of extending an already existing subsidy aimed at the better off to those less fortunate. It also has the implication that higher education subsidies can be further reduced without making anyone worse off, since one potential use for the grant could be to pay for tuition and living expenses while acquiring further education.

## 4   Why inheritance tax?

The logic of the argument so far suggests that we could usefully link our potentially popular spending proposal with reforms to a hitherto unpopular and inefficient tax – inheritance tax. Hypothecating, or earmarking, inheritance tax revenues to capital grants could provide the means for rehabilitating a despised tax. It also has an obvious popular appeal: the wealth of one generation is visibly spread around so as to fertilize the growth of the next.

Inheritance tax is a misnomer in the UK. What we have is a tax on estates that bears no relation to the amount any individual inherits, either from the estate in question, or over a lifetime. And the tax is largely voluntary. The Inland Revenue estimates that in 1995 total marketable personal wealth stood at £2013 billion. This measure excludes wealth that cannot be realized, such as accrued pension rights. In contrast, the yield from inheritance tax is pitiful, just £1.7 billion in 1997–98. Wealth passes almost untaxed between generations through lifetime gifts, through exempt items such as agricultural land and forestry, and through devices such as discretionary trusts that can defer tax liabilities for decades.

It is against this scale of wealth transfer that suggestions such as capital grants should be measured. There are approximately 650,000 eighteen year olds in Britain, so it would cost £6.5 billion to give them each £10,000. The current yield of £1.7 billion would only pay for about £2,500 per eighteen year old, but though this might be better than nothing, we argue later that a capital grant may need to be bigger if it is to be used wisely. Yields, and hence the grant, could be increased in subsequent years by reforms that have long been on economists' agendas, but that have lacked popular support. These include shifting the basis for the tax from the donor to the recipient, and extending it to include lifetime inheritances and gifts. This would encourage the wealthy to pass on their wealth to those who have not already been substantial beneficiaries, as by so doing they could reduce the taxman's take. The system would require that everybody had a lifetime gift and inheritance allowance, say of £50,000, which could be received free of tax. Thereafter tax could be levied at progressive rates to maintain incentives for wealth to be spread around. A review of exempt items and Trust law should also be undertaken to broaden the base of the tax.

In theory receipts could collapse with such a tax if bequests were directed only to those who had not used up their inheritance tax allowance. However, if that occurred a fairer distribution of inherited wealth would have been achieved, and there would be less need of an additional system of grants. More likely, however, is that wider bequests would happen mainly at the margins, as people would continue to want to help their own children first. As they did so they would be taxed to pay for grants for those less fortunate. It would not be necessary to impose penal rates of inheritance tax to finance a substantial reallocation of capital. Indeed an ideal system would have rates that most regarded as reasonable, to minimize incentives for avoidance or evasion.

What would these rates be? The inadequacies of the existing inheritance tax mean we have limited information about the extent of wealth bequeathed or given on a year-by-year basis. Inland Revenue figures show the net value of estates of people who died in the year to 31 March 1995 was £21.75 billion. Of this, £12 billion was in estates bigger than the Inheritance Tax threshold of £150,000 applying for that year, £3.2 billion was tax exempt, as this amount was left to surviving spouses, and other reliefs and exemptions reduced the chargeable figure to just £7.3 billion. Tax paid was £1.4 billion, a yield of just 6 per cent on the net value of the estates.

How big could the tax base be if all lifetime gifts were included, all reliefs other than those to the surviving spouse abolished, and trust law significantly tightened? It is not possible to give any firm estimates, but it would be surprising if the value of estates and lifetime gifts made in a given year were together less than £30 billion today, particularly given the substantial increases in house and share prices. On that basis a reformed inheritance tax would need to yield around 20 per cent to finance £10,000 per young adult, perhaps 25 per cent if bequests to surviving spouses are ignored. This is far from penal taxation. Moreover, if higher education subsidies were reduced *pari passu* (as they should be if equity is to be maintained), the savings from this could also be used to finance the grant, and the inheritance tax rate could be lowered yet further. Since the participation rate of the relevant age group in higher education is now running at just over one third, this means that the average inheritance tax rate could be lowered to under around 14 per cent – or 17 per cent if bequests to spouses are ignored. Alternatively, the rate could be kept at 20–25 per cent and the savings in higher education spending could be used elsewhere within the education budget or for other public services. In short, there is every opportunity here to levy a modest tax on gifts and bequests, and still make sure every young person has the capital needed to get off to a good start.

The insignificant contribution of inheritance tax to financing public spending, and the sense of the state as inherently wasteful, have meant that avoiding such tax has never attracted much moral opprobrium. The ease of avoidance of inheritance tax reflects the lack of public support for it (Fabian Society, 2000: 54–5). But if the proceeds of the tax were visibly distributed through capital grants, perhaps that perception could change.

## 5   Should the grant be unconditional?

Political support for the scheme would depend not only on its method of finance but also on what happens at the other end: what the recipients of the grant did with the money. The intention of our scheme is to encourage investment and hence the accumulation of capital (financial, physical or human). Hence grants must be spent on investment opportunities. There would be no surer way to lose popular and political support for a system of capital grants than with a few well-publicized cases of young people blowing their grants on cocaine or wild holidays.

The size of the grant may in itself be of importance here. While it may be tempting to launch such a scheme with a small grant to introduce the idea, there is a danger then that it is seen to be insignificant by the recipient, who might then feel quite justified in 'blowing it' for a bit of fun. The sum needs to be seen as significant, providing a one-off opportunity that justifies careful consideration. Instinct says that a grant of a thousand or two may fall between stools, being insufficient for most worthwhile investments. So our objective is a grant of £10,000.

It would be possible to make a respectable case for this level of grant to be given unconditionally on the grounds that ultimately adults do have to take responsibility for their own lives, and that young adults have to learn to do so. As it is, there would be plenty of social pressure on 18 year olds not to blow their grants; to add to that pressure by confining the grants to only certain kinds of spending might be seen as unacceptable state paternalism. But an element of paternalism is commonplace when moneys are passed on nowadays. Few parents would entrust tens of thousands of pounds to the very recently adult. They might well put money aside, but pass it on only when convinced it could be well spent. Public moneys need handling in similar ways.

Administratively, capital grants could be paid into a special account held in the individual recipient's name either in a local commercial bank or in a local branch of a network of publicly owned savings institutions set up by the Government specifically for this purpose. The account would have a special name: since its purpose is for the 'Accumulation of Capital and Education', suggesting the simple acronym ACE. ACE accounts would be handled by a set of trustees, whose purpose would be to approve the spending plans of individuals before releasing any capital: hence individuals would only be able to draw money from the account to spend on approved purposes, as defined by the trustees.

Having quality ACE trustees would clearly be important to this aspect of the scheme. For they would not only have to vet the spending plans, but also ensure that the money was spent in the way proposed. They could be specially employed by the local institution to vet the spending plans of all the grants being given out by that branch; alternatively they could be drawn from panels of local business people and other community leaders, on a voluntary basis, perhaps through the Business in Community scheme.

What sort of investment purposes should they approve? One obvious possibility is *higher and further education*: a way of accumulating human capital and hence increasing an individual's value to the labour market. The grant could be used to contribute to the fees and maintenance costs for a university education, or to the costs of more vocational forms of training. To ensure compliance, it could be paid through the educational institution concerned, in much the same way as the present student grant and loan scheme. Another use for the grant might be for the *down payment on a house or flat purchase*. Unpublished research by Gavin Smart suggests that for many poor people the down payment is the biggest obstacle to home-ownership: once the down payment is made, people have a commitment to their homes and usually manage to keep up the mortgage payments regardless of any income or employment problems they encounter. Again to ensure compliance, the payment could be made directly to the vendor. The grant could also form part of the *start-up costs of a small business*. The development of a business plan and its approval by the trustees would be essential – which makes it the more desirable to include local business people among the trustees. What should happen if no worthwhile uses are proposed for an individual's ACE account? One option would be for the grant to be put towards a *personal or stakeholder pension*. The pension schemes could be drawn from an approved list, and payment made directly from the ACE account to the scheme.

Such arrangements could not prevent all abuse, and it would be pointless to pretend otherwise. Assets bought through trustee-approved distributions must at some future date be saleable, and use of the proceeds could not easily be monitored. It is not unheard of for the offspring of the wealthy to fritter away their fortunes; and it will always be in the nature of some of the recipients of our capital grant to do so. What counts is that everyone gets their opportunity. Thereafter, as in many other aspects of life, it should be up to them.

## 6   Should the individual also contribute?

One possible objection to the scheme concerns the fact that its receipt does not depend on any actions on behalf of the recipient. It might be thought better to have a scheme that requires some form of matching contribution to the ACE account from the individuals themselves or from their families. So, for instance, the government could offer to match personal or family contributions at a rate of, say, £1 grant for £1 contribution, or at a higher (or lower) rate.

Matching grants have the advantage of encouraging people to help themselves and such schemes are being implemented in the US (Kelly, Gamble and Paxton, this volume). They also mobilize private resources and thus reduce the cost of the scheme to the state. However, matching grants favour those who can contribute more and who are likely (although not necessarily) to be among the better off. To overcome this, the matching rate could be varied with the income of the family (as in some of the US schemes – see Kelly, Gamble and Paxton, this volume): higher for poor and lower for better-off families, and perhaps even dropping to zero for the very well off. Varying the matching rate in this way might make the scheme more politically acceptable but would have the disadvantages already discussed of requiring a means test. It might be better to have the same matching rate for all, but instead to cap the total amount of grant received by any one individual and to count it for lifetime inheritance and gift purposes. The well-off would repay their grants as further bequests came their way, and were taxed at progressive rates.

## 7   What about disincentives?

We have seen that the scheme could offer a number of positive incentives, especially towards greater capital accumulation by the poor. But are there also major disincentives associated with the scheme – aspects that would discourage otherwise socially or economically desirable behaviour? For instance, might not the tightened-up inheritance tax discourage parents from saving for their children, or even from working quite so hard to benefit their families? Might not the existence of the grant itself lead parents to cut back on what they were planning to give to their children? And might not the recipients of the grant be discouraged from saving for themselves?

These seem unlikely dangers. For effective inheritance taxes to weaken the economy in this way, taking care of the next generation would have to be the main motive force for individual achievement. The tendency of the ambitious to delay having children and forge their careers first would seem to suggest that other factors matter more. Also the amounts involved are not that great – especially when compared to the massive inheritances received by a few lucky children under the current situation, which almost certainly do have a discouraging effect on their subsequent work and savings activities.

## 8   Conclusion

In the UK, the present Government is implementing a rather impressive set of measures for alleviating poverty. But it also needs to devise a longer-term strategy for spreading opportunities more widely and so heading off poverty before it occurs. A scheme such as the one we propose here could form a crucial part of such a plan.

The idea that every 18 year old could receive £10,000 from the state could become the cutting edge of a wider ambition to increase opportunity and reduce privilege through capital distribution. The key is to link this potentially popular spending proposal with reforms to a hitherto unpopular and inefficient tax – inheritance tax. Hypothecating inheritance tax revenues to capital grants could help rehabilitate a much-despised tax. However it could only succeed if accompanied by measures to ensure that the sums given out do not go to waste. The price of equal opportunity could be acceptance of an ongoing paternalism, well into adult life.

# Notes

1. The ideas here were first presented in Le Grand and Nissan (2000).
2. Both of the present authors had the idea of a capital grant financed from inheritance tax independently. Indeed one of us published exactly this proposal over ten years ago (Le Grand, 1989). However, as with a number of other imaginative innovations in social policy (such as education vouchers), in fact the idea seems to have originated with Tom Paine, who argued that everyone reaching the age of twenty-one should receive the sum of fifteen pounds sterling out of a 'national fund' financed from an inheritance tax (Thomas Paine, 1797). In more modern times in the UK a similar idea was put forward by the economist Cedric Sandford in the early 1970s (1971: pp. 250–4) and discussed by A. B. Atkinson in his pioneering work on wealth inequality (1972: 233–6). The Institute of Public Policy Research has recently produced a major review of schemes designed to promote asset ownership which contains much useful material on the importance of asset ownership in determining life-chances (Kelly and Lissauer, 2000). The idea of some kind of capital grant to people at the beginning of their working lives has also been extensively discussed in the United States. Michael Sherraden of Washington University in St Louis has proposed setting up what he calls *Individual Development Accounts* – optional, earnings-bearing, tax-benefited accounts in the name of each individual, initiated as early as birth and restricted to specific purposes (Sherraden, 1991: ch. 10; compare Kelly, Gamble and Paxton, this volume; and Fabre, this volume). Finally, Bruce Ackerman and Anne Alstott have put forward a more ambitious idea – a stakeholder grant of $80,000 to everyone at the age of twenty-one with a high school diploma and no criminal record – that is closer to what we are proposing (Ackerman and Alstott, 1999, 2003; also Ackerman, this volume).
3. PEPs (*Personal Equity Plans*), introduced in 1986, offered people the opportunity to invest in stocks and shares and to enjoy dividends and capital gains on these assets tax-free. TESSAs (*Tax-Exempt Special Savings Accounts*), introduced in 1990, gave people the chance to open up savings accounts (one per person) with banks or building societies in which they could save up to £9000 over five years with no tax payable on the interest or bonuses on these savings. Both schemes were phased out following the budget of July 1997 and have been replaced by a new tax-privileged saving instrument, the ISA (*Individual Savings Account*) which is intended to do more to increase long-term saving amongst low-income households (Kelly, Gamble and Paxton, this volume).

# 3
# Stakeholding and Individual Ownership Accounts[1]

*Gavin Kelly, Andrew Gamble and Will Paxton*

## 1  The current distribution of wealth and assets in the UK

There has been a revival of interest in the UK in asset egalitarianism in general and individual ownership accounts in particular in recent years. One reason is that inequality appears to be increasing once again. The new inequality is particularly marked in the ownership of assets. Assets are a stock of resources accumulated over the past and held in different forms such as savings accounts, housing, stocks and shares and pensions. Wealth refers to the net worth of assets held by an individual or household (for example, housing) and may include non-marketable forms of wealth such as pension rights. Financial wealth refers to non-pension and non-housing assets, including deposit accounts, savings and investments but not including balances in current accounts or the value of life insurance policies.

During the post-war period in the UK there has been a gradual reduction in wealth inequalities driven by a range of factors including higher home-ownership rates and strong rises in housing values. Considerable wealth equalization occurred between the late 1930s and the end of the 1970s. Before World War II the top 5–10 per cent owned over 75 per cent of overall wealth, which fell to below 40 per cent in 1976. Nonetheless, wealth inequalities still remain acute (94 per cent of all wealth in 1999 being held by the top 50 per cent of the population) and continue to outstrip income inequalities by a large margin (see Figure 3.1) (Inland Revenue, 2001). The most recent evidence, moreover, suggests that after a long period of stability wealth inequalities may now be starting to grow again (Paxton, 2002). It is certainly the case that the patterns of wealth holdings are increasingly reinforcing income inequality, as income from assets plays a larger role in explaining overall income

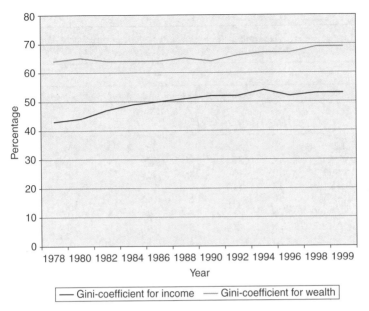

*Figure 3.1*   The Gini-coefficients for wealth and income between 1978 and 1999
*Source*: Inland Revenue Statistics, 2001 and Office for National Statistics, 2000/01

distribution. Indeed, since 1979 the contribution that investment income makes to income inequality has increased almost fourfold (Clarke and Taylor, 1999).

In addition to these very high levels of wealth inequality in the UK, one of the most significant trends during the 1979–97 period has been the *greater polarization of asset holding* between different groups in society, particularly the growth in the proportion of households without any asset ownership at all, doubling from 5 per cent in 1979 to 10 per cent in 1996 amongst the population as a whole and by 10 per cent to 20 per cent for 20–34 year olds. There are also high numbers of 'asset poor' – those with very low levels of asset holdings. From Table 3.1 it can be seen that low levels of investment and low financial wealth are most pronounced amongst younger age groups. Whilst it is important to bear in mind the role of life-cycle effects (we would expect the young to have lower wealth holdings than middle-aged groups) the figures are still striking. Out of those 21–24 year olds who *do* have some assets, 60 per cent have financial wealth of under £500, which only falls to 41 per cent for the 35–44 age group.

*Table 3.1*   Liquid savings by age groups, UK

| A | Age group with no savings or financial investment products (%) | | | | | | | |
|---|---|---|---|---|---|---|---|---|
| | Total | 16–20 | 21–24 | 25–34 | 35–44 | 45–54 | 55–64 | 65 + |
| | 26 | 36 | 36 | 29 | 25 | 22 | 21 | 23 |
| B | Age group with saving or investments, and declaring a value (% in each wealth band*) | | | | | | | |
| | Total | 16–20 | 21–24 | 25–34 | 35–44 | 45–54 | 55–64 | 65+ |
| Up to £200 | 27 | 48 | 41 | 32 | 27 | 21 | 16 | 19 |
| £200–£499 | 14 | 20 | 19 | 17 | 14 | 11 | 10 | 11 |
| £500–£999 | 12 | 15 | 14 | 14 | 13 | 12 | 10 | 11 |
| £1000–£2499 | 13 | 11 | 14 | 14 | 15 | 14 | 12 | 12 |
| £2500–£4999 | 9 | 4 | 7 | 9 | 10 | 11 | 10 | 10 |
| £5000–£9999 | 8 | 1 | 3 | 7 | 8 | 10 | 11 | 10 |
| £10,000–£19,999 | 7 | 1 | 2 | 4 | 7 | 10 | 11 | 10 |
| £20,000–£29,999 | 3 | – | 1 | 1 | 3 | 4 | 6 | 6 |
| £30,000+ | 6 | – | – | 1 | 4 | 7 | 13 | 11 |

* Excludes 'don't know' and 'refused' (12% and 21% of respondents respectively)

*Source*: Financial Research Survey, NOP, 1996

The form in which financial wealth is held also varies considerably across social groups: 47 per cent of wealth held by those in the highest wealth decile is in equity-related products (for example, stocks, shares, unit trusts) compared to just 2 per cent of wealth of the lowest decile, who are far more dependent on National Savings products and other low-risk, low-return savings schemes. These different types of assets have generated very different returns for their holders. For example, £100 invested in government debt in 1978 was worth £188 in 1996 compared to £630 if the same amount was invested in the FTSE 500. This helps to explain the growing importance of asset-holdings in over-all income inequality.

## 2   Alternatives to asset building

### 2.1   Income transfers

Even if it is accepted that policy-makers should be concerned about the underlying trend in assets, many argue that measures which directly target asset building are not the most appropriate policy response. Two arguments are often made in support of an exclusive focus on income transfers. First, it is contended that asset-holdings simply reflect income patterns. The best way of boosting asset building is therefore to increase the incomes of the asset-less; why not spend resources on income-related measures or further skills and training initiatives? The second argument is that patterns of asset-holding reflect life-cycle transitions: saving is a way of smoothing levels of consumption over the life-cycle as income ebbs and flows. Low asset holding today may simply indicate that individuals are earning less than they expect to in the future.

There is of course an element of truth in both of these arguments. Asset-accumulation *is* related to income. Life-cycle factors *are* very important. But there are important points that these arguments fail to pick up. First, there are 'lumpy costs' involved in climbing onto the asset-building ladder. Mortgage companies often require down payments and banks require collateral for loans for new business start-ups. Slightly higher income flows are unlikely to be as effective a means of addressing these issues as an asset-based approach. The role of policy should therefore be to provide a hand-up onto the asset-building ladder. Second, the life-cycle effect on savings, though important, can only explain part of the variation in asset holding across different social groups. At each and every stage of the life-cycle there are significant minorities among the population who hold no assets at all.

Third, having the opportunity to invest one's own financial asset in a house, in learning, or in a business start-up fosters a sense of autonomy and responsibility and allows people who normally have to focus on the immediate circumstances to plan ahead. It helps liberate disadvantaged people from the tyranny of short-term time-horizons. Finally, and perhaps most significantly, there is an emerging body of evidence which sets out the independent effect of asset-holding on key life-chances over and above the impact of income-levels. Evidence suggests that holding an asset has positive social and psychological effects, which leads to these improved life outcomes (Bynner and Paxton, 2001). Again, this suggests the benefits of measures which seek directly to stimulate asset building.

The advocates of asset-based policies regard them as supporting rather than supplanting income- and skills-based approaches towards widening opportunity and reducing inequality. Indeed some asset-building strategies rely on people saving from current income, and consequently they require a simultaneous bolstering of income-based social policies. Similarly increased opportunity will not be achieved by investment in asset-based policies alone; it is only part of a wider policy response which includes investment in education and skills.

## 2.2   Loans

Some will also argue that government should help move people onto the asset-building ladder through the use of targeted loans (for example, subsidized loans for learning, first-time home buyers, new firms and so on) rather than through individual accounts. Given that both loans and assets are ways of resolving some capital market failures they are, to some extent, substitutes for each other. Moreover, loans are often likely to be a cheaper policy response to particular market failures. But an asset-building strategy does have important additional advantages.

First, there is little evidence that loans have a similar beneficial effect to asset holding on the social, psychological and economic outcomes outlined above. Second, an asset-based approach is more openly redistributive: making loan facilities available to everyone does not in itself reduce wealth inequalities in the way that a universal asset-strategy does. Finally, it is difficult to see how a loan system could be devised to change radically the number of low-income people undertaking risky forms of investment. At the moment repayment of government-sponsored loans for risky forms of investment (for example, higher education) tends to be heavily income-contingent; indeed this has been presented as the basis on which loans are compatible with social equity. They tend to work well when most of the group undertaking the risky investment go on to earn enough to pay the loan off. Herein lies the problem. On the one hand, if the main purpose of the loan is to encourage those on below-average incomes to make a risky investment, then an income-contingent repayment system may not be viable (that is, if many of the participants do not go on to earn high enough incomes to pay the debt off). On the other hand, if the loan is not income-contingent then many low income and risk-averse individuals will refuse to bear the risk of the investment. Loans are a useful policy tool but they will not open up new opportunities in the same way that assets do. Individual ownership accounts are therefore likely to become an essential tool for governments that seek to check or reverse the current tendencies towards greater inequality.

## 3   Assets for the 'haves': the policy legacy in the UK

It has long been the case that public policy in the UK has sought to promote individual asset accumulation of one kind or another. Asset-based policy has been a central feature of the welfare state, presided over by governments of both left and right. The defining feature of these policies is that they are primarily geared towards the affluent, what

Richard Titmuss termed the fiscal welfare state. Home-ownership was promoted through some form of mortgage interest tax relief (MIRAS) since the 1920s, and was given a particular boost in the 1980s by the Right to Buy policy of the Conservatives. Personal and employer-based pension plans benefit from tax advantages which are remarkably regressive – it is calculated that half the benefit of pension tax relief goes to the top 10 per cent of taxpayers, with a quarter going to the top 2.5 per cent (Agulnik and Le Grand, 1998). Employee share ownership, a policy which obviously excludes those in the public and voluntary sectors, has also been encouraged through the tax system (a policy which has enjoyed support across the political spectrum). Similarly, the accumulation of financial assets has been encouraged through favoured tax-treatment for savings products. As these initiatives suggest, there is nothing new about the *principle* of government seeking to encourage asset building. The issue is what type of asset accumulation should be promoted, and whether policy should be targeted at particular groups.

Even before the announcement of explicit asset-based policies (which we return to below) there were some indications that the Labour government elected in 1997 was setting about a different approach to asset building. MIRAS was scrapped thereby removing a substantial public support to asset building by middle-income groups. An asset-based approach was used to promote training for the low-skilled in the form of *Individual Learning Accounts* (ILAs). These provided a one-off government match of £150 for a £25 individual contribution to their accounts. Although they were recently suspended, mainly because of fraud, there are plans afoot for a second-generation ILA. This could overcome the previous problems and also make them more of an explicit asset-based policy.[2] Though this chapter is not considering pensions it is noteworthy that the government is attempting to address pensioner poverty through a *State Second Pension* that aims to extend state second pensions to those on low incomes. In addition the new *Stakeholder Pensions* were designed to reach those on low and middle incomes by improving standards of quality and cost control and increasing national insurance rebates. There are however, question marks over whether stakeholder pensions will reach their intended target group and whether the current incentives to save are either appropriate or represent value for money.

There is a wide range of asset-related tax reliefs that are a considerable expense to the exchequer (Table 3.2). Policies introduced since 1997, such as *Individual Savings Accounts* (ISAs) continue the long-standing tradition of relying on tax reliefs to provide incentives for low-income

Table 3.2    Selected tax expenditures

| | Estimated cost (millions) | |
| --- | --- | --- |
| | 1998–1999 | 1999–2000 |
| Private pension schemes | 11400 | 12900 |
| Profit-sharing schemes | 190 | 210 |
| Discretionary share option | 110 | 90 |
| Savings-related share option schemes | 490 | 420 |
| Personal equity plans | 1000 | 1000 |
| Individual savings accounts | 0 | 100 |

Source: Ready Reckoner, 1999

Table 3.3    Penetration of ISAs according to income

| Household income | Total* | ISA holders | Penetration (%) | Share of total ISA holders (%) |
| --- | --- | --- | --- | --- |
| Sub-total | 14051 | 681 | 5 | 100 |
| Up to £2499 | 225 | 0 | 0 | 0 |
| £2500–£4499 | 1301 | 8 | 1 | 1 |
| £4500–£6499 | 1460 | 21 | 1 | 3 |
| £6500–£7499 | 842 | 17 | 2 | 2 |
| £7500–£9499 | 887 | 33 | 4 | 5 |
| £9500–£11,499 | 906 | 46 | 5 | 7 |
| £11,500–£13,499 | 824 | 34 | 4 | 5 |
| £13,500–£15,499 | 702 | 46 | 7 | 7 |
| £15,500–£17,499 | 780 | 36 | 5 | 5 |
| £17,500–£19,999 | 832 | 44 | 5 | 6 |
| £20,000–£24,999 | 1334 | 82 | 6 | 12 |
| £25,000–£34,999 | 1803 | 118 | 7 | 17 |
| £35,000–£49,999 | 1238 | 101 | 8 | 15 |
| £50,000+ | 917 | 95 | 10 | 14 |

* Excludes 'don't know' responses (4432); refusal to answer responses (5324)
Source: Financial Survey, NOP, September 1999

groups to save. The difficulty with this approach is that it will have only a limited impact on those with the lowest incomes, many of whom pay little or no tax, while the affluent gain disproportionately. As we can see from Table 3.3, ISAs, which were specifically geared to increase savings levels among those on lower incomes, are concentrated among those on middle and high incomes: 58 per cent of ISA holders are on incomes of £20,000 or more, compared to 4 per cent held by those on incomes of less than £6500. A large proportion of payments into ISAs have also been made in cash and it is thought that savers are depositing the maximum amount. This leads to the conclusion that ISAs are encouraging current savers to save more, rather than attracting new savers. Despite

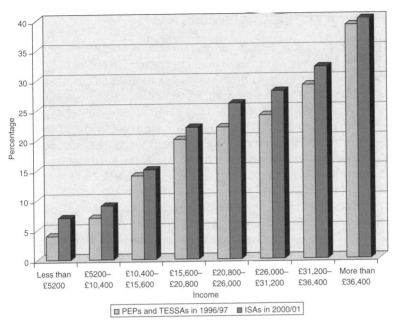

*Figure 3.2*  ISA penetration compared with PEPs and TESSAs

*Source*: Authors' own analysis of FRS data

attempts to make ISAs more attractive to people on low incomes, the penetration of ISAs in 2000/01 in low-income groups has been very similar to that which their predecessors, PEPs and TESSAs achieved in 1996/97 (see Figure 3.2). It is debatable whether the cost of tax relief on ISAs is the best use of public resources since relatively high earners are the principal beneficiaries of these programmes.

What seems to emerge from this shifting pattern of policy measures is the idea that there was some disenchantment with the traditional approach to asset building. The realization has grown that traditional approaches towards asset building have not benefited the disadvantaged. As shown above, the percentage of British adults without *any* assets increased dramatically during the Conservative years – the era of so-called 'popular capitalism'. The strategy of trickle-down asset accumulation failed. Reversing the underlying trend towards greater asset-inequality will require a different approach from the tax-relief route favoured in the past. This is a route that, as we shall see below, the UK government has tentatively started to take.

## 4   Options for an asset-building strategy

The heart of such a strategy will be some form of individual ownership account. There are a number of different options to consider, along with the best way to implement them, both technically and politically.

The first issue is whether such accounts should be universal or targeted. A universal scheme would offer grants to everyone of a particular age group, in order to foster a sense of economic citizenship. Every individual when they become a young adult is guaranteed the right to a share of the nation's wealth and can use it to shape their own life-chances. This will provide every citizen with at least a stake in the market economy and no one will be excluded.[3] Those who favour a targeted approach view asset building instead as a new way of redressing entrenched wealth inequalities and of ensuring that the opportunities that flow from asset ownership are extended to disadvantaged groups. Why would government seek to subsidize asset building for the son of the Duke of Westminster when he is likely to be on a high income and benefit from considerable inheritances? Should not these scarce resources be directed towards the asset-poor? The primary purpose of targeting, reflected in the US *Individual Development Accounts* and the UK *Saving Gateway*, which we outline below – is *not* to foster a common sense of economic citizenship or to institutionalize intergenerational equity, but to combat asset-exclusion and spread opportunity to the poorest. Targeting can take a number of forms: a matched-fund system, an initial capital endowment, or a combination of both.

A second issue is how individual ownership accounts should be funded – whether out of general taxation or from a wealth tax based on inheritance or (more effectively) lifetime gifts. The latter is recommended by both Ackerman and Alstott (1999) and by Le Grand and Nissan (2000, this volume; also Le Grand and Estrin, 1989) on the grounds that it would foster inter-generational equity and erode hereditary privilege and would help legitimize universality as rich families (whose children would benefit from the asset) would be seen to be paying a fair share towards the fund.

A third issue is what the assets can be used for – whether the choices should be restricted or unrestricted. Libertarians favour as few restrictions as possible, allowing individuals the freedom to make their own choices and mistakes. This would reduce administrative costs to the minimum, but many advocates of individual ownership accounts believe that there would be serious problems of legitimacy if a substantial proportion of young people used their grants (funded with taxpayers' money) to support decadent life-styles. This leads to conditions being placed on the purposes for which the accounts can be used to ensure that public money is spent on activities likely to generate real social gains in the form of improved life-chances.[4] An alternative approach is to help people cope with life-transitions, such as having a baby, setting up a home, coping with divorce or bereavement, although one problem with such a life-cycle approach is moral hazard: the policy may set up perverse incentives for individuals to take a course of action that they would not otherwise have adopted. This would be the criticism, for instance, if an asset-account were made available to individuals who were made redundant or got divorced.

A fourth issue is the age at which individuals should be able to access an individual ownership account. If an asset-building policy simply takes the form of a matched saving system for existing adults (for example, IDAs and the *Saving Gateway*) then an age needs to be selected at which individuals (or third parties) can start to contribute to and access the fund (for example, at the age of 18 for ISAs). But some asset-policies may involve the state (and other family members) making a payment into a fund before the beneficiary has reached an age when they are able to use it. For instance, the state may wish to make a payment into a 'children's fund' at the point when a child is born which cannot be accessed until the child reaches 18 (as with the *Child Trust Fund* outlined below). Alternatively, the state may want to make a payment to 18 year olds, a 'young adult fund' that can be immediately accessed by all 18 year olds (or left to accumulate). In either case 18 seems a reasonable age for the beneficiary to be able to start to use the funds.

There are a large variety of ways of designing an asset-building strategy, but the main choice is between targeted individual development accounts and universal opportunity funds. Both these approaches are reflected in the US and UK debates.

## 5   Targeted individual development accounts

### 5.1   The US experience

The debate about extending asset ownership is more established in the US than in the UK. In the US, asset-building programmes have been operational for nearly two decades. The strategy adopted thus far in the US, and to a lesser extent in Canada, has been the targeting of asset-building policies at low-income adults in the form of *Individual Development Accounts* (IDAs) (Regan, 2001b).

IDAs are a policy instrument that seeks to encourage asset-accumulation among low-income individuals in disadvantaged localities (Sherraden, 1991). They are savings accounts that accumulate funds for specified personal development purposes such as post-secondary education, training, starting up a business or home ownership. An individual contribution to the account triggers a matched contribution, in varying ratios, by the state government, business and/or non-profit sources. The IDA programmes are typically administered by local voluntary or non-profit-making organizations. These are small-scale but highly innovative schemes, which while still in the process of early evaluation have expanded in number and there are now approximately 15,000 IDA account holders across the US.

The first federal legislation providing for IDAs came as part of the *1996 Personal Responsibility and Work Opportunity Reconciliation Act* which legitimized state involvement in funding IDAs and stipulated that individuals participating in programmes would not forfeit their eligibility for other means-tested forms of government assistance. Under the Act, states were authorized to use funds from their *Temporary Assistance for Needy Families* (TANF) block grants from the federal government in order to create community level IDA programmes and to match individual deposits in IDAs. In each state wanting to develop IDAs, the Department for Economic Development (or other relevant state department) was made responsible for soliciting proposals from community development organizations interested in implementing the local IDA programme.

More recently the *Assets for Independence Act* (1998) provided funding for the establishment and evaluation of demonstration projects designed to investigate the effects (social, civic, psychological and economic) of asset-building initiatives. This scheme – dubbed *The Downpayments on the American Dream Demonstration* – involves monitoring 13 pilot projects, which provide IDAs for 2000 people. The Act made $125 million available over the five-year demonstration. Over 90 per cent of federal money allocated to support IDA schemes is directed towards providing matching funds for programmes.[5] Non-profit organizations are permitted to match participants' savings anywhere from $0.50 to $4.00 for each dollar of earned income saved. The federal match then equals the non-federal/private one. There is a limit of $2000 federal contribution to any individual IDA over the course of the programme. The *Assets for Independence Act* specifies that up to 9.5 per cent of the federal funds received by the demonstration projects should be reserved for economic literacy programmes, together with project administration and evaluation.

The Act further stipulates that eligibility for the *Downpayments on the American Dream Demonstration* programme should be determined in one of two ways: either on the basis of eligibility for TANF or through qualification for the *Employment Income Tax Credit 1* and meeting a further capital means test. Policy guidelines for states, developed by the Center for Social Development, recommend that IDA programmes are designed to encourage saving amongst individuals with a household income at or below 200 per cent of the federal poverty level, or 80 per cent of the median income in the given locality. By November 1999, it was estimated that 27 states had passed IDA legislation for TANF recipients and/or low-income citizens and that nearly 200 community-based IDA programmes had been initiated or were in the planning stages in the US.

Some important pointers for policy development are emerging from the evaluation of key characteristics of IDAs, which were identified by research into the initial stages of the American Dream Demonstration (Sherraden, Page-Adams and Johnson, 1999). First, IDAs appear to be most successful in promoting asset accumulation among disadvantaged groups where they combine a stable and experienced sponsoring organization; a good programme plan; financial literacy programmes for participants; flexible implementation of any pre-saving requirement and a one-to-one relationship between an IDA adviser and IDA participants. The glitches found in the IDA pilots illustrate some familiar problems of establishing community partnerships: fundraising, specifying the design of programmes and managing organizational relationships. In addition, more in-depth studies found a strong demand for intensive assistance, the need for culturally specific advice, continuing support for business development, the need for flexibility and support to reassess IDA goals and the importance of transparent notification of savings levels and targets.

Despite their widespread popularity, current IDA schemes are often highly localized and targeted towards the needs of a specific neighbourhood or community group. Each IDA programme participating in the American Dream Demonstration targets a certain population from within the pool of eligible recipients. The *Women's Self-Employment Project*, for example, is directed towards African-American women and micro entrepreneurs already affiliated to the self-employment programme. The Heart of America Family Services organization runs an IDA programme in Kansas City that targets area residents and specifically the Latino population.

There have been several attempts, by the Corporation for Enterprise Development (CfED), which monitors IDA activities throughout the US, to get legislation through Congress to bring IDAs into the federal tax code. Currently, matching funds that are provided under the Assets for Independence Act are not taxable, although interest on individual deposits is taxed. A new act – the *Savings for Working Families Act* – is currently going through Congress. If implemented this will provide $6 billion in federal tax credits to incentivize financial institutions to match IDAs and the private sector to invest in IDA programmes. CfED would also like to see a full revision of asset limits, or capital limits in UK parlance, which are found in public assistance programmes.

## 5.2   The UK experience

In the UK, though the debate on asset-building strategies is more novel, there has been some striking progress recently. In 2000, asset-based welfare moved into the policy limelight with the publication of policy proposals by two think tanks, the Institute for Public Policy Research and the Fabian Society. Following this in the lead-up to the last general election the government announced two significant asset-building policy proposals – the *Child Trust Fund* and *Saving Gateway*. The former will break new ground when implemented, being the best example of a universal opportunity fund. The latter draws more directly on the US experience with IDAs.

The *Saving Gateway* is a targeted policy for low-income adults. Through matching people's saving, probably at a rate of pound for pound, it will provide incentives for low-income adults to develop a saving habit and accumulate an asset. The policy was announced in April 2001 and pilots, due to run for two years, started in August 2002. In many ways the *Saving Gateway* has very similar characteristics to IDAs. Only certain low-income groups will be eligible for the accounts, which will run only for a restricted length of time, most likely five years. Drawing on the successful characteristics of IDAs, there will be an important role for trusted local organizations in the delivery of the *Saving Gateway*. Many people in the target group will be wary of mainstream financial organizations and community-based organizations will be important in ensuring that those who should benefit most are reached by the policy. Similarly, the importance attached to financial education as part of IDA programmes will be replicated in the UK context, and the *Saving Gateway*, while first and foremost a tool to help people accumulate assets, will also be used to increase financial literacy and confidence.

There are also fundamental differences between the *Saving Gateway* and IDAs. The most glaring concerns restrictions on the uses for any funds accumulated. Where IDAs direct spending towards on-going investment such as education, in Britain a more libertarian approach has been adopted and people will be able to spend the funds how they like. The government has argued that as the name suggests, the *Saving Gateway* should be thought of as a *gateway* to other savings, helping people to develop a savings habit and to give them a kick-start in asset accumulation.

The second difference regards, not the structure of the account itself, but instead the method of targeting the policy. Although CfED and others would like to deliver IDAs nationally, they remain locally administered area-based policies. The *Saving Gateway* pilots are similarly area-based, but the objective in the UK is ultimately to roll the policy out, making it available nationally to all people who qualify on income grounds. This raises questions about how the successful IDA model, which relies on a locally based, resource-intensive and flexible approach, can be replicated on a larger scale. The pilots will, among other things, be exploring how partnership models between financial institutions, the government and local community-based organizations can be developed which could ensure universal coverage across the country.

Other concerns raised about the *Saving Gateway* will also be addressed in the pilots. One regards the impact of the strong incentives provided by the matching. It would be perfectly rational for people on low incomes to go into debt in order to save into the *Saving Gateway* and receive the matched payments. After repaying any credit the net impact on the asset-holding of the account holder would be reduced. This has been recognized and attempts, in the form of limiting the level of monthly deposits, have been made to structure the policy such that borrowing to save is difficult. Also, while IDAs would appear to suffer from the same problem – even more so it would be thought in programmes with higher match rates – there has been no evidence of widespread borrowing to save in the US. It is also possible that there will be little new saving as people simply transfer financial assets that they already have or simply continue to save as they would have done anyway even without the matched incentive. This still means that people will increase their level of asset holding, though it reduces the likelihood that new savers will be created.

There are a number of generic disadvantages with the IDA and *Saving Gateway* approaches. They share some of the difficulties of means-testing – low take-up among some groups and the exclusion of individuals who fall the wrong side of the income cut-off or just outside the designated area. There is also a disincentive issue. If programmes are geared towards groups who are out of work – those most likely to be the asset-poor – similar provision would have to be available for those on low wages. More generally, IDAs and even a nationally available *Saving Gateway* will remain heavily targeted with a narrow focus. The evidence from the US is that while IDAs have been successful in beginning the process of asset accumulation, the poor still find it difficult to accumulate significant savings. The drawback of the approach is that it would involve fairly substantial administrative change for a relatively small gain. There is also the possibility that if the asset policy is focused too narrowly on those at the margins it may, however mistakenly, be seen simply as rewarding 'failure'. Excluding the majority of the population from the asset-building policy may be unduly unambitious. If the objectives of asset egalitarians are to be achieved and asset-based policies are to make a substantial contribution to creating a genuine stakeholding society then a more fundamental policy is needed to complement the IDA–*Saving Gateway* approach. There are, after all, many young adults from low-to-middle income families who would also benefit greatly from having access to assets.

## 6   Universal opportunity funds

The second approach to asset building would be an *Opportunity Fund*, either some form of *Children's Saving Account* or a *Young Adult's Fund*. These policies would not be tightly focused and could be available for all children or young adults allowing people to start their life with an asset that they can draw on. They would foster a sense of common citizenship by granting all people a financial stake in the society in which they live. This strategy might be seen as an alternative to the IDA approach. In fact the two would complement each other. IDAs address asset poverty and asset exclusion in the short term and *Opportunity Funds* would more fundamentally allow all people to start their lives with a stakeholding fund.

The main difference between the two *Opportunity Funds* is the time when individuals would receive a state endowment. In the case of a *Children's Saving Account* the universal endowment would be paid into an account when a child is born. Over time this would accumulate into a considerable fund and at a given age people would have access to the funds. In the UK this focus on building up assets for children also runs with the grain of the government's child poverty pledge. The distinctive feature of the *Children's Opportunity Fund* is that it seeks to influence the savings behaviour of *parents* as well as the ultimate beneficiary of the fund (the child). It fosters intergenerational investment and the creation of opportunities through bequests from parent (and grandparent) to child, forging a new parent–state compact on the provision of opportunity for 18 year olds.

*Young Adult's Funds* cut out the saving element and provide a universal endowment at the age of 18, and thereafter the individual would make her own contributions. Common to both these approaches is the aim of influencing adults' attitudes towards their *own* futures: promoting self-improvement, personal responsibility and risk-taking. It would mean recasting the economic contract between the individual and the state, and providing a new tool to use to improve opportunity for all.

One of the advantages of a universal policy is that it appears to make it easier to win political support. It is seen as simplifying the administration, and makes it easier to justify to the wealthy by emphasizing common citizenship. Smaller grants if they involved matched funding would require means tests which would pose difficulties and do not necessarily ensure that the middle classes 'buy in' to the policy (Kelly and Lissauer, 2000; Edwards, 2000). In the longer term, if the UK were to move towards annual individual self-assessment for tax, as in the United States, greater opportunities are opened up. Individuals would provide the Inland Revenue with information on their income and capital on an annual basis, including their *Opportunity Fund* contributions. The Inland Revenue could then pay out matched contributions on asset accounts at regular intervals.[6]

## 6.1 The US experience

In the US there has been debate but little progress on *Universal Opportunity Funds*. Variants of both *Children's Savings Accounts* and *Young Adult Funds* have been mooted as have other large-scale asset-building policies. The most ambitious of these came as part of the Democrats' new asset-building agenda, which formed the centrepiece of President Clinton's 1999 State of the Union address. The proposal was for *Universal Savings Accounts* (USAs), funded from the budget surplus, which would be a key part of the effort to 'save' social security. Given that USAs were about the accumulation of savings for retirement they are in some respects quite distinct from the asset-building initiatives discussed in the rest of this chapter. But they are worth outlining as their proposed scale offers a useful contrast to the highly localized and (as yet) small-scale IDA initiatives.

The proposed scheme involved using a system of matched savings accounts to provide pensions for those on low incomes and those without occupational pension plans in which each participant would have received an automatic government contribution to their USA every year in the form of a refundable tax credit. For example, a single taxpayer, with income below $50,000 (gross) or a head of household with income below $75,000 would, under the proposal, have been able to claim up to $400 of matching tax credit. This tax credit would also be available for each partner (between the ages of 18 and 70) in a married couple with family earnings over $5000 and less than $100,000. The automatic credit would have been phased out between $40,000 and $80,000 of adjusted gross income. In total up to $1500 each year could have been contributed to USAs from a combination of personal, voluntary and matching contributions (Perun, 1999).

The USA proposal was truly ambitious and innovative.[7] The White House claimed it would potentially have led to 73 million people who had not been participating in employer-provided pension plans, being eligible to establish savings accounts. The proposal represented the possibility of a highly progressive and nationwide asset-building strategy. The scale of the proposal was, however, a hindrance and was criticized on the grounds of cost, complexity and practicality. USAs would have required a new independent administrative structure to keep and establish the investment programme for the millions of small accounts that would be created.

During the 2002 presidential campaign both candidates proposed large-scale asset-building policies. Al Gore's, which was called Retirement Savings Plus (RSP), drew on some of the features of Clinton's USA proposal. Generous matching funds were included, at rates of up to 3 : 1, which would have been used to provide funds for home ownership and higher education, as well as retirement. George Bush also proposed, but has yet to try and implement, a large increase in the number of IDAs. Interestingly the asset-building agenda in the US is increasingly a bipartisan issue. The right are attracted to notions of increasing personal responsibility and independence while the left support the redistributive implications of asset-based approaches.

In the US, debate on child- or young-adult-focused opportunity funds has been more limited than in the UK. Ackerman and Alstott have proposed the introduction of stakeholder grants for all young adults at the age of twenty-one, to the tune of $80,000 (Ackerman and Alstott, 1999). More recently CfED have proposed a demonstration of a children's savings accounts, which they have called *Saving for Education,*

*Entrepreneurship and Development* (SEED) accounts. The accounts will be intended primarily to help finance post-compulsory education, training and the development of other significant assets, they will provide new-born children with an endowment and then match subsequent deposits from low-income families. A pilot for SEED accounts is of course a long-term project and it seems unlikely that in the near future the US will adopt a large-scale children's or young adults' savings account.

## 6.2 The UK experience

If universal opportunity funds appear a distant prospect in the US, in the UK they are close to becoming reality. At the same time as the Fabian Society proposed a universal young adults' opportunity (Le Grand and Nissan, 2000; Le Grand and Nissan, this volume) the Institute for Public Policy Research (IPPR) developed a proposal for *Children's Opportunity Accounts*. Similar to the proposed SEED accounts, under the scheme all newborn children would receive an initial endowment of £1000 and subsequently children on low incomes would have their savings matched by the state. It was left open as to whether there should be restrictions on the uses for funds that had accumulated by the age of eighteen (Kelly and Lissauer, 2000).

These proposals provoked considerable interest and immediately prior to the 2001 General Election the government announced its intention to establish a *Child Trust Fund*. The core aim of the *Child Trust Fund* (CTF), or the 'baby-bond' as it has been dubbed by the media, is to build the assets of *all* children so that when they turn eighteen they have a fund to invest in their future. After two government consultation papers the full structure of the policy is beginning to take shape (HM Treasury, 2001a,b):

1. It is a universal policy, providing an account and endowment for all newborn children.
2. The State will make an initial endowment of £500 for children from low-income families and £300 for children from wealthier families.
3. Additional top-ups at ages 5, 11 and 16 will be made by the government. Again these will be progressive with £100 for the poor and £50 for wealthier children.
4. The money will be managed by financial services companies.
5. Families, friends and children themselves will be able to make voluntary contributions.
6. There will be no access to the funds before the child turns eighteen.

7. Young adults will be able to spend funds as they like.
8. Important links will be made with financial education in schools, which is now part of the national curriculum.

The eventual size of the fund accumulated will differ depending on a number of variables, including the level of individual contributions and the nominal growth rate assumed. However, a typical fund for a child from a low-income background at the age of eighteen would be approximately £3000–£4000.[8] While this will not necessarily significantly shift overall wealth distribution, it will have an important impact on levels of asset holding among young adults. As we have seen at present many in this group have either very small assets or none at all.

As with the *Saving Gateway*, UK policy-makers have opted for having no restrictions on the uses of funds accumulated in the CTF. This is in contrast to the US, where many assume that there should be restrictions and that financial assets accumulated should be channelled towards positive investment, be it in training, education, housing or enterprise. Although there are libertarian justifications for having no restrictions, practical considerations have been more important. Policing the expenditure of 650,000 children turning eighteen each year and avoiding fraudulent use was seen as problematic. In the UK, policy-makers opted for the most administratively simple approach.

This does not mean that restrictions could not be considered for future policies, be they in the UK or elsewhere in the world. As with IDAs, direct payments could be made from Funds to providers of educational services or mortgage companies. Alternatively vouchers could be issued. If people were to exercise the entrepreneurship option, they could present a business case stating how the funds would be used and there would need to be a monitoring system, which would involve some bureaucratic costs but could be based on existing structures. If restrictions were adopted, unspent funds could be invested in a personal pension or transferred to someone else's fund at a specified age (say 50). This would have two benefits. First, it would have the advantage of not penalizing those who, for whatever reason, planned to but then were not able or inclined to 'invest' in themselves. Second, it would cut down on the likelihood of people squandering their funds on 'investment' programmes that they are not committed to in order to avoid the funds being reclaimed by the state.

The CTF has raised other issues and has not been without its critics (Wakefield and Emmerson, 2001). Many of the debates apply to universal opportunity accounts generally and would be repeated if and when similar policies were introduced around the globe. One fear is that universal opportunity accounts would be seen as a reason for the government to withdraw from supporting people in other areas. For example, if all children are ensured access to a lump sum when they turn eighteen then it might be possible for the state to withdraw further from supporting people in higher and further education. In the US the SEED pilot proposals explicitly state that one of the uses for funds will be 'post-secondary education'. Undoubtedly, some people may use the CTF to meet the costs of higher education. Whether or not this is a problem is debatable. Receiving an asset at eighteen could reduce barriers to entry into higher education. But it is true that the CTF will be dwarfed by student debt which is now on average £10,000 (Barclays Bank, 2001), which means that the interaction between policies for student finance and asset building for young adults needs careful consideration, if a coherent and progressive asset-based approach is to be fashioned across public policy.

## 7  Funding individual ownership accounts

The cost implications for individual ownership accounts can be considerable, particularly for the Opportunity Funds. The proposal by Julian Le Grand and David Nissan would cost £6.5 billion (this volume). The Ackerman–Alstott (1999) proposal would be more expensive again. On top of this, for some proposed schemes there would be the cost of the matching funds component of the Fund which would depend on the ratio selected, the nature of the taper used, and the level of uptake.[9] The CTF will cost in the region of £400–£600 million, which while less than more ambitious options is still a considerable amount of money for a government to spend with no immediate tangible return. Although the CTF will not be funded through a linked reform, some have pushed to join up debates about individual ownership accounts to specific funding mechanisms.

The more limited schemes could be funded from top-rate tax reliefs on pension fund contributions, or the current tax reliefs on *Individual Savings Accounts*. The more ambitious proposals could be funded through a large increase in the current return from inheritance tax, by moving away from taxing estates on death (which has become largely a voluntary tax and yields very little) to taxing lifetime gifts. Tony Atkinson set out how this might be done some time ago (Atkinson, 1972). The principle of such a tax is not a problem, but the political will to implement it certainly is. It would be difficult, but not impossible, to build the kind of consensus which would be required, but it would have to overcome strong opposition from defenders of property rights who would represent the proposed fund as a fundamental infringement of the liberties of existing wealth holders, and who would point to the additional administrative costs of collecting the tax. On the Right at the present time there are calls for inheritance taxes to be abolished altogether, certainly not increased.

There are two visions of society in conflict here. The first stresses the 'rights of property' and in particular the rights of individuals to pass on their wealth to their families. These rights are paramount, and much more important than the obligations of a common citizenship. Robert Skidelsky, reviewing Ackerman and Alstott (1999) has argued that inequality of income and wealth, however great it may be, is never a justification for interfering with the outcomes of the market (Skidelsky, 2000). But although some additional taxation of wealth would be required, even in the most ambitious scheme – that of Ackerman and Alstott – the tax rate would not rise above 50 per cent. This would still enable very large sums to be passed on by individuals to their families. By contrast, the intention of the proponents of asset egalitarianism is not to ensure equal shares, or even equal starting points, but merely that every individual is guaranteed a 'minimum starting point'.

## 8   Building on small beginnings

The role of individual ownership accounts in welfare policy is establishing itself as an integral part of contemporary policy debates. In the US *Individual Development Accounts* have been up and running since the early nineties and in the UK the announcement of the CTF and *Saving Gateway* is of far-reaching importance. Yet this is not the end of the debate. The use of and debate about individual ownership accounts has only just started. The principle that ownership of wealth and assets must be a concern for policy-makers has been established. The role that targeted individual development accounts or universal opportunity accounts can play is now an active part of policy debate and raises a number of questions. In some ways, the most important aspect of a large-scale policy proposal like the CTF is not the value of the fund proposed at present. Instead it lies in the framework and principle it establishes. Once all children have a state-sponsored account from birth further progressive policy development can be considered.

It would be possible, for example, to consider the role that non-financial credits could play in the accumulation of funds. Rewarding voluntary work with such credits would help achieve two objectives, increased levels of civic involvement and also larger assets being accumulated in the CTF. It could also be possible to integrate different individual accounts into a more coherent structure. Children's savings accounts, individual development accounts, pensions and learning-focused accounts could all be brought together to provide a unified scheme covering different uses. Lastly, once the infrastructure and the principle have been established it is, of course possible for the value of funds to be increased. While some proposals for large endowments appear to be politically impractical at present, if more moderate and practical policies prove popular and effective this could change.

If the many streams of asset egalitarianism, from the civic republicanism of Thomas Paine and Thomas Jefferson in the late eighteenth century, through to the market socialism and market egalitarianism of contemporary thinkers, are to become reality, then the role of individual ownership accounts must continue to be explored and expanded. The green shoots of a fundamental shift in western public policy are just appearing. If nurtured with new ideas and political commitment they could grow and achieve the vision of *ownership for all*.

## Notes

1. This chapter draws on the more detailed analysis in Gavin Kelly and Rachel Lissauer (2000).
2. One problem with ILAs is that the £150 is a one-off public contribution to kick-start the fund and it is a 'virtual' rather than a 'real' pot which only comes into existence when the funds are spent.
3. Some universalists do rule out some categories of people such as those with a criminal record or those who failed to graduate from secondary school (Ackerman and Alstott, 1999: 49–53).
4. The libertarian versus paternalism debate on assets mirrors that on the relative merits of a citizen's income and a participation income (see Oppenheim, 1998).
5. The federal component of the funding for any given IDA project must not exceed the non-federal element, the latter comprising both local state funding and private and voluntary sector contributions.
6. Of course there are also a number of disadvantages to moving to annual tax assessments – such as loss of tax revenue, universal testing and joint taxation (Meadows, 1996).
7. It is also noteworthy that USAs would give individuals the right to select between several different investment strategies for the funds in their accounts.

8.  This assumes voluntary deposits of between £50 and £100 a year and a nominal growth rate of 7 per cent (using the guidelines issued by the Financial Services Authority to companies providing pensions and ISAs).
9.  There would, of course, be savings to the Exchequer in the form of reduced dependency on benefits as a result of assets policies working.

# 4
# Sneaking up on Stakeholding[1]

*Robert E. Goodin*

## 1 Introduction

Public policy-makers fall into ruts more easily than most. 'Path dependence' is the technical term. But that is often an overly generous description, suggesting as it does that there might be some objective forces at work (such as the effort involved in retraining all trained touch-typists out of the QWERTY keyboard, for a famous example). Rutted thinking in public policy more typically stems from a simple failure of imagination. Nowhere is this more evident than in relation to the problem of poverty.

If the problem is to prevent people from falling into destitution, then there are many different points at which public policy could conceivably intervene. Welfare policy in most countries is presently in the rut of intervening at the last possible moment: the pattern is to wait until all of a person's other income has been in and counted, and then to provide means-tested public programmes of income support at just the point at which they would otherwise slip into poverty. But it does not take any massive feat of imagination to see that there are various earlier points in the process at which public policy might alternatively intervene. One obvious early-prevention strategy would be for the state to undertake to ensure that (a) everyone has a job and (b) every job pays a living wage (Goodin and Le Grand, 1987: ch. 10). That was the classic 'full employment' strategy – now forsaken and politically all but forgotten – that was practised, however imperfectly, throughout the period of High Keynesianism. In many places, it was an ideal that was paid little more than lip service. But, some such policy was actually implemented (with a gendered twist) in Australasia throughout most of the twentieth century. There, a 'male-breadwinner's welfare state' operated through policies of (virtually) full employment (for working-aged men) and Industrial Arbitration systems to ensure that every worker's wages were sufficient to support a family of four (Hancock, 1979; Castles, 1985, 1997).

More generally it may be said that, if our goal is *income adequacy*, then there are as many potential sources of 'adequacy' as there are of 'income'. People can derive income streams from the labour market, from returns on capital or from private or public transfers. Thus, as Scandinavians have long emphasized, active labour market policies are as much anti-poverty programmes as public programmes of transfer payments (Moene and Wallerstein, 1995). So too, libertarians say, is private charity (Green, 1993) or, Confucians say, are families taking care of their own (Jones, 1990). And so too, advocates of a property-owning democracy from de Tocqueville onward have said, is the allocation of capital in such a way that everyone's income from capital is adequate to meet their basic needs on a recurrent basis (de Tocqueville, 1966 (1835) vol. 1: ch. 3; vol. 2: chs 17, 21; Krouse and McPherson, 1988: 94–5; Goodin, 2001a).

It is that latter sort of strategy upon which I shall be concentrating here. Rawls expresses the basic idea ably, albeit as an afterthought to his own larger theory of justice:

> Property-owning democracy avoids [impoverishment], not by the redistribution of income to those with less at the end of each period, so to speak, but rather by ensuring the widespread ownership of productive assets and human capital (that is, education and trained skills) at the beginning of each period. ( ... ) The intent is not simply to assist those who lose out through accident or misfortune (although that must be done), but rather to put all citizens in a position to manage their own affairs on a footing of a suitable degree of social and economic equality.          (Rawls, 2001: 139)

*Stakeholding*, as that proposal has come to be called in contemporary policy discourse, can be implemented in various ways. It can be done after the modest fashion of the British Labour government's 'Baby Bonus', a small sum put inaccessibly on deposit for a long time, which eventually will grow to become a substantial capital lump sum by the time the child has reached adulthood. Or it can be implemented in a bold fashion right from the start, after the fashion of the proposals by Ackerman and Alstott (1999) or Le Grand and Nissan (this volume; also Nissan and Le Grand, 2000), with everyone upon coming of age being given a large capital sum, financed through inheritance taxes.[2] Put positively, the point is to give everyone 'equal opportunity', a fair start in life. That, clearly, is an emphasis of political philosophers from de Tocqueville through to Rawls. Put negatively, from the jaded policy-maker's perspective, the point of making those capital transfers up front is to obviate the need for continuing income support payments subsequently. The state, it is hoped, can 'get out of the welfare business', by making bold up-front capital transfers instead.

Here I want first to introduce a note of realism on that latter score. There are all sorts of good reasons for giving everyone a decent start in life, but expecting that good start to obviate any need for 'the welfare state as we know it' is not one of them. State programmes of income support (whether of basic income or some other more conditional sort) are still going to be needed, even after we have adopted state programmes of lump-sum capital transfer (even of the most unrestricted basic capital sort). Advocates of stakeholding ought to be realistic on another score, as well. Public policies themselves almost invariably start small and grow. No country is likely to implement the full basic capital programme – together with the death duties required to finance it – all of a cloth, right from the start. What we need are political stepping-stones toward that goal.

Consider the cognate case of basic income. It is now pretty well accepted, among the more realistic advocates of such schemes, that the best they can hope for in the foreseeable future is a more conditional, activity-tested form of *participation income*. So too with proposals for basic capital. Although that would be paid with no strings attached – as unconditionally as basic income would ideally be – political realities probably dictate that it be introduced in a conditional form in the first instance. The particular form of conditionality I shall be suggesting could be dubbed *project capital* – capital paid to people on condition they specify how the capital will be used to help them become self-supporting. And if merely asking them what they are going to spend the money on is not sufficient to make the scheme politically palatable to the broader public, I have another suggestion for a further condition that might be harmlessly added as well.

The larger point is that political realism dictates that we be reasonably modest in our claims as to what unconditional capital grants will do for us: specifically, they will not prevent altogether the need for continuing income transfers as well. And we ought to be reasonably modest in what sort of capital grants we seek: in the first instance, we probably ought to be prepared to content ourselves with some more conditional forms of capital grant, letting the idea of public transfers of capital sink in before taking the next steps, making those grants less and less conditional in form.

## 2   What happens when you lose your stake?
## The continuing need for income support

One fundamental fact to hold in mind about stakeholding is that stakes are wagered, and wagers are lost. Any gambler knows as much. That palpable fact is all-too-easily elided by advocates of stakeholding who allow us to imagine that those lump-sum capital transfers can substantially substitute for continuing income-support policies.[3] This is not a criticism peculiar to stakeholding proposals; the same could be said for advocates of social insurance. Throughout the first half of the twentieth century, they harboured similar hopes that social insurance could substantially substitute for means-tested poor relief. And the same can be said of those who are currently advocating private pensions as a substitute for public ones.

The problem with all those schemes, seen as substitutes for rather than supplements to public systems of income support, is that there will always be a certain proportion of people who fall through the cracks. For one reason or another, their income from those other sources – social insurance entitlements, or private pensions, or whatever – will leave them below the poverty threshold. At that point the residual programmes carried over from the earliest poor laws must kick in, providing social assistance to people whose own means are inadequate.

The reasons people fall through cracks in social insurance or private pensions have largely to do with programme design, which we might hope to be able to redesign programmes to eliminate. Thus, for example, there is an obvious problem in how to vest the old-age social insurance entitlements of people who are not themselves in paid labour and making contributions toward their own social insurance. We conventionally fix that in large part by deeming non-employed spouses and dependants to be covered by the contributions of the waged spouse. That covers most people, but not all: some people are both unemployed and unpartnered; and some employed people's spouses are themselves unemployed as well. Many countries simply give up at that point and accept that those people will be burdens on the general social assistance system in old age (just as during other periods of their lives). But other countries try to 'fix' social insurance to cover them as well. In the Netherlands, for example, the social security agency providing the unemployed with their current benefits also contributes toward their old-age social insurance pension, as if it were their employer.

Whereas there might be some hope – however chimerical – of papering over the cracks in those sorts of schemes through programme redesign, there would seem to be less hope in the case of stakeholding. Of course programme design matters there, too; and stakeholding may well pose certain fixable problems in that regard. For example, the stake may not – indeed, in the programme's early years probably will not – be large enough to yield an adequate income stream, even if invested wisely. That obviously is a fixable problem (intellectually, if not politically). The deeper problems we are likely to encounter with people falling through the cracks of basic capital schemes are less amenable to programme redesign. It is an absolutely essential element of stakeholder proposals to provide people with capital grants that they are to use as they please to generate an income stream. The scheme is therefore inevitably susceptible to bad choices, or to good bets gone wrong. There is no way to design those risks out without changing the essential nature of the stakeholding proposal (Ackerman and Alstott, 1999: 213; Le Grand and Nissan, this volume).

With stakeholding as with social insurance and private pensions and all other schemes, when the first tier entitlements are exhausted the state will have to step in with supplemental income assistance to prevent people from falling into serious hardship. The state will have to do that – or else let people fall into hardship. Some stakeholding advocates might be prepared to do just that, letting happen whatever may. 'After all', they may say, 'people had their chance and muffed it; they cannot expect to have a continuing call on state resources' (Ackerman and Alstott, 1999: 194–6). But that latter is a distinctly unattractive approach. In the long run, it is probably politically unviable, as well. Notice that even Americans determined to 'end welfare as we know it' only repealed Aid to Families with Dependent Children. The poor law remained on the books (albeit of each of the fifty separate states). Conceivably, general stakeholding might change public attitudes, making people less tolerant of those who had a decent stake that they then recklessly blew than they now are of those whom they reckon never had a fair chance. The point remains that, even where, as in the US in recent years, the rhetoric of 'equal opportunity' clearly dominates the rhetoric of 'equal results', people are still given social assistance to tide them over when they have recklessly squandered their unemployment cheque.

## 3   Making stakeholding politically palatable: the case for conditional capital grants

The first note of political realism introduced above was: 'Don't oversell the stakeholding proposal, pretending it can do things that it can't.' The second note of political realism to which I now turn is: 'Don't push too hard; settle in the first instance for small steps that will encounter less political resistance, but which will set us inexorably on the path toward full stakeholding.' We know where the political sticking points with stakeholding are likely to come from, judging from objections encountered by cognate schemes for unconditional transfers of public monies such as basic income. The first seemingly inevitably worry is, 'Where is the money coming from?', as evident from replies to van der Veen and Van Parijs (1987). The second seemingly inevitable worry is, 'Isn't it socially irresponsible to give people something for nothing?', as evident from replies to Van Parijs (2001; see more generally van der Veen and Groot, 2000).

The most famous stakeholding proposals – Ackerman and Alstott's (1999) and Nissan and Le Grand's (2000) – are both certainly vulnerable on the first score. Both schemes would rely upon wealth or inheritance taxes to raise the substantial sums required. Intellectually honest and ethically defensible though it may be to say so, doing so is politically suicidal. Inheritance taxes have long been the 'third rail' of tax policy: touch them, and you are dead, politically. Say what you may about how the taxes might not have to be all that high, and say what you may about generous tax-free thresholds (Le Grand and Nissan, this volume: 35–7; Nissan and Le Grand 2000: 7–9), that basic fact of tax politics is likely to remain. And as regards Ackerman and Alstott's proposed wealth tax, the reassurance we feel at being told 'no fewer than twelve countries in the OECD tax wealth annually' is immediately undermined by the devastating caveat, 'although only Denmark and Sweden have imposed rates as high as those we recommend' (1999: 100).

The Ackerman-Alstott scheme is vulnerable on the second score as well. They are insistent on the proposition that funds disbursed under their scheme should be available to people to use just however they please:

> In our many conversations on the subject, somebody invariably suggests the wisdom of restricting the stake to a limited set of praiseworthy purposes – requiring each citizen to gain bureaucratic approval before spending down his eighty thousand dollars. Won't this allow us to redistribute wealth and make sure the money is well spent?

This question bears the mark of the welfarist mindset. The point of stakeholding is to liberate each citizen from government, not to create an excuse for a vast new bureaucracy intervening in our lives. If stakeholders want advice, they can buy it on the market. If people in their twenties cannot be treated as adults, when will they be old enough? (Ackerman and Alstott, 1999: 9)

Whilst admitting the principle, Le Grand and Nissan (this volume: 37) are politically more realistic: 'there would be no surer way to lose popular and political support for a system of capital grants than a few well-publicized cases of young people blowing their grants on cocaine or wild holidays'; so they make their grants payable only upon approval by trustees of local worthies – smacking uncomfortably of the Poor Law Guardians of old.

## 3.1 The basic proposal

Asset building is increasingly popular as an anti-poverty strategy (World Bank, 2001: ch. 5). Pursuant to that, there are many different proposals for capital grants from the public purse.[4] Here I shall focus on one particular version proposed, but never implemented, by Australia's then-Minister of Social Security, Peter Baldwin in 1995. The particular merit of that proposal over many others lies in its greater political feasibility, being both strictly conditional and literally costless to the national Treasury.

The proposal itself came poorly packaged. It came in a meandering paper, unfortunately entitled *Beyond the Safety Net*. (Bad imagery: in every circus I have seen, the only thing beyond the safety net is the cold, hard ground.) It was unfortunately phrased as if it were a matter of 'borrowing against one's future social security entitlements' (Baldwin, 1995: 48–9). In private discussions with Departmental officials, it became clear that there was no intention that entitlements to future income support from the social security system would be in any way reduced for people who received such a capital grant, should they subsequently suffer financial hardship. The paper, Departmental officials were privately at pains to emphasize, was written wholly by the Minister himself and printed at his own expense. In short, it is hardly surprising that the innovative proposal never got anywhere near being approved by Cabinet, much less implemented in the dying days of Keating's ostensibly Labour government.

Still, the thinking underlying the proposal is interesting and deserves a much wider airing that it ever got, in Australia much less anywhere else. The idea is this. Invite people who have been on unemployment benefit for 12 months or more to submit to the Department of Social Security proposals for how they might get off unemployment with the assistance of a modest capital grant – something in the order of one or two years' worth of unemployment benefits. A skilled tradesman might propose buying the tools of his trade, if he had been using his previous employer's and did not have a set of his own. Some people might propose setting up a company, others buying a fish and chip shop. The Department would vet the proposals, and if they thought the proposal had a serious chance of success the individual would be given the capital grant.

The calculations underlying the proposal were these. The longer you are unemployed, the longer you are likely to remain unemployed. Unemployment is not like a queue, where the longer you have been in it the sooner you will be out of it. Just the opposite: the long-term unemployed are more like decreasingly fresh goods on the florist's shelf, more likely to be passed over the longer they have already spent on the shelf (Budd, Levine and Smith, 1988: 1071). Statistics suggested that during this period in Australia people who had been unemployed for one year could expect, on average, to be unemployed for another four years.[5]

Now, suppose you gave selected individuals a capital grant, out of the Department of Social Security budget, equal to two years' worth of their unemployment benefits. Suppose the bureaucrats are only moderately good at picking winners: half of those to whom they give grants fail, and fall back on unemployment benefit; but the other half make a success of it and are off unemployment benefit for good. Given that those people would otherwise have remained on that benefit for four years, the Department has broken even. It cost no more to give the capital grants than it would have done to pay them unemployment benefits. And, of course, if the Department manages to pick winners at a higher rate, or if people would have been on unemployment benefit for more years in the absence of that intervention, then all the better.

## 3.2   Political feasibility

Such policies stop well short of constituting anything like basic capital, which (like the basic income which it parallels and for which it might partially substitute (Ackerman and Alstott, 1999: 210–16)) is supposed most fundamentally to be unconditional in virtually every respect. Conditional capital grants of the sort here in view would be doubly conditional. They would be conditional, firstly, upon the *unemployed for a year test.* They would be conditional, secondly, upon the *good project test* (as in Le Grand and Nissan, this volume). Unfortunate though conditionality might be from a principled perspective, it does serve to make those sorts of grants politically more palatable. The first condition, together with established sociological facts about the way labour markets work, underpins the calculation as to how much might potentially be saved by the Treasury in getting these people off unemployment benefits. The second condition reassures us that capital will be concentrated on those most likely to succeed, and hence most likely to yield such savings.

Politically, this is one of the great selling points for conditional capital grants: they are costless. More precisely, conditional capital grants will cost the Treasury no more than existing policies of income support for the long-term unemployed. And from the point of view of the national economy as a whole, of course, such transfers will contribute to economic growth rather than constituting the drag on it that economists so often say that welfare payments are. From the point of view of the recipients, of course, financial independence and the potential for a substantially higher standard of living than unemployment benefits provide makes the conditional capital grant much preferred as well. It is, in short, a classically win–win proposition: no one loses; everyone gains.

That is why this is such a good way to 'sneak up' on basic capital. Advocates of basic capital may regard it as a (very small) first step in that direction, and embrace the proposal for that reason. But you do not have to be an advocate of basic capital to embrace the proposal in view. You merely have to be a believer in efficiency: given however much or little we are spending on public support for people incapable of supporting themselves, those public monies should be spent as efficiently as possible; they should provide as much support to people as possible within the budget constraints. If paying some of the money to people in the form of project grants rather than as day-to-day income support will have the longer-term effect of making those people more self-supporting, then that is the best way of spending the money to maximize the bang for the buck. Even the most hard-nosed efficiency expert who does not care one whit about basic capital must readily concede that point.

## 3.3   A variation that is even more politically feasible

In what is aptly called 'the mean season' (Block et al., 1987), win–win might not be enough for some electorates. It is not enough that the public purse be protected; mean-spirited voters want to ensure that no one gains anything more than they strictly deserve. It is particularly important to them that no one is seen to be getting something for nothing. That is the main complaint against basic income (White, 1997, 2000a; Widerquist, 1999; Goodin, 2001b, 2002). In the case of basic income, the solution is to make sure that the recipients give back something in exchange for the 'free lunch', in the form of socially useful participation of some sort or another. Insofar as some such payback is politically required by mean-minded electors, not content with merely making capital grants conditional on some acceptable proposal for how to sue the money, or with repayment of the grant out of one's estate when one dies (Ackerman and Alstott, 1999: ch. 5), there are certain further things that can be done to make 'basic capital' schemes politically more palatable.

Suppose we model conditional capital grants on the sorts of public student loan schemes in place in the more generous places in the world. Suppose, like Australia, we do not require recipients to repay until after they have begun earning more than average weekly earnings. Suppose we made the 'loan' interest-free up until that point. Suppose, furthermore, we guarantee that – come what may – recipients would not have to start repaying until ten years after the first such grant was made to them. The upshot of such a scheme would be to reassure mean electorates that no one is getting something for nothing, at least insofar as anyone who could (easily) repay will be required to repay. But at the same time, recipients are not being put under a very great hardship. After all, these are people who when they got the grant would have been earning (mostly in state benefits) somewhat less than half the average weekly earnings; so getting their earnings up to fully the average weekly earnings would be quite an improvement for them. And guaranteeing that they would not have to start repaying for fully ten years from the date of the grant puts the whole issue of repayment well beyond the planning horizon of most people, thus providing a further guarantee that the requirement of eventual repayment will not be a disincentive to uptake.

As an aside, I should say that I commend this strategy of 'delayed repayment' or 'delayed withdrawal' in the design of means-tested social benefit programmes more generally. Culture of poverty theorists tell us that poor people have a much shorter planning horizon than is rational in terms of discount rates implied by objective factors such as interest rates, risk and uncertainty, and so on.[6] But if so, why not take advantage of that for social policy purposes? Why not let these known psychological propensities wipe out the problems of incentives, tapers, withdrawal rates and poverty traps that so befuddle hyper-rational economistic designers of means-tested benefit programmes?

## 3.4 The next natural extension: taking care of the kids

This proposal for conditional capital grants is hitched to issues of long-term unemployment, leading us to think first and foremost of recipients as being people of prime working age. But strictly speaking there is no need for that. So, for example, when older people fall out of work, they too become a charge on the public purse, whether that charge is couched in terms of pensions or disability benefits which are so often paid pending their reaching pensionable age (Kohli et al., 1991). Some of those older people might have good ideas on how to start up a business, if only they had a bit of capital to hand. There is no reason they should not apply, and receive, conditional capital grants on the same basis as anyone else, whatever their age.[7] And so long as their public pensions cease if their businesses succeed, then those grants would once again be cost-neutral to the Treasury.

Rather more needs to be said about the other end of the age spectrum. Proposals for stakeholding strive above all to ensure equal opportunity in the sense of a fair start in life for everyone. They are in that way aimed principally at youths on the cusp of adulthood. But if that is the ordinary target group of basic capital proposals, my conditional capital grant variation seems ill suited to hitting that target. Instead of giving people a tidy lump sum on their eighteenth birthday, my scheme would require that recipients suffer fully a year's unemployment before applying. Instead of ensuring everyone gets a good start, my initial variant on this policy would apply only to those who have got off to a bad start; and furthermore, it would provide an incentive (insofar as the capital sum is an attractive prospect) for everyone to get off to a bad start.

Here is the variation on my conditional capital grant scheme that I would propose to take care of this special case of young adults. Recall that unemployment rates among youth are very high: often twice or three times that of people of prime working age. Recall further that unemployment leads to unemployment: having been unemployed once makes you statistically more likely to be unemployed again; having been unemployed for longer makes you statistically more likely to remain unemployed longer still. Finally, unemployment leads to crime, incarceration and still larger costs to society, counted purely in terms of a prisoner's room and board. Far from being a welfare-state laggard, the US actually spends about the same proportion of its GDP on welfare as any other OECD country and has about the same proportion of people on welfare, once you come to see the US Federal Prison System as America's own peculiar form of 'indoor relief' (Western and Beckett, 1999).

Given all that, there is a compelling case for preventing young adults from starting off down that track at all. We can winkle out the relevant statistics: what are the chances of an 18-year-old being unemployed? if unemployed, what are the chances of that unemployment being long-term or leading to incarceration? if that transpires, what would be the costs to Treasury? Having done those sums, we can – just as with those who are already long-term unemployed – calculate what it would be worth to prevent that. Then we can, in the same fashion as before, determine what the odds are of grant assessors picking winners among the proposals submitted to them, and pay each successful applicant a conditional capital grant in that amount. Youngsters would on this proposal be required to submit proposals, just like anyone else, specifying what they would do with their capital grant and how that would make them financially self-sufficient thereafter. In many cases, that would amount to investing in their human capital. Indeed, we might roll education grants that are already being paid to students in further education into this scheme: they are a clear instance of precisely this logic (Ackerman and Alstott, 1999: 51–7). But even people with high human capital need a bit of financial capital to start up a successful enterprise; and people with even modest human capital can often make a success of things, if only they are provided with a bit of physical capital.

The repayment scheme that I have floated for conditional capital grants in general is, as I have said, modelled on the repayment requirements already applied to higher education loans across several jurisdictions. So, in a way, the conditional capital grant scheme more generally might be seen as merely an extension of the 'human capital grants' we currently pay to students in higher education. Why should conditional capital grants be available for only one particular form of human capital, when a variety of other forms of human, physical and financial capital might serve essentially the same social function?

## 4   Conclusion

Friends of basic capital will be as disappointed with these proposals for a conditional capital grant, as friends of basic income are with proposals for mere participation income. It is not universal; it is not unconditional. And that is a pity. But more is the pity, politically that is probably the best we can do, for now.

The great virtue of these more modest schemes is that they just might be politically possible. Furthermore, far from being a dead end, there is then a natural dynamic by which they can and probably will subsequently be expanded in more universal and less conditional ways. Once the programme has been shown to work for kids and the long-term unemployed, mid-career workers will start asking why they have to wait fully a year in dole queues before they become eligible; and that will be a question asked not just by workers who have fallen unemployed but also by all those who, in the newly flexible labour market, reasonably fear they might. Once project assessors get some experience in assessing proposals, they will become more confident and less conservative in their judgements of what might work; and, while they will rule out some projects even more firmly than before on the basis of that experience, we might reasonably expect them to become ever more open to novel proposals once their baseline success rate with 'tried and true' sorts of proposals is assured. Finally, further down the track, we might start thinking of even larger conditional capital grants; of the state's grant taking the form not just of a loan but of an equity share. The state might thus become a shareholder, with a beneficial interest in the activities of the person and the enterprise s/he created, guaranteeing not to sell its interest for a specified period of time (or not to sell it all at once, or whatever).

Who knows exactly where it might all lead? But a programme of conditional capital grants would be a small, politically feasible step, well worth taking in its own right in terms of the impact on both the long-term unemployed and the national Treasury. And the next steps that most immediately follow seem to lead down a slippery slope toward the sort of basic capital that, in principle, we would most like to see.

## Notes

1. This chapter has roots in a 1995 workshop convened by the Australian Institute of Health and Welfare, jointly with the then Department of Social Security, to discuss Baldwin (1995). I am indebted to Diane Gibson, Peter Saunders and public servants protected by anonymity for discussions at that time. The present version was written at Nuffield College, Oxford and the LSE and presented to the American Political Science Association Annual Meetings, Boston, August 2002. I am grateful, then and later, for comments from Bruce Ackerman, Brian Barry, Jurgen De Wispelaere, Keith Dowding, Julian Le Grand, Carole Pateman, Robert van der Veen and Stuart White.
2. Precursors include Le Grand (1989) and Snower (1993: 711–13), and further back Tom Paine (Ackerman and Alstott, 1999: 181–2) and nineteenth-century theorist François Huet (Cunliffe and Erreyghers, 2003).
3. As Le Grand and Nissan's contrast (this volume: 29–31) between 'preventive' and 'curative' welfare states might seem to suggest.

4. Many summarized by Le Grand's and Nissan (this volume) and Kelly and Lissauer (2000). Start-up grants are widely discussed in the US, especially in recent years; they have long been an element of Scandinavian active labour market policies. Unlike the Baldwin proposal to be discussed below, those other grants would typically entail additional costs to the Treasury; and they would typically come in the form of loans that recipients are expected to repay, often on vaguely commercial terms that would be far less generous than would be the case on the plan I float below as a variation on the Baldwin proposal.

5. Divided roughly equally between this and probable successive spells which a previously long-term unemployed person could statistically expect to experience over his or her working life, and which the capital grant is supposed to prevent once and for all. That was the basis upon which Departmental calculations proceeded, anyway. For academic discussions of these issues, see for example, Chapman, Junankar and Kapuscinski (1992).

6. Actually, I would argue that the objective uncertainties surrounding life at the bottom are such as to make a much higher time-discount rate rational for them than for others: but that is a further argument, not strictly necessary for the case here being made.

7. In calculating their chances of succeeding, we may (or may not) want to allow assessors of project proposals to take into account age-related statistics on the success rates of projects undertaken by such people.

# 5
# Freedom, Reciprocity, and the Citizen's Stake[1]

*Stuart White*

> the social state is advantageous to men only if all have a certain amount, and none too much.
>
> Jean-Jacques Rousseau, *The Social Contract*[2]

## 1  Introduction: what kind of stake is just?

A democratic social order is one in which individuals can mutually affirm the social arrangements in which they live as respecting their standing as free and equal citizens (Rawls, 1993; Cohen, 2003). For freedom and civic equality to be genuine, citizens must have a reliable claim on resources, on terms that do not compromise their independence. The policies and institutions of developed welfare states obviously go a long way towards meeting this goal. But it is not clear that they go far enough. While preventing a good deal of deprivation, these policies and institutions are often targeted at relieving the symptoms of underlying asset inequality, rather than reducing this inequality itself. As such, they do not necessarily provide the less fortunate with the dignity and self-confidence that can flow from asset ownership (Bynner and Paxton, 2001). Moreover, such policies and institutions often come with conditions and requirements that limit the immediate freedom of action of those they assist. Hence, there is a growing interest in what might be called *citizen's stake policies*: policies which do aim to give citizens assets or their equivalent in the form of guaranteed income streams, and so enable economic cooperation to proceed on a footing of real equality between independent individuals. One way of providing this citizen's stake is to pay each citizen a guaranteed, but non-mortgageable stream of income received periodically throughout his or her life. In the British context, this idea is referred to as a *Citizen's*

*Income* (CI). There is no reference to any standard of basic need in the usual definition of CI. But most advocates of CI propose as a long-term goal the introduction of CI set at or close to a level sufficient to meet a standard set of basic needs (though, in Britain, advocates of CI usually exempt housing costs from coverage by a CI). They envisage that many, though by no means all, other welfare benefits (and tax reliefs) would be integrated into this CI.

Arguably, however, a democratic social order ought also to be governed by a principle of productive reciprocity. Those who share in the social product should, as an expression of their respect and concern for their fellow citizens, conceived as equals, make a contribution to this product (at least if they are productively capable). As John Rawls puts it: 'all citizens are to do their part in society's cooperative work' (Rawls, 2001: 179). This principle of reciprocity creates a problem for CI advocates. Wouldn't a CI allow citizens to share in the social product without meeting this contributive obligation? If so, would it not permit citizens to treat others unjustly?

This paper continues an exploration I started in earlier work (see especially White, 2002, 2003a) as to how we might reconcile concerns for freedom and productive reciprocity in the design of a citizen's stake-policy. I shall proceed as follows. Section 2 explains in more detail the sense in which I think a concern for freedom supports a CI. Section 3 explains the value of productive reciprocity and considers some responses to the objection that a CI would allow citizens to enjoy income in violation of this principle. In sections 3 and 4 I then consider other variants of the citizen's stake designed to address concerns for both freedom and reciprocity. Section 4 briefly discusses the proposal for a Development Grant. Section 5 outlines the proposal for a Time-Limited Citizen's Income. Section 6 concludes.

## 2   Citizen's income and individual liberty

The value to which proponents of CI most frequently appeal is that of liberty (Van Parijs, 1995; Fitzpatrick, 1999). The basic idea is that liberty has material/economic preconditions and that a CI secures these preconditions. If one takes as a normative premise the idea that individuals have a right to liberty then it might be argued that a CI is justified as a way of securing this right. This germ of an argument can be elaborated in different ways. Here I shall focus on what I think is the most compelling elaboration of the freedom-based argument for CI.

It is important to appreciate that poverty reduces liberty quite directly. Let us say that one lacks the liberty to do some action if others can intervene, with the power of the law behind them, to make you desist from doing this action. Now any action requires some external resource. Even passive meditation, for example, requires a space in which to meditate, and this space is an external resource. If someone has full private ownership of an external resource, that means he/she can legally prohibit others from using this resource and can, therefore, prohibit others from performing any action which requires this resource. For example, if I fully own a particular space then I am legally empowered to make you desist from performing any action, such as meditation, in this space. Now imagine that every external resource in the world has some private owner (that is, someone who has full private ownership rights in the resource). Imagine, finally, someone – call him Jim – who is suddenly thrown into this world without any private ownership rights in any external resources. It follows from what we have said thus far that Jim is not only poor but, in virtue of his poverty, unfree to do anything. He is radically unfree because every time he tries to act, he must lay claim to some external resource which belongs to some other person, and that person can force Jim to desist from using this resource, and thus from performing the action which requires this resource. There is, therefore, no action he can perform which someone somewhere is not legally empowered to prevent or stop. Jim's absolute poverty translates into an absolute lack of liberty (here I follow Waldron, 1993b; see also G. A. Cohen, 1997).

Jim's case might seem a little extreme, but, as Jeremy Waldron has explained, the situation of many homeless individuals in contemporary capitalist societies is arguably not far removed from that of the imaginary Jim (Waldron, 1993c). Consider something as basic as the freedom to sleep. A homeless person is not free to sleep in any privately owned place because he is not free to be in those places. To be sure, homeless people are free to be in public spaces, such as public parks and pavements. But if the local authority passes a law, as many city authorities in the USA have done, that forbids citizens from sleeping in these public places, then the homeless are not free to sleep in these places either. Wherever a homeless person lays down his head, someone somewhere is legally entitled, under the realistic assumptions we have made, to make him or her move on. The homeless individual thus lacks the liberty to do something as basic as sleep.

Now if one thinks that all individuals have some sort of entitlement to some modicum of this simple negative liberty, then one must recognize how this implies an entitlement of some kind to the external resources that, we can now see, are essential to this kind of liberty. A CI is one way we might secure for all the resources necessary for such liberty. Having said that, however, we must acknowledge that this line of argument does not clearly pick out CI as against other ways of providing a basic safety net for all. We could also secure a modicum of basic negative liberty for Jim through a means-tested welfare payment, or, assuming that Jim is able to work, by a system of guaranteed jobs. Is there, then, a way of strengthening the liberty argument specifically for CI?

Go back to the case of Jim. According to one school of thought, what makes Jim unfree is not merely the *actual* interference he suffers at the hands of property-owners eager to move him off their property, but also his thoroughgoing *vulnerability* to such interference. Perhaps some property-owners desist from preventing him from using their property to perform basic actions like washing or urinating or sleeping. But in the world we have imagined, Jim can only ever perform such actions with the permission of the relevant property-owners. He therefore lives under the shadow of interference even when he is not actually subject to it, and merely to live within this shadow is in itself a constraint on one's freedom (Pettit, 1997; Skinner, 1998). Pettit (1997: 85–7) explains that to be subject to the arbitrary will of another in this way 'is to suffer an extra malaise over and beyond that of having your choices intentionally curtailed. It is to have to endure a high level of uncertainty (. . .) [that] makes planning much more difficult (. . .) and [it] is to have strategic deference and anticipation forced upon you at every point.' It is this conception of freedom – freedom as non-dependency – that Jean-Jacques Rousseau is getting at when he writes (in his *Discourse on Inequality*) that the worst thing that can happen in human relationships is 'to find oneself at the mercy of another' (Rousseau, 1984: 125). Now surely if any principle is basic to a democratic social order, in which people are to live together as free and equal citizens, it must be that no person should have to live 'at the mercy of another'. Economic deprivation can clearly produce dependency of this sort and this fact reinforces the case for some sort of safety-net (Pettit, 1997: 158–63). But it might be further argued that the distinctive unconditionality of a CI offers crucial added protection against dangers of dependency. For the unconditionality of the CI means that payment of the income grant is not subject to anyone's discretion. This in itself diminishes one's subjection to potentially arbitrary power exercised by welfare bureaucrats. In addition, it may well strengthen one's ability to resist would-be dominators in other spheres such as employment and in the home. The point is that one can rely on the income from a CI to be there, and immediately, in a way one typically can't in a more conditional welfare system in which eligibility tests have to be satisfied before any benefit is paid. And this makes it that much easier for the employee (or wife) to walk out on the abusive employer (or husband). If one thinks that freedom includes non-dependency, and that universal freedom should be a primary goal of social policy, then one has a strong reason for preferring a CI to other possible ways of providing a safety-net. (See White, 2003b, for further discussion of this issue.)

# 3 Citizen's income and distributive justice

That a CI promotes non-dependency is an attractive reason to support CI. But, as I intimated above, CI is not morally unproblematic. A standard objection is that a generous CI will allow citizens to live off the labours of their fellow citizens without making, or showing any willingness to make, a productive contribution in return. It would allow people to share in the social product in violation of a principle of productive reciprocity, and would thus permit people to take unfair advantage of – to exploit – others (see Elster, 1986; van Donselaar, 1997; White, 1997).

The idea that economic justice centrally requires some kind of productive reciprocity between citizens, so that income entitlements track productive contributions, is one that can be elaborated in different ways, and some of these ways are distinctly non-egalitarian. The particular conception of reciprocity to which I am appealing here is what one might call the *fair-dues conception of reciprocity* (see White, 2003a: ch. 3). According to this conception of reciprocity, if the economic institutions of a society are sufficiently just in other respects (in particular, sufficiently egalitarian in opportunities and rewards for work) then all those who claim a share of the social product available to them under these institutions have an obligation to make a decent productive contribution to the community in return. The basic intuition is that, in the context of an otherwise sufficiently fair economic system, each of us should 'do her bit'.

Far from being inegalitarian, something like this conception of reciprocity has often featured in egalitarian accounts of economic justice. The classic socialist slogan, 'From each according to ability, to each according to need', can be understood as expressing one version of this idea: in the context of institutions that reward workers according to need, all have a duty to work according to their ability. A version of the fair-dues conception of reciprocity can also be seen in John Rawls's theory of justice. As Rawls has made clear since the publication of *A Theory of Justice*, the minimum income share to which citizens are entitled under the difference principle is not something to which citizens are entitled regardless of their willingness to work (Rawls, 1974, 1993: 181–2, n9, 2001: 179). Only those willing to meet a minimum work requirement are entitled to this income share. For Rawls (2001: 179), this 'expresses the idea that all citizens [sharing in the social product] are to do their part in society's cooperative work', that is, contribute to the community in return for sharing in the social product.

Reciprocity of this kind can be seen as expressing precisely the same underlying ethic of mutual concern and regard as the egalitarian commitment to protect people from serious disadvantage. The fundamental intuition is that if we are members of a given political community, and we share in the social product created by our fellow citizens, then, as a matter of respect for them, we have an obligation to make a reasonable effort to see that they benefit from our membership of the community as we benefit from theirs. If our contributive capacity is relatively low, then we are not obliged to exhaust ourselves trying to return exactly the benefit we have received. But we are obliged to make a good faith effort to give something back, given the contributive capacity we have. Other citizens have a right to expect this much from us, and we therefore treat them unfairly if we choose not to honour this expectation. At the same time, while the demand for reciprocity seems appropriate in the abstract, we must be attentive to the specific circumstances in which the demand is pressed. If the economic system is structured in a way that unfairly makes some citizens significantly worse off than others, then those who benefit from this injustice surely do not have the right to expect as much, by way of productive contribution, from those who have been disadvantaged as they otherwise would. Thus, only when society is sufficiently just in other relevant respects can we begin to think in terms of a uniform contributive effort that can reasonably be expected of every citizen.

The problem with the CI proposal is that it would apparently allow people to claim a non-trivial share of the social product without satisfying a reasonable expectation of personal productive contribution to the community. To put the point in Rawlsian terms, CI is a way of structuring access to the minimum share available under the difference principle which allows citizens to claim this minimum without making the corresponding productive contribution in return.

More than anyone else, Philippe Van Parijs has wrestled with this objection (Van Parijs, 1995). Van Parijs defends CI as a cashing out of each citizen's right to an equal share of 'job assets'. The gist of the argument – I summarize brutally, but not, I think, unfairly – runs as follows: citizens' life-chances are affected by their access to jobs. As egalitarians, we should regard each citizen as having a right to an equal share of available job assets. We cannot literally carve up the jobs and give equal shares of them to each citizen, but perhaps we can give people the cash equivalent: we can give each citizen an equal, per capita share of the value of these job assets (financed from a tax on those who hold the assets). We should pay each citizen a uniform income grant financed from a tax on the employment rents attached to job assets.

For this argument to persuade it is not enough to think – as surely we ought to think – that justice requires compensation for those who are *involuntarily* excluded from employment (as part of a more general policy of seeking to prevent or correct for brute luck disadvantage). That moral consideration supports a policy of targeted grants to those who wish to work but can't, not a uniform CI. For Van Parijs's argument to persuade we have to accept that justice requires that each citizen be allocated an equal share of society's available jobs *regardless of his or her relative willingness to work*. But the moral force of this claim is far from obvious, precisely because it seems to ignore a concern for productive reciprocity. If we think that the conception of fair-dues reciprocity does capture an important aspect of economic justice, then, in thinking about how we distribute assets that confer access to the social product, it is surely relevant to consider the kind of work preferences that people have. If people are going to be allocated such assets, and, thereby, access to the social product, they ought to have work preferences consistent with meeting the obligations they have as a matter of fair-dues reciprocity. By extension, the value of these assets should not be taxed and distributed indiscriminately to all as a CI, but distributed only to those with the right sort of work preferences. (For a related argument, to which I am much indebted, see van Donselaar, this volume.)

What, though, about resources that are not the product of one's fellow citizens' labours, but, say, of past generations? Are we, perhaps, entitled to a share of these resources regardless of our willingness to make a productive contribution to the community? After all, they are produced by past generations, and it seems odd, at first sight, to say that we have some kind of obligation to reciprocate the dead for what they have given us. On second look, however, this idea does not seem quite so crazy as it sounds. Of course we do not have an obligation literally to reciprocate the dead for what they have left us with. But it is perfectly intelligible, and plausible, to say that we should match their efforts for us by making a similar effort for future generations. Each generation has a collective obligation to ensure that it leaves the next generation a sufficiently generous level of resources and collective opportunity, to make good what it uses up from the inheritance of past generations. And each of us, as a member of a given generation, has a duty to do our bit, productively, in the creation of an adequate replacement product (or to reciprocate those who produce it). We escape such obligations only if we are willing to forgo our presumptive right to a share of the social inheritance. Thus, as with job assets, I do not think we can straightforwardly include these inherited resources in the pool used to finance a CI on the grounds that our entitlement to them carries no corresponding productive obligations (here I follow Vandenbroucke, 2000: 40).

Finally, what about natural resources? Again, these are not produced by our fellow citizens, so is it fair to insist that entitlement to them be conditional on willingness to work? Imagine ten people arrive on an uninhabited island with a supply of land. Nine of them wish to use the land for productive purposes. A tenth wishes merely to bask in the sun and live off wild fruit. Do we feel comfortable saying that this tenth person has no right to a share of the island's land merely because he/she does not wish to make productive use of it? If not, then we seem to be accepting that individuals *do* have some resource rights – rights to land – that are unconditional on their willingness to make a productive contribution to their society. However, even in this case important caveats must be entered. Granted that everyone is entitled to some land in such a case, it does not necessarily follow that they are entitled to *equal* shares of land. It is perfectly conceivable, as van Donselaar argues, that an equal division will allow some non-workers to capture 'parasitic' rents off those who work (see van Donselaar, 1997, this volume).[3] Moreover, if someone like the tenth person in our hypothetical island example enjoys his/her right to some share of land more securely because a legal and political system has been put in place to define and enforce this right, does he/she not owe something to the community as a contribution to covering the costs of this system? How do proponents of a CI propose that this obligation be met? And presumably this entitlement is, again, regulated by a concern for intergenerational equity so that if someone uses their land share in a way that diminishes its utility to future generations, then he/she must somehow generate an adequate replacement for this (or reciprocate those who do so).

## 4   Responding to the reciprocity concern 1: the development grant

Some proponents of CI do think that a CI, in and of itself, may create a problem of objectionable free-riding or parasitism. However, they reply that while this exploitation objection is a *valid* objection, one which points up a real moral cost of CI, it is nonetheless not a *decisive* objection. It is not decisive because the prospective moral cost from CI is outweighed by the prospective gains, in particular, to freedom. Whereas some proponents of CI, such as Philippe Van Parijs, defend the view that CI is best from the standpoint of social justice, proponents of this second, more concessionary view, such as Brian Barry, hold that CI is the most reasonable second-best from the standpoint of social justice – at least for societies like our own here and now (Barry, 1997, 2001). And they hope that the evident benefits of a CI for personal freedom, and the priority generally accorded to this value in liberal democratic societies, can win people over to the proposal in spite of its apparent weakness from the standpoint of reciprocity. The concessionary response can be strengthened further by showing how, in certain respects, a CI might actually help individuals better to satisfy their reciprocity-based obligations, for example by making it easier to take part-time employment rather than stay unemployed (for more on this argument, see White, 2002, 2003a: ch. 7).

I am quite sympathetic to the concessionary reply to the reciprocity objection, but there are at least two problems with it. The first is a philosophical problem. We can only point to the benefits of a CI to justify or excuse the moral cost it allegedly carries, if it is the case that no other policy instrument will produce these same benefits at this or equivalent moral cost. It is possible, however, that there are some variants of CI, variants which depart from the pure form of CI in specific ways, that will secure the same benefits at less cost. If so, we should surely prefer these variants over the pure form of CI. Moreover, turning to the second problem with this reply, it is far from clear that the appeal to personal freedom on its own *will* win political support for a radical citizen's stake policy like CI if this policy is seen to flout norms of productive reciprocity. The establishment and maintenance of a generous citizen's stake policy will require considerable social solidarity (Van Parijs, 1995: 226–33). There is, however, a body of evidence which suggests that solidarity is more readily built and maintained in support of social programmes that are seen to be respectful of the demands of productive reciprocity.

This point is central, for example, to Theda Skocpol's recent discussion of what makes for successful innovations in American social provision (Skocpol, 1997; see also Bowles and Gintis, 1998, 1999). Reviewing a number of successful social policy initiatives, including public schools, benefits for Civil War veterans, Social Security, and the GI Bill of 1944, Skocpol considers what features these initiatives had in common that explains their success. She argues that one key feature in this regard is their consistency with a norm of reciprocity:

> The most enduring and popularly accepted social benefits in the United States have never been understood as poor relief or as mere individual entitlements. From public schools to Social Security, they have been morally justified as recognitions of or as prospective supports for individual service to the community. The rationale of social support in return for service has been a characteristic way for Americans to combine deep respect for individual freedom and initiative with support for families and due regard for the obligations that all members of the national community owe to one another.
>
> (Skocpol, 1997: 111)

According to Skocpol, 'liberal Democrats' in the United States have suffered a 'political impasse' in enacting new social policy initiatives for many years because since the 1944 GI Bill they have abandoned 'the long-standing formula for successful American social provision – giving support to people who are seen as contributors to the community, whatever their social class' (Skocpol, 1997: 118).

So, what are these variants on the pure CI policy that address both the concerns for personal freedom and reciprocity? I shall consider two possibilities here which I think are worth serious attention.

One possibility I think worth exploring is the idea of what we might call the *Development Grant* (also van Donselaar, this volume). The development grant is not a periodic, non-mortgageable income, but a lump-sum capital grant akin to that proposed by Ackerman and Alstott (Ackerman and Alstott, 1999). In contrast to their proposal, however, use of the Development Grant is restricted to specific purposes such as education, training, or establishing a new business. One example is the scheme recently proposed in Britain by Julian Le Grand and David Nissan (this volume; also Nissan and Le Grand, 2000). This has much in common with Robert Haveman's earlier proposal for a 'universal personal capital account for youths', and with a number of other more recent proposals in the USA (Haveman, 1988; Unger and West, 1998; Halstead and Lind, 2001).

Obviously, under the Development Grant, citizens have less immediate choice as to how to employ their capital grants as compared with a proposal like that of Ackerman and Alstott. One might try to defend this on two distinct grounds. Firstly, one might defend the restrictions on paternalistic grounds. Again, we come back to the distinction between manifesting our concern for freedom as a concern to prevent dependency and as a concern to respect freedom of choice. Like a CI, though in a different way, the Development Grant takes a stand in favour of the first of these alternatives. The restrictions on use of the grant can be seen as a way of limiting the risk of 'stakeblowing' and resultant dependency – as limitations on freedom of choice intended to preserve freedom as non-dependency (for further discussion, see White, 2003b). Secondly, many of the uses which are mentioned in Development Grant proposals, such as education, training, and the establishment of new businesses, are related to productive participation in the community. Citizens are thus encouraged and, to some extent, constrained, under these proposed schemes to use their grants in support of their productive contributions to the community. In this way, as Skocpol recommends, social support is connected with service. The historical, agrarian parallel is the idea of giving people rights to land on condition that they make productive use of this asset endowment, the model adopted in the United States in the 1867 Homestead Act (a model which William Simon calls a social-republican property right: see Simon, 1991). The Development Grant is a contemporary variant on this farmer, yeoman model of the citizen's stake. Thus, on the face of it, the Development Grant might seem a particularly attractive option in that it seems to be good for freedom (as non-dependency) *and* for reciprocity. The choice apparently forced upon us by CI seems to be wholly avoided, and we get the best of both worlds.

However, the Development Grant has some obvious drawbacks. One drawback is the probable administrative cost of the proposal. It will cost society resources to monitor individuals' compliance with the use-restrictions it places on the grant. Some of these restrictions may be quite easy and cheap to monitor (for example, use of the grant for higher education purposes). Other permitted uses, such as setting up a business, may be much harder and expensive to monitor. This drawback is not necessarily decisive, however. Such costs mean that society has to pay something for having a Development Grant rather than an unconditional lump-sum scheme like that proposed by Ackerman and Alstott. But society may regard this price as worth paying for the benefits it gets from opting for the Development Grant over this alternative: extra security, at the individual level, against the risk of 'stakeblowing'. A second drawback with the Development Grant is that the restrictions on how such a grant may be used make it less effective than a CI as a possible cushioning device which individuals can use to help them through difficult periods when they might face financial difficulty and, therefore, increased risk of dependency. If we could be confident that the responsible uses to which the grants are put would always result in individuals having good opportunities in the marketplace this might not be something to be too concerned about. But we cannot be sure of this. Citizens could quite conceivably use their grant in responsible ways, for example to acquire specific skills or set up a new business, but then find that these investments fail: the skills become unexpectedly outmoded by a new turn in technological development, or the business which looked a promising bet flounders in the face of an unanticipated change in consumer demand. Once again, I am not sure this is necessarily a decisive argument against having a Development Grant at all, but I think it sufficiently strong to make it worth considering what other forms of citizen's stake policy might offer us a way of bridging the concerns for freedom and reciprocity.

## 5   Responding to the reciprocity concern 2: time-limited citizens' income

At this point it may help to take a step back for a moment and remind ourselves of the existing terms of the debate over 'welfare reform' in liberal capitalist countries such as Britain and the USA. Putting to one side the libertarians who would like to scrap all forms of welfare, at one extreme in this debate are those who advocate a welfare system in which benefits are both work-tested and time-limited, that is, available only for a limited period over the course of a whole working life. This is the workfare model exemplified in the United States in the 1996 Personal Responsibility and Work Opportunity Reconciliation Act. At the other extreme, are those who advocate welfare benefits that are neither work- or participation-tested nor time-limited. Proponents of a pure CI, as replacement for most other welfare benefits, fall into this second camp. But we certainly do not have to choose between these two extremes. One alternative that we might explore would be to develop an income support system that has two tiers. The first tier, which I will call the conventional tier, is work- or participation-tested, but not time-limited. So long as one continues to meet the relevant work or participation conditions, one continues to receive the relevant benefits. So, for example, those who are out of work will be eligible for unemployment benefits, and will have to satisfy job search requirements as a condition of receiving benefit, but provided that they do meet these requirements there will be no termination of benefit. People who make a good-faith effort to find work will not be penalized by termination of assistance should they have the misfortune to fail to find work within a fixed time period. In addition to benefits for the unemployed, this first conventional tier of income support might include refundable tax credits for the low paid, subsidies for certain categories of care worker, and so on. The second tier of this proposed two-tier system of income support consists of a *Time-Limited Citizens' Income*: an income grant that one can choose to draw on without satisfying a work/participation-test (or means-test) but which can only be enjoyed for a fixed number of years (one, two, three?) over the whole course of one's working life. For example, individuals might have a right to draw up to a maximum of £20,000 in CI over the course of a working life, with, perhaps, a maximum of £8000 drawable in any given year. This second tier of income support is not work- or participation-tested; but it is, in effect, time-limited. A modest Time-Limited CI is proposed here, then, not as an alternative to conventional welfare, but as a vital supplement to it.[4]

From the standpoint of the public values that have framed our discussion in this paper, freedom and reciprocity, there is apparently much to be said for this two-tier model of income support relative to the alternative workfare and pure CI models. The concern for reciprocity is obviously addressed by making the benefits available under the first tier work- or participation-tested. In contrast to the contemporary workfare model, however, we also address the concern for freedom as non-dependency by refusing to impose a time-limit on support of this kind: as said, potentially vulnerable citizens are not going to be thrown to the mercy of others if, through no fault of their own, they fail to find employment. And, of course, the concern for freedom as non-dependency is also addressed by supplementing the first tier of work- or participation-tested support with the Time-Limited CI. Prudently managed, a Time-Limited CI could provide individuals with crucial financial independence in periods of difficulty which might otherwise expose them to dependency. If individuals go through periods of crisis and transition – due to divorce, or changes in jobs or careers – they can look to their Time-Limited CI to provide crucial support, helping them to get through these transitions constructively rather than floundering vulnerably in desperation. Of course, they could also look to the first tier of support. But if the conditionality of the first tier creates problems – perhaps the nature of the crisis or transition is such that the individual in question cannot meet the relevant eligibility conditions for conventional welfare in the short-run – then they can trigger this second tier of support to help them through. At the same time, because this CI entitlement is time-limited, it cannot be used to underwrite a life-style of long-term withdrawal from productive contribution to the community, and this aspect of the proposal addresses the concern for reciprocity.

Of course, a Time-Limited CI also has some drawbacks. In particular, it is essentially an instrument to help people manage crises and transitions. It could be used to facilitate new business ventures, or investments in human capital, but is not really aimed at supporting asset-building activities of this kind which can help in the long run to bolster an individual's material security. For this reason, it may be advisable to regard it as one element (albeit an important one) in a citizen's stake policy, rather than as sufficient in itself.

## 6   Conclusion: the merits of 'hybridity'

I have argued in this paper that citizen's stake policies ought to address two basic moral concerns, a concern for freedom (understood to include a concern for non-dependency), and a concern for productive reciprocity. While the CI proposal has obvious and strong attractions in terms of the concern for freedom, it has drawbacks in terms of the concern for reciprocity. One possibility, of course, is that we simply have to accept these drawbacks for the sake of doing what is effective for personal freedom. But before we jump to this conclusion, we should first consider other forms of citizen's stake policy that potentially go further towards bridging and reconciling these two concerns. One possibility is the Development Grant discussed in section 4; another is the Time-Limited Citizens' Income, understood as the second tier of a two-tier system of income support, discussed in section 5. A further possibility, not considered above, is a hybrid form of citizen's stake which combines a Development Grant and a Time-Limited Citizen's Income (both operating, moreover, against the backdrop of a range of more conventional welfare programmes). To be concrete: imagine, for purely illustrative purposes, that on maturity each citizen receives a Citizen's Account with an initial real value of something like £40,000 in today's prices. This account is divided into two parts. The first part, of, say, at least half the total value of the initial Citizen's Account, is a Development Grant, akin to the account proposed by Nissan and Le Grand. Citizens would be free to use the funds in this account to help finance a range of activities that are broadly related to productive participation in the community, such as education, training, and the establishment of a new business. The second part is a Time-Limited CI: a sum, perhaps not interest-bearing but inflation-indexed, that citizens are free to draw down at their discretion to supplement income from other sources, subject perhaps to restrictions on how much they can withdraw within a given time period.[5] Such a hybrid would serve freedom, both in the sense of non-dependency, and in terms of making freedom of occupational choice effective; and it would respect the concern for productive reciprocity. I cannot, and do not, claim that a hybrid of this kind is uniquely consistent with the concerns for freedom and reciprocity. Specific policies seldom follow so simply and straightforwardly from basic value commitments. If, however, we are to give due weight to both concerns in the design of a citizen's stake policy (understood largely as a complement to, rather than substitute for, much conventional welfare policy), then a hybrid of this kind has much to recommend it as a long-term aim.

## Notes

1. I would like to thank Bruce Ackerman, Selina Chen, Jurgen De Wispelaere, Keith Dowding, Jane Lewis, Erik Olin Wright, Will Paxton, and Karl Widerquist for comments on earlier versions of this chapter and/or on its topic that I have found helpful.
2. Rousseau (1994: 62).
3. Van Donselaar argues that a just distribution of external resources depends on the 'independent interest' that people have in making use of these resources (that is, their interest in using the resources independently of the use that others wish to make of them). To distribute a given asset to all equally, regardless of the pattern of independent interests, will allow those who end up with more resources than they have an independent interest in using to extract 'parasitic' rents from those who have an independent interest in using more than an equal share. Arguing along these lines, van Donselaar claims that a just distribution of external assets is not necessarily a strictly equal one, but one that shows equal respect for the independent interests each individual has in using the relevant assets. See van Donselaar (1997; this volume).
4. Some ongoing work by Will Paxton and Sue Regan at the Institute for Public Policy Research (London) on 'Life Accounts' as a form of 'asset-based welfare' points in a similar direction. See Regan (2001a); Paxton and Regan (2001).
5. I set out and defend such a hybrid at more length in White (2003a). See also White (2003b) for a detailed discussion of the merits of such a hybrid from a paternalist perspective (as opposed to the justice-based perspective adopted in this paper).

# 6
# The Stake and Exploitation

*Gijs van Donselaar*

## 1 Who shall inherit the earth?

The question 'Who shall inherit the earth?' seems to be an ancient question. At least there are ancient answers to it. Jewish, Christian and Muslim scriptures are in agreement not only that the earth in its entirety belongs to its creator but also that not just anyone can be a legitimate inheritor of it, or even of a share of it. There are serious conditions to that. The Psalms state, and the Qu'ran cites approvingly, that it shall only be God's servants and the virtuous, who will inherit the earth.

I skip a few long ages. With John Locke modernity seems to have changed the conditions for legitimate inheritorship. The virtuous have been replaced with the industrious, or as some may prefer to say: industry is turned into the sovereign virtue. In any case Locke's theory of so called original acquisition, whatever its many puzzles and complexities, implies that the earth shall belong to those who work on it, that the fruits of the earth shall go to those who work at all, and not to those who are idle and lazy. This in its turn has been the dominant answer for some time now.

But ever since Tom Paine wrote *Agrarian Justice* there has also been a subversive undercurrent of thought on social and economic justice that relies on a challenge of the very idea that there should be conditions at all attached to the right to inherit the earth, be it industry or virtue, or industry as a virtue, or whatever. And recently that undercurrent has surfaced and gained in force. The idea is that all people have a natural right to an equal share of the natural resources of the world, and that, once this idea is properly understood, it follows just as naturally that all people ought to have a social right to an equal share of the *value* of the natural resources.

Two recent books on social justice vigorously and resourcefully deliver an argument to this effect (Van Parijs, 1995; Ackerman and Alstott, 1999).[1] In this chapter I will first summarize, and challenge, Van Parijs's argument for basic income and with it I will challenge Ronald Dworkin's view of justice as equality of opportunity on which it builds. I will suggest that the ancients were basically right: there ought to be conditions to inheriting the earth, and I will even grant Locke that industry has something to do with that. My point is that no person, simply in virtue of her being a person and without further motivation, can claim that she is wronged if her government fails to provide her with a labour-free income. Then I will see where the argument against basic income leaves us with regard to the other proposal: the stake. Based on my view of legitimate earth-inheritorship I will try to defend a version of the stake-holding idea that differs from Ackerman and Alstott's in about every relevant respect: its justifiable level, the liberty it should provide to stakeholders, and the way it should be financed.

Before I turn to a discussion of basic income let me point out one significant negative feature of both proposals, that is: what they are not. Neither basic income nor the stake is intended to compensate people who have comparatively meagre innate talents to the effect that they have low or even no earning capacity from wage labour or as independent providers of services on the market. Ackerman and Alstott insist that the Stake is not a poverty programme and that their 'first concern is not with safety nets but with starting points; not with misfortune but with opportunity' (1999: 8). Van Parijs argues for a (rather ungenerous) income transfer system *besides* basic income, which is especially targeted at those who (even with a basic income) are universally believed to be the very worst off in society, the downright handicapped. This is what Van Parijs (1995: 58–88) calls 'the principle of undominated diversity' which, interestingly, is an elaboration of an idea first formulated by Bruce Ackerman (1980: 116). However, basic income and the stake would in themselves be as justified for a population that consisted of entirely equally talented persons as they are claimed to be in our world with its differences in this respect. Basic income and the stake are both presented as a consequence of individual liberty rights per se; to put it bluntly: they have nothing to do, at least not in their philosophical motivation, with compassion for the suffering, or 'charity'. The authors offer their respective proposals as a natural implication of a commitment to equality of opportunity but it is clear that the real commitment they have in mind is to equality of *external* opportunities: stuff that is not tied to persons (and *to* which persons are not tied). It is of some importance to realize this from the outset, and I will return to this matter to point out the consequences of this commitment.

## 2   Equality of resources and basic income

Ronald Dworkin's interpretation of equality of opportunity is sufficiently well known to warrant just a sketchy account of it: unproduced natural resources are to be divided equally, and the criterion of equality is that of non-envy. People acquire bundles of resources in such a way that no one will prefer the bundle of another person to his own. In a group of shipwrecked people washed ashore on an island, *auctioning* the various resources could bring about such an envy-free distribution of resources, as follows. A divider hands each

> an equal and large amount of clamshells, which are sufficiently numerous and in themselves valued by no one, to use as counters in a market of the following sort. Each distinct item (...) is listed as a lot to be sold, unless someone notifies the auctioneer (as the divider has now become) of his or her desire to bid for some part of the item, including part, for example, of some piece of land, in which case that part becomes itself a distinct lot.                    (Dworkin, 1981: 286)

Another way to achieve the same distributive result would be to give all persons the same amount of each of the various resources under consideration, and then let them trade among each other at equilibrium rates (Varian, 1985). Those who are under-supplied in one type of resource will try to purchase additional shares of it from others in exchange for things they presently hold but do not value. So, we allow each to use an equal amount of token money, 'clamshells', to express her priority over the various resources under auction, or we begin by giving everyone an equal share of all resources, which will then be tradable – the outcome will be the same.

In order to point out the problem in this approach to justice I will begin by carrying through some radical reductions: let us consider a population of only two persons dividing only one resource between them.[2] There are four plots of land. The four plots are equally large and equally fertile, but they do in fact require an investment of labour to make them productive of consumable goods – as land usually does. We need not worry about the nature of these consumable goods; they may be various or of one kind, that does not matter. But to make things easy I will refer to these goods for short as 'income'. Land produces income only when people work on it. Now what would be an equal distribution of this land over the two persons? The answer seems simple enough: each should have two plots.

But let us now consider the eventuality that one of the two persons is a relatively lazy person in that he is not very willing to invest a lot of labour in the land to make it produce income. He puts a high value on sitting in the sun without working, and he has no great desire for income. As matters stand he would choose a trade-off between leisure and income (a leisure–income bundle) such that only one plot of the land would suit him perfectly. He doesn't want any more. And suppose the other person had appetites that were much more on the side of income than on the side of leisure. She doesn't mind working hard if it means that in the little remaining leisure time she can consume a lot of income: with three plots of land she would exactly achieve her favourite leisure–income bundle. Following Philippe Van Parijs, for reasons soon to be apparent, I will call these two persons 'Lazy' and 'Crazy'.

Under the equal distribution of land, Crazy will be under-supplied because she would like to have more, and Lazy will be over-supplied because he holds a plot of land that he has no use for. So the equal distribution seems to be very inefficient. But it need not be so. Crazy might of course try to purchase some additional land from Lazy. What she should do is offer some of her income to Lazy in return for the use of his spare share. Should they agree on a price then Crazy will not do as well as she would have done with three plots in her own initial possession but she will certainly do better than if she does not purchase additional land at all. Lazy, of course, will do better if he can hire out, or sell, his surplus land, because that will give him additional income. In the two-person case there will be room for negotiations about the price of the land between Lazy and Crazy since there is a range of income-to-land exchanges that will be efficient. So the two will have to bargain their way out, but whatever the bargaining result, both will be better off than if each were stuck with his or her own initial share. The result will represent a so called Pareto improvement compared to the initial situation of equality.

This result can be generalized over situations involving more persons and more types of resources, and the man who did the generalization is Philippe Van Parijs. I quote at some length from *Real Freedom for All*. Like us, he considers an initial equal distribution of external 'assets' as it would follow from Dworkin's doctrine:

Crazy may be desperate to use more than her plot of land, while Lazy would not mind being deprived of some or even all of his in exchange for part of what Crazy would produce with it. This directly yields the following suggestion. There is a non-arbitrary and generally positive legitimate level of basic income that is determined by the per capita value of society's external assets and must be entirely financed by those who appropriate those assets. If Lazy gives up the whole of his plot of land, he is entitled to an unconditional grant at a level that corresponds to the value of that plot. Crazy, on the other hand, can be viewed as receiving this same grant, but as owing twice its amount because of appropriating both Lazy's share of land and her own. Thus, in our society of Crazies and Lazies, the legitimate level of basic income is just the endogenously determined value of their equal tradable right to land.          (Van Parijs, 1995: 112–13)

Of course, as Van Parijs explains, we need not actually go through this cumbersome procedure of an in-kind provision of shares of land, and oil wells, and fishing grounds, and copper mines, and then organize the resource-to-income market. We just have to design the tax and transfer system that will mimic the outcome of such a hypothetical market. Equality of resources, then, if we accept it, must lead to the introduction of an unconditional basic income, financed through taxation, and which, in essence, means that it is a transfer of income from those who work hard to those who work not so hard, or not at all. Unconditional basic income is an income at the level of the commercial value of an equal share of resources, that each is entitled to regardless of her willingness to work, and we should add: regardless of whether or not she is actually disadvantaged by the fact that others *are* working very hard.

## 3  The challenge

This brings me to the challenge. Equality of tradable resources, and hence unconditional basic income, is exploitative or, in the terminology of David Gauthier (1986: 191–232), 'parasitic'. It allows some persons, the Lazies, to take advantage of other persons, the Crazies.

In its simplest formulation Gauthier's (1986) idea of parasitism, or of taking advantage can be stated as follows:

Person A has a parasitic relation with another person B (or: A takes advantage of B), if A is better off than she would have been in the absence of B, while B is worse off than he would have been in the absence of A.

It is not difficult to see what is objectionable in parasitism or exploitation: many offences that form the hard core of the criminal law are exploitative in Gauthier's sense. Consider the standard cases of robbery and theft, rape, breach of contract, or extortion and fraud. In all such cases offenders give themselves access to goods, or benefits, that they would not have had without their victims, while these would have been a lot better off without the offenders. Likewise, slavery would be an exploitative practice and, indeed, so is Feudalism: large landowners exploit their exclusive property rights to let tenants work for them, consume their product – part of their so-called 'surplus labour' – but make nothing available to the tenants. The landowners have control over resources and others have to buy or hire what would have been freely available otherwise.

But then neither is it very difficult to see why equality of tradable resources, and hence basic income, is also exploitative in Gauthier's sense: it is nothing but 'equalized Feudalism'. This can be demonstrated on the two-person case we considered above. Crazy is interested in three plots of land, Lazy is interested in only one, so actually there is no such thing as *scarcity* in the natural supply of resources. Though, seemingly, Lazy and Crazy are making rival claims to resources, because they both need a measure of resources to attain their favourite leisure–income bundle, there is in fact no controversy between them. Suppose we give one plot of land to Lazy and one plot to Crazy; from that moment onward it is no longer true that they *both* value additional resources. Only Crazy values additional resources, Lazy does not.

But equality of resources creates scarcity of market supply. Crazy will be demanding an additional plot to her initial equal share, which she will have to buy from those who are over-supplied. But then it is obvious that she is doing worse than she would have done in the absence of Lazy, whereas Lazy himself is doing better than he would have done in the absence of Crazy, since, through the sale of his surplus land, he acquires (additional) income without working for it – as if he were a Medieval liege lord.

We can generalize this conclusion to the many-person multiple resource situations, and the basic income policy. People will have diverse interests for resources depending on their willingness to sacrifice leisure. So, starting from equality, some will have surplus shares that they may want to trade for labour-free income. Those who are under-supplied will want to buy additional resources, and equilibrium prices will emerge, for example, for land. The sellers of land will tend to do better than they would have done in the absence of those who now buy their land, but the buyers would have had larger unencumbered shares of land in the absence of those who now hold equal shares that they do not need. Buyers will tend to do worse than they would have done had the land been less scarce. In fact the Lazies exploit the scarcity of the land itself. Had it been less scarce, they would not have made such a good price for their surpluses. There is a very simple way to demonstrate Lazy's perverse interest in scarcity. Suppose Lazy and Crazy had been sitting on an island with four plots of land, to be shared equally and the ship the *SS Justice in Progress* comes by. The captain offers to improve their situation: he can take them along, but only both of them, and drop them off at a nearby island that is similar to theirs in all respects except that it has six plots of land, not four. Crazy, of course, will gladly accept: equality will then grant her a third unencumbered plot. But will Lazy? No. He would rather stay where he is; on the bigger island, equality would rob him of a convenient labour-free income from Crazy's efforts.

We may also put it thus: equality of resources allows the Lazies to exploit their capacity to be a nuisance to others. It allows them a claim on something for which they have no 'independent interest' and the only reason they have to maintain their claim is that they may sell what they cannot use to those who do have an independent interest in it. First they stand in another person's way (they are given the right to do that) and then they offer to step aside in return for income. Their behaviour is comparable with that of the man who stands in the queue at the post office, or puts himself on the hospital's waiting list for cardiac treatment, with the single purpose of selling his place to one who gets there later. 'Mischief, made vendible, increaseth', said Thomas Hobbes. Nuisance, made vendible, increases too. The corresponding legal foul, I believe, would be that of 'extortion': to inflict or threaten harm in order to sell the relief of it.

What I am basically suggesting here is that we have to confront an *impossibility theorem*: given that preferences for leisure and income may be diverse, we have no guarantee that a distribution of external resources is at once

1. free of envy;
2. free of exploitation;
3. Pareto-optimal in the resulting allocation of leisure–income bundles.

Any two, but not all three of these features may be compatible. Setting aside for the moment that we might want to settle for distributions that are not Pareto-optimal, the theorem implies that a serious choice between exploitation-freeness and envy-freeness is forced on philosophers of justice, even egalitarian ones. Van Parijs's argument for basic income highlights the urgency of that choice. His argument implies that the desirability of envy-freeness always has priority over the objection against exploitation, and that is a view that I find deeply contestable.[3]

I need to address a further consideration however. As I claim that it is by no means clear that the end state of *envy-freeness* is a good reason to argue for substantial transfer payments from hardworking persons to lazy persons, I do not claim that there can never be a reason for justifying transfer payments at all. I cannot elaborate on such a justification here but the concept of exploitation, defined as narrowly as I have done, is not offered as one that should exhaust all legitimate moral concerns. Compensatory transfer payments, for instance, in support of the well-being or autonomy of people who are somehow lacking in innate productive talent, or ability to function well, can be justified with a reference to how their life would go in some objective sense in the absence of support. But such a reference is characteristically lacking from the justification of basic income. Indeed, as I pointed out, concerns for the effects of differential internal capacities are taken care of in Van Parijs's theory by the 'principle of undominated diversity', and *that* principle (or something like it) is not under discussion, or criticism, here.[4] But lazy people may be as talented as, or more talented than, some of the others and under equality of external opportunities they would still acquire the (bargaining) power to enforce transfer payments. A person may want to work but he cannot; a lazy person can work but prefers not to. The difference is crucial in my appreciation of their position as beneficiaries of a tax and transfer system. It is clearly the element of deliberateness in the latter's attitude, the element of *seeking* to live off the efforts of others, which is the truly objectionable feature in the justification of basic income as a fundamental social right. To exploit, surely, is an active verb.[5]

## 4   Justifying a stake

So, where do my considerations of basic income so far, leave us with regard to the other proposal: the stake? Is it an implication of my argument that equality of external opportunity cannot justify the idea that modern society should adopt a general responsibility that all young persons get some fair start in life? Or to be more precise: that this general responsibility, even if a *willingness*-to-work condition were imposed on recipients, could not stretch beyond the actual provision of pathetic bits of land from which pathetic little incomes could be obtained? I shall argue that this is not so. I think that equality of opportunity can justify a *version* of the stakeholding idea, although I am certain that Ackerman and Alstott would not recognize that version as their own proposal.

In the following I will try to indicate, but only in a very sketchy way, what can be done, and what cannot.[6] I will point out a fundamental ambiguity in Ackerman and Alstott's argument for the stake, and I shall argue that they also misrepresent the 'liberty' of the stakeholder. In both cases it is indeed the problem with the proper justification for transfer payments that should lead us to more restrictive views than Ackerman and Alstott have developed.

Let us return to Dworkin's Virgin Island and what equality of opportunity has to say about it, again starting with land as one of the few directly accessible resources and again assuming equality of innate talent, for the sake of argument. Of course it is quite possible, in fact it seems inevitable, that some of the equally talented castaways will say to the others: look here we can all work as farmers on a restricted piece of land, allowing all of us a pathetic income, but would it not be much better if we also had blacksmiths and carpenters making our tools, millers graining our flour, and what about that chunk of gold that sits there in the mountain? Shouldn't one of us try to get it out, so that we may have jewellery? Would not we all be much better off if only some of us continued farming on more extensive stretches of land while the others specialized in other productive activities so that we might exchange our products and services (some of which will again lead to efficiency gains in farming itself, so that even more persons can devote their efforts to other things)? And then of course others would say: yes, very well, and let us also have doctors and musicians and lawyers and philosophers and designers of paper napkins.

Out of the general acclamation of this smart idea, its prospect of higher consumption levels, there would arise a general agreement on an arrangement which allowed some to spend some years of their lives on the acquisition of complicated skills that could be put to use, other than farming. During those years these students would have to be maintained through the productive work of the farmers, and only after that could they acquire an income through the sale of their skills and products. But besides demanding total coverage of their student years, those non-farmers would obviously insist that their income position would more or less keep pace with that of those who continued to farm, indeed allowing differences among themselves only to compensate those who engaged in 'onerous' trades, such as, according to Adam Smith, that of a butcher (Groot, 1999: 75). No reason why some would profit more extensively than others from a voluntary division of labour, in which – since all are equally talented – each position could have been taken by each of the persons involved. There is, then, a level of mutually advantageous labour division that requires all or some to acquire skills that are needed for specialization but that does not necessarily presuppose that some are more able in either exercising or acquiring such skills.[7]

So the insistence is in fact that through the acquisition of skills and training the students get something that is as productive of income as the shares of land that the farmers continue to hold, that is: as valuable. And this valuable thing comes about as an investment from the farmers during the student years of the others, and naturally this valuable thing will be substantially more valuable, more productive of income, than the original tiny bits of land. So all have a share of, what may be called, the means of production but these means are now of various kinds, some have physical external resources, and others have acquired skills and know-how. And some in all probability have combinations of those. All right, let us call this share of the means of production, in whatever form, their 'stake'.

I take the liberty to bring in another 'creation myth'. The Yoruba, an African people, have a legend that reports that in the beginning of all things the Gods offered mankind a baffling choice: they could either have eternal life or they could have offspring. According to the Yoruba, mankind chose not to forgo the joy of having children. Now, the Yoruba being obviously right about this, the original generation of contractors on Dworkin's Island would certainly have agreed that all should be free to have children, and we may assume that all parents would want to provide a share of the means of production to their children. But this poses a new problem.

The parents all have a share in productive resources, but these are of various kinds, roughly: some have acquired skills; others have physical, external shares of nature. But skills tend to perish with those who have them, whereas physical resources do not. Some means of production have a higher natural 'inheritability'. This implies that a system of private inheritance would favour those who have physical resources: a farmer, if he dies, can leave his land to his child but a doctor, if she dies, cannot leave her education to her child in the same way. If the child is going to be a doctor too it will have to go through the process of being educated again just like her mother, and during those years she will need support and funding, just like her mother did. If we leave it up to the mother to pay for this, it effectively implies that she will pay her child's stake out of her income, while a farmer can consume all of his income, just passing on his stake, in kind as land, to his child. This would seem to be unjust because it means a system of private inheritance would arbitrarily burden some parents, and not others, with the provision of the stake of their children.

However, we may stipulate that this effect is to be foreseen before the original intra-generational labour dividing contract is made, and most probably those who are destined to become skilled workers will insist that they shall not be burdened on their own with their children's education just as farmers are not *burdened* with the provision of their own children's stake; they will insist that their children should be admitted to enter the contract on the same conditions as all those who are now present, which means with access to a stake of roughly equal value as the stake of all the others, financed by all who already have a stake. A most convenient arrangement would be of course, if all were to be taxed – farmers and doctors alike – for the provision of the education of the next generation of skilled workers. Thus a next generation's right to a stake is naturally included in the earlier generation's contract.[8] This, I believe, is how far the idea of equality of opportunity may take us.

But how far is that? Well, in any case it may be further than some assume. Robert Nozick says:

> Fourier held that since the process of civilization had deprived the members of society of certain liberties (to gather, pasture, engage in the chase), a socially guaranteed minimum provision [a stake?] for persons was justified as compensation for the loss. But this puts the point too strongly. This compensation would be due those persons, if any, for whom the process of civilization was a *net loss*, for whom the benefits of civilization did not counterbalance being deprived of these particular liberties.             (Nozick, 1974: 178–9)

But this puts the point too weakly. The compensation would be due to those persons for whom the process of civilization was a net loss compared to the (productive) opportunities that *would* have come their way if they, and the long series of their ancestors, had never been robbed of their legitimate original equal shares in the natural resources to begin with.

## 5   The tax base

Nevertheless, let us now turn to a demonstration of how an appeal to equality of opportunity *simpliciter* may go astray. We do so by relaxing the equality of innate talents condition. Let us envisage the possibility that, at some stage in the development sketched above, two couples, A1&A2 and B1&B2 start with equal external opportunities, with stakes, say at a value of 2S, and that each couple has two children, a1 and a2, and b1 and b2 respectively. However, A1&A2 are extremely talented compared to B1&B2. They accumulate bits of their annual income to the effect that, in the course of their lives, they manage to turn their original stake of 2S into an aggregate wealth of 4S, which they would like to leave to their children, whereas B1&B2, though very responsible parents, just succeed in maintaining their wealth at the original level of 2S which is what their children would get through private inheritance. Now, since the two couples of parents start with equal external opportunities there is nothing in the idea of stakeholding itself that justifies transfers of income from the talented couple to the less talented couple. But for their children the situation is different: if we allow for a system of private inheritance, a1 and a2 will get 2S each, while b1 and b2 will get only 1S each, and so their external opportunities will be unequal, and call for redistribution. Would Ackerman and Alstott share this conclusion? It seems they would as they remark that '(i)n our society, starting points are irrevocably shaped by parental wealth and position. But no one deserves his parents' (1999: 23). But, then, no one deserves his (lack of) talents either, and if *desert* (in this sense) is to be made into a justification of transfer payments the whole distinction between internal capacities and external opportunities, and hence the distinction between justifying stakeholding and justifying 'poverty programs', will evaporate.

But why would Ackerman and Alstott want to make such a distinction in the first place? Why is it so important – in the name of equal citizenship – to share external resources while not so important to share talents? My guess is that this distinction is driven by an intuitive grasp of a distinction of the following sort. It may be that I have no share in your talents but it does not follow that I have been *deprived* of a share in them. It is not as if your talents would have been my talents if they had not been yours. However, if I do not share in your external natural resources, such as land, that have an existence which is independent of your existence, then it *is* the case that I have been deprived of them, in the sense that if they had not been yours they (or greater shares of them) would have been mine.

More fundamentally there are cases of so-called 'brute luck' where the good luck of one person is causally related to the bad luck of another, and there are cases where this is not so. Differences in innate capacities belong to the latter category. It is your brute good luck that you are talented and my brute bad luck that I am not, but it is not the case that I am untalented *because* you are talented. Why is this distinction relevant? At least one reason may be found in the problem of justifying transfer payments. If we redistribute the fruits of talent, I may reap (some of) the fruits of a talent that would have been absent in your absence, and you may lose (some of) the fruit of your own talent because of me. And that, as I argued before, would require an entirely different justification than if we require you to compensate me for the fact that you have disadvantaged me by excluding me from the use of the earth. Indeed the latter can be thought of as a form of redress while the former cannot. Again, I am not saying that there can never be a justification for non-redress transfers; I believe there frequently *is* such a justification, but a mere appeal to equality of external opportunities is not it. It has nothing to do with the question of who shall inherit the earth, it has nothing to do with 'starting points' and hence it has nothing to do with the justification of stakeholding.

Ackerman and Alstott insist that equality of external opportunity is a matter of public concern while 'charity is best left to churches, unions and community organizations' (Ackerman and Alstott, 1999: 183). But were they to identify wealth *as such* as the tax base for policies that should equalize *intra*-generational starting points, they would not be able to maintain the distinction. Everything I have said so far about talents is also true about parents. It seems implausible that if your parents had not been *your* parents, they would have been my parents. The wealth they saved (above and beyond their own fair stakes) would not have existed in your absence because they saved it for you, and it would certainly not have gone to me. Siblings may have ugly conflicts about (this part of) the inheritance; others have no claim to begin with.

And then there would be what some may consider even worse: our original two couples of parents may well have been equally talented, and started out with equal stakes, but one of these couples may simply have taken a different view of what they would *like* to do for their children, saving more of their income (and consuming less than they might have) for the purpose of passing it on as (additional) wealth to their children – such differences *do* exist after all. Again, the children would have unequal opportunities and equality of opportunity within the generation of the children would again call for a tax on and transfer of wealth. So the tax on wealth-at-death is not only an indirect tax on talent, it is also a tax on love.[9]

Of course, the fact that the *exercise* of freedoms upsets the *patterns* of freedoms is well known, not only at the gate of the basketball stadium, but also across generations, and this is a reality that can only be avoided by allowing *lesser* freedoms to all generations. Ackerman and Alstott do not think through these conceptual complexities and ambiguities of their ideal of justice to the end. They *are* perfectly aware of the injustice of interfering with the results of people's choices. If starting points were fair and some of us decided to work, innovate, and accumulate while others spent more on leisure and consumption, we would not challenge the ensuing distribution merely because the innovative savers had accumulated much more than the leisurely consumers. To the contrary, the ensuing distribution would simply be testimony to the diversity of ideals that motivate free men and women in a just society (Ackerman and Alstott, 1999: 96).

The real problem they should solve is how to respond when such a diversity of ideals in generation X *translates into* a gross inequality of starting points in generation X + 1. If our parents deserve their wealth and may do with it as they like, but we do not deserve our parents, then what? They want to steer clear of the libertarian position, and they are right to do so insofar as libertarianism is characterized by the denial that there is *some* wealth which cannot be attributed to some persons in particular. The other extreme to be avoided is not so much utilitarianism or the 'welfarist mindset', but the idea that *all* wealth has a more or less anonymous origin and therefore should be up for collective grabs and redistribution, even if only on behalf of the next generation. It is not obvious that they always steer clear of that position too, at least not in the theory behind their proposal; the reference to 'not deserving one's parents' should certainly put us on the alert.

It may be rejoined that Ackerman and Alstott do not *in fact* propose to tax all wealth but that they restrict taxation by the pay-back requirement. People should (only) pay what they have received themselves (plus interest). How does the (restricted) pay-back condition of generation X relate to the ideal of having equality of starting points in generation X + 1? What *makes* the starting points within a certain generation fair? Is it that none of these starting points sinks below a certain level compared to the (similarly justified) starting points of previous generations or is it that these starting points are (sufficiently) close to equality compared to each other? Ultimately the philosophical problem Ackerman and Alstott fail to address is whether theirs is a historical-entitlement conception of justice or an (egalitarian) end-state conception of justice. The first, I acknowledge, may involve insurmountable practical problems, and a myriad of assumptions and counterfactuals, and it may require estimations that are to a large extent arbitrary. Yet a version of that conception seems inevitable if we are committed (as Ackerman and Alstott seem to be) to a distinction between starting points and outcomes. The second conception may be simpler to apply but it creates an immediate and obvious injustice to some within the present generation of parents.[10]

## 6  The liberty of the stakeholder

Let me try instead to draw some brief conclusions, from my observations in the first half of this chapter, about the form of the stake. Since the stake is justified as a share of each in the means of production, to be used productively through the application of labour to it, as farming is applied to land, it is obvious that it is a requirement of justice, and not only a matter of paternalist worries, that people do not 'blow' their stake. To put it somewhat bluntly: since one cannot eat land, and since one cannot drink education, one should not be allowed to spend the stake on consumer goods. Proper precautions should be taken to ensure this will not happen. The pay-back requirement that Ackerman and Alstott attach to the stake is therefore not only to be appreciated as an obligation to future generations, but also as a guarantee that some stakeholders will not simply (and deliberately) live off the efforts of the members of their own generation.[11]

But as such the pay-back requirement, however effectively enforced, is insufficient. It follows from my discussion of Van Parijs's argument for basic income, that stakeholders are not at liberty to put their stakes in a bank, live off the rent for the rest of their lives (or use that rent just to top their income from other sources) and then at the end of it cheerfully deposit an equivalent of the original stake back into the fund with a clear conscience. Again, in such a case the stakeholder has not used her stake productively; she has allowed others to use it productively and taken a profit from that, but that only demonstrates that *she* never contributed to the surplus that is generated with the help of the stake. She merely took money for getting out of the way of others, while she shouldn't have been in their way in the first place.

Ackerman and Alstott are too indiscriminate when it comes to their view of what people may use the stake for. *The Stakeholder Society* contains a number of suggestions of, in their view commendable, uses of the stake that are not irresponsible in the sense of wasteful but still definitely at odds with the basic idea that stakes are justified only as shares in the means of production. One of their 'profiles of freedom', for instance, suggests that a person might use the stake to buy a house to live in (1999: 69), and elsewhere they mention that the stake may be kept in stock in a 'rainy-day fund' (1999: 29). But if one buys a house with the stake, and just turns in the house at the end of one's life, then again one uses the stake only to increase one's own consumption level without contributing to the source of that increment. It means that one simply lives in a house that is bought with money that stems from the productive activities of others. There is a crucial difference between someone who does this and someone who uses his stake to buy an education, and then uses his *increased income* from his acquired skills to buy a similar house. The difference is that the latter's increased income indicates that he, through the use of his stake, contributes to an increment of the cooperative surplus from labour division, and that he is not just tapping that surplus, as if the stake were the source of a crypto-basic income. And keeping the stake in stock for hard times means that you keep it to eat it, and will not pay it back – as Ackerman and Alstott say you should. Of course we may be concerned about the fate of people who cannot find affordable housing, and about people's protection against hard times, but *these* are the concerns of poverty programmes, 'charity' if you wish, and safety nets, not of stakeholding.

## 7 Design

So how should we design a stake system which does what it is justified and required to do? Here we may reach a crossroads: some will think that the best way to make sure that the stake is indeed a means of production is to offer it in kind, by creating an (almost) freely accessible, highly refined educational system, tailored to society's (expected) needs, and maintained and controlled by government agencies – a system such as is in place (not altogether unsuccessfully, but always under pressure) in many European welfare states. Others will insist that the market will have to do its work in education as anywhere else. They would rather have students control their own funds with which to purchase (prolonged) education as they see fit, inducing competition on the supply side.

Moreover, Ackerman and Alstott have identified a group of persons who have concluded that higher education (and perhaps wage labour) 'is not for them' (1999: 56) and who would rather start a small business of their own. These people would have to make considerable investments in their improved productivity but their legitimate needs would not be covered by the in-kind delivery of higher education. Now, in itself this need not knock out the idea of the in-kind provision of stakes, but I am not denying that it calls for socioeconomic innovation: a group as just mentioned could be accommodated, and indeed sometimes is accommodated, by granting them so-called 'starter subsidies' for young entrepreneurs. Naturally candidates would have to qualify by producing a sound business plan just as if they were to turn to a commercial bank. But the subsidy would otherwise be unencumbered. A system like this could be developed in a more robust way than we are acquainted with anywhere yet.

Still, if we want to drive the liberty of the stakeholder to the maximum, we should perhaps best think of the stake as a *voucher*; indeed think of it as 'shadow money' that is earmarked and can only be spent in a number of ways, to purchase education, machines, tools and other productive facilities, or indeed, *land*: in quantities and combinations as the purchasers see fit, but subject to conditions that should guarantee that the stake is not highly likely to be wasted or otherwise abused. These conditions and their effects, their strictness or lenience, the level of intrusiveness of our government they imply, the blunders they avoid or allow, will of course be the subject of perpetual debate and change over time, but that is one of the complexities we should not hope to avoid if we do not want the arrangement to degenerate into a 'mistakeholder society'. This voucher system is certainly not as elegant as the proposal of Ackerman and Alstott, but it should be clear by now that – other than in science and dress – elegance is an uncertain virtue in politics. I assume that even within the most liberalized stake system (indeed even if the stake *were* provided in green dollars) we would require educational institutions to be certified somehow, before their agents start persuading eighteen year olds that they are about to enter a future of bliss. There is no reason to waste the stakes (and lives) of perhaps hundreds before the market identifies an impostor while an experienced civil servant sees through him right away.

Nor is there any reason for society to provide stakes to its citizens and then wait until at the end of their lives, perhaps and who knows, some of the sufficiently successful stakeholders prove to be sufficiently friendly and grateful to have the decency not to go on a cruise around the world. Financing the stake out of a tax on inheritance may seem to have a certain symbolic value, one generation taking care of a next, but really, relying on citizens' hoped-for exalted sense of community to solve a problem that will obviously have the structure of the production of a public good (with a very powerful temptation to free ride), it again signals that Ackerman and Alstott have an ambiguous view about justice on the 'input side' of the stake. Of course they gesture at measures that should counter free riding or its effects (taxes on large pre-death bequests and an additional annual 2 per cent tax on wealth, regardless of its origin), but I think the solution must really lie elsewhere.

Because even as a symbol I think the inheritance tax would be a mistake: people reach the age of maturity every day. Generations come in cohorts and not in discrete blocks of, say, 25 years. That they get their stakes is a collective responsibility of all who already have a stake and take advantage of it, not just a responsibility of the novices' grandparents. And if we appreciate the stake for what it is, namely as a share in the means of production that should be used productively, it is also obvious that 'pay-back time' starts as soon as pay-off time has arrived, that is: as soon as the stakeholder starts earning good money. Hence the logic of its justification suggests that the stake be financed through an income tax, which would at once and conveniently remove excessive business opportunities for cruise organizers, as well as some of the injustices indicated before.

Let me, finally and after all these doubts and criticisms, prove myself to be more generous (to stakeholders) than Ackerman and Alstott are, in one respect. I have been puzzled by their remark that the stake should be paid back *with interest*. They have calculated that acceptance of a stake of eighty thousand dollars would involve a commitment to pay back the equivalent of roughly a quarter of a million dollars! Why? To whom would this interest be owed? To the members of one's own generation? No, they have fair stakes themselves and have no further claims. Would it be owed to members of the next generation? No, they will get their stakes if old stakes are decently paid back, and they too have no further claims. And isn't it odd to hail the stake because it will free students from the necessity to turn to commercial banks to finance their education, and then ask for interest on the stake itself? So what can be the justification for squeezing rent out of people's fair stakes? I do not think there is any.

I have argued that people have no unconditional right to the fruits of the earth, that is, to basic income, because they have no unconditional right to a share of the earth itself. But now the boot is clearly on the other foot: if people meet the conditions and are entitled to inherit a fair share of the earth then they are also entitled to all the fruit they produce with it. Surpluses belong to people who are entitled to produce them.

# Notes

1. In many ways *The Stakeholder Society* is a political pamphlet written for the American home market, and at times I feel that the patriotic pep talk obscures the exact philosophical position of its authors. However, the importance of the fundamental moral principle it invokes to justify the stake, equality of opportunity, is of course perceived in other countries as well: I will therefore treat this book as if it, like *Real Freedom for All*, were addressed to an audience that is capable of a sense of justice which does not necessarily require the waving of a flag.
2. The following analysis of the argument for basic income, and the criticism thereof, is an excerpt of chapter 4 (entitled, 'Clamshell Rent') in van Donselaar (1997). I have omitted various subtleties and distinctions from my presentation here that are not directly required to grasp the general spirit of my argument.
3. A similar concern has been stated by Stuart White (1997), who argues that what is essentially lacking from the basic income social scheme is an element of reciprocity. See for a discussion of this type of argument, van der Veen (1998).
4. Elsewhere (van Donselaar, 1998) I have argued against Van Parijs that there is no single consistent conception of 'opportunity' that may at once warrant a commitment to 'self-ownership' and transfer payments to the lesser talented; here too a choice cannot be evaded.
5. Note that a handicapped person who would be entitled to support, would not have a reason to sabotage the enlargement of the aggregate stock of resources; she has no interest in scarcity of resources since her entitlements are not positively (and are perhaps even negatively) related to such scarcity. She would not object to society's transfer to a larger island, as would a lazy person under equality of resources.
6. In the next paragraphs I reach conclusions that are similar to those of Den Hartogh (1995).
7. Of course the doctors, lawyers, philosophers and designers of paper napkins in our world will tend to say that such a presupposition is needed to explain their highly valued contributions to the social surplus. However that response may indicate part of the problem we are trying to address here. Would their contributions have been *as* highly valued if all with similar talents had been given access to the same educational facilities as they enjoyed? The scarcity of their *acquired* skills does not prove the superiority of their *innate* talents.
8. There are alternative routes to this conclusion that are not dependent on Yoruba preferences. I will not explore them all, but here is one suggestion: all in the first generation will want (or have) to retire from work at old age. If they want to continue to live, others, young persons, will have to work in order to produce their 'pensions'. But to be able to do so these young persons will need stakes.
9. Of course any tax will affect what people can decide to do, and hence what they can decide to do for their children, but a tax on inheritance seems to *single out* people's desire to do something for their children, for what other motive could they have to accumulate bits of their income to last beyond their graves? (Admittedly, they might also want to support some lofty cause, keep their art collection intact or have their name attached to an important university chair – but nevertheless.) Philippe Van Parijs (1995: 125–30) is clearly aware of the love tax as a consequence of equality of opportunity, but it is hard to determine what he concludes from that (1995: 92).

10. What I have said about the grounds for constraining the level of the stake has nothing to do with an *incentive argument*. It affects the principle of maximin or leximin opportunity as much as a principle of equal opportunity. It may well be that if we take a cut of more than, say, 60 per cent of each inheritance (over and above the value of their original stakes) parents will no longer bother to save additional wealth for their own children. This would be counterproductive for all in the next generation, and Pareto-wisdom suggests a switch to lower tax rates. It is my point however that even these lower rates may not be consistent with the distinction between talents and land, or love and resources.

11. And this is a sufficient reason why persons who do not (intend to) have children are in no different position with regard to the pay-back requirement than those who do.

# 7

# The Stake: an Egalitarian Proposal?[1]

*Cécile Fabre*

## 1 Introduction

The word 'stakeholding' has become one of the most often used, and perhaps one of the least clear, of all the terms recently coined by left-wing politicians, journalists and academics in search of a coherent political and economic programme. Broadly speaking, to give people a stake means to empower them as economic agents. Proposals have ranged from conferring on workers rights of participation in the management of firms, to reforming the political system and the workplace and to overhauling the welfare state.[2] Individuals, it is argued, have a fundamental interest in deciding what to do with their life, and they should therefore be given the means to control the environment – economic, social and political – within which they make such decisions.

My aim in this paper is to examine the normative principles which underpin one aspect of stakeholding, namely welfare policies. It is commonplace to point out, in academic and political circles, that although welfare expenditures have increased manifold since 1945, the gap between rich and poor has widened in the last 30 years and many people on welfare cannot get out of the poverty trap. The welfare state, or so it is argued, has benefited those, the middle class and the working poor, who need it least, and let down those, the unemployed poor, who need it most: in short, it has failed to meet its objectives.

In the eyes of some social policy specialists, the welfare state has failed because it has focused on redressing income inequalities and overlooked the fact that lack of assets, or so it is alleged, is a much more important cause of poverty than lack of income. From this diagnosis, a number of policy proposals have been put forward, two of which warrant close scrutiny. Bruce Ackerman and Anne Alstott (1999) in the US, and Julian

114

Le Grand and David Nissan (this volume; also Nissan and Le Grand, 2000) in the UK, have suggested that each citizen should receive a one-off payment, or a stake, upon reaching majority, for them to go to university, buy a house, start a business, or other purposes. Others, such as Michael Sherraden (1991) in the US, and Gavin Kelly and Rachel Lissauer (2000; also Gamble, Kelly and Paxton, this volume) in the UK favour the creation of savings accounts, sometimes known as Individual Development Accounts. Those accounts are credited by their holders, with means-tested matching contributions from the state, local authorities, charities, businesses, and so on.[3]

Both proposals differ from yet another recent and radical suggestion, the unconditional basic income, whereby individuals should receive a monthy income throughout their life, whether or not they work (Van Parijs, 1995). Whereas the unconditional basic income has been discussed mostly in academic quarters, the stake and IDAs have attracted a lot of attention from policy-makers, particularly from quarters located in the so-called Third Way. In this paper, I focus, first, on the proposals themselves and on what they purport to achieve (section 2); I then examine the ways in which they are funded (section 3). I argue that, in various ways, they fall short of their goals.

## 2 Equality of opportunity and stakeholding

Both the stake and IDAs are meant to ensure equality of opportunity. By equality of opportunity, advocates of the proposals have in mind a broader ideal than what Marxists are fond of ridiculing as bourgeois equality. Under bourgeois equality of opportunity, people are equal if they are not legally discriminated against by others (such as potential employers, civil servants, retailers, and so on) on grounds of race, gender, and social status. Under the more generous ideal of equality of opportunity which the stake and IDAs seek to bring about, people are equal if their chances of leading a fulfilling life are not jeopardized by poverty.

### 2.1 Failures to give equality of opportunity

Do the stake and IDAs bring about equality of opportunity? The stake is supposed to ensure that the young have an equal opportunity to implement their conception of the good life. And yet, individuals have different conceptions of the good life, some more costly than others; as a result, although they are all given the same amount of money, which gives the impression that equality obtains, some of them, in fact, will not be able to implement their conception of the good.

Ackerman and Alstott explicitly claim that these differences between individuals are a matter of choice: if you decide that you want to set up a business which takes up 90 per cent of your stake and which will not yield a high income for many years, you cannot complain that the remaining 10 per cent will not buy you a house; and you do not have a claim to extra funds against Joe Smith, who has very inexpensive preferences and who therefore can save and invest most of his stake (Ackerman and Alstott, 1999: 96). That claim draws on Ronald Dworkin's (1981) ideal of equality of resources: in Dworkin's view, equality requires that individuals each be given an equal amount of resources for them to bid for the goods they need in order to implement their conception of the good. Inequalities which result from people's choices are not condemnable at the bar of justice, whereas those which result from factors they are not responsible for are condemnable.

The problem, of course, is that quite often these preferences are not a matter of choice. It is not always a matter of choice that I want to go to university and spend most of my stake in that way: I may have been brought up in the expectation that I would go to university; I may be the kind of person who needs, as opposed to prefers, the stimulation and challenges of academic pursuits, and so on. Moreover, I may not always be responsible for the fact that my conception of the good is beyond my financial means, or uses up most of them. Suppose that Paul loves photography, which is an expensive hobby, and that Fred loves fishing, which is a cheap hobby: the inequality between them which results from Paul not having the resources to pursue photography should be of concern to the egalitarian (Cohen, 1989). Thus, one has reasons, on egalitarian grounds, to modify the proposal and, instead of giving the same sum to everybody, to give each a sum which is tailored to the cost of what is unchosen in their conception of the good, and which is sensitive to the fact that they have virtually no control over how much it costs and over their having, or not having, the resources to implement it.

Moreover, if what matters for professed egalitarians is that people should not be disadvantaged by factors outside their control, they should subscribe to a different, more radical egalitarian ideal, one which includes, amongst constraints on individuals' opportunities, not simply legal discrimination and poverty, but also natural disadvantages such as poor health and lack of remunerative talents. Le Grand and Nissan are silent on that point, but Ackerman and Alstott recognize that these are obstacles in the way of people's chances to lead a fulfilling life. Yet, their position on health care is ambiguous: whereas it is clear that the state should take financial responsibility for people with severe mental and physical disabilities, it is not clear whether individuals with lesser disabilities should be expected to use up part of their stake towards medical insurance or towards extraordinary medical expenses (Ackerman and Alstott, 1999: 96, 38). If people have to incur such medical expenses for reasons which are beyond their control, then I contend that it is unfair, at the bar of equality, to ask them to use part of their stake to that effect. Moreover, neither Le Grand and Nissan nor Ackerman and Alstott have much to say on differential productive talents. And yet, Ackerman and Alstott, at least, insist that the stake will bring about genuine equality of opportunity (1999: 96). Insofar as the proposal does not make provision for compensating people who have less by way of remunerative talents, I doubt that it will achieve what it sets out to achieve: Le Grand and Nissan, more realistically, are less ambitious in that they see their proposal as decreasing inequalities, rather than eradicating them. Thus, equality of opportunity, understood as that ideal whereby people's chances of leading a fulfilling life are not adversely affected by their social and familial background, is not radical enough. If what matters for egalitarians is that people should not be disadvantaged by factors which are beyond their control, then the lump sum they receive should compensate them for all such disadvantages.

There is another and, in my view, more fundamental problem with the stake. It is meant to help young people by providing them with an equal starting point: Ackerman and Alsott explicitly say that it is not meant to protect them against whatever misfortune may befall them in the course of their life (1999: 8, 87). Le Grand and Nissan seem to agree on that point, since they do not suggest that people receive a grant at various stages in their life. And yet, one may come to lack equal opportunities at a later stage through sheer bad brute luck, even if one had equal opportunities to start with. Surely that should be of concern to an egalitarian. Although the stake is not meant to replace standard welfare services but rather to supplement them, and although people are therefore not left without a safety net at any time, a proposal which allows for large brute-luck based inequalities between individuals in the course of their life is not an egalitarian proposal. A just proposal (as opposed to 'congruent with current American or British views on distribution') is one whereby individuals would receive at the beginning of their adulthood a lump sum tailored to their conception of the good, and would continue to receive throughout their life what they need in order to implement it, provided they are not responsible for not having been able to use their stake as they should have done.

IDAs, by contrast, fare better on that count than the stake, for they allow people to build assets over time, and to use them so as to weather various crises. They are more sensitive to life-cycles, and to the fact that resources are needed afresh at the beginning of those cycles, than the stake. For example, individuals need certain resources in early adult-hood in order to buy a house, get married, start up a business, have chil-dren; later on, they might need further resources to put their children through college, weather the cost of a divorce, and so on; finally, in their early sixties, they might need yet further resources to get through the first steps of retirement. IDAs allow them to adjust to these various changes in their circumstances better than the stake does. In that respect, incidentally, they are quite close to unconditional basic income.

Although some proponents of IDAs are aware of this particular strength of their proposal, they qualify it and point to what they think is one of its perverse effects. Thus Kelly and Lissauer claim that IDAs might provide people with an incentive to make bad, or rash, decisions, for example, getting a divorce, which they would not have made had they not had a financial incentive to do so (2000: 18). Perhaps they would. Conversely though, without access to assets at various points in their life, they do make decisions which they otherwise would not make, for exam-ple staying single for lack of enough resources to move out of their par-ents' home, instead of getting married and moving in with their spouse.

IDAs, thus, provide people with resources at various stages in their life. However, they are vulnerable to a number of objections at the bar of equality, which the stake escapes. First, whereas under the stake all indi-viduals (except convicted criminals) are entitled to a certain amount of resources for them to use in a responsible way (a point to which I shall return below), individuals have access to IDAs only if they decide to con-tribute to them. This supposes that they have enough to contribute in the first instance. Of course, they could receive help from their parents, grandparents, friends, and so on. But equally, they might not. In fact, the proposals for IDAs, as they are formulated, leave open the question of who counts as rich or poor. Is the child of wealthy parents rich even though he himself, in his own name, and as a young adult, may be poor? To regard him as rich and to assume that he would get help from his family should he wish to open an IDA, overlooks the fact that his family may not, after all, be generous towards him. Even if, empirically, there are good reasons to believe that individuals will be able to open an account, the system should be designed in such a way as to ensure that those who, through no fault of their own, are not capable of contributing anything are still in a position to have access to assets.

Relatedly, Sherraden, in particular, points to the benefits of IDAs for households and individuals interchangeably. But one can be asset-poor in an asset-rich household, just as one can be income-poor in an income-rich household. The distribution of resources within households, thus, is a crucial incident of individual well-being. To be sure, individuals can open an IDA irrespective of their familial situation. But there is no guarantee that they will be able to take up that opportunity. An income-poor woman who has had to give up working to look after her children and who can just make do with what her income-rich or asset-rich partner gives her for household expenses is unlikely to be able to save enough to build herself a nest egg over time.

Furthermore, and most importantly, although the government would match, up to a point, contributions from the poor, it remains likely that IDAs would mostly benefit those who are already well-off or whose families are well-off. For consider the following. Suppose that the government matches contributions to IDAs up to 100 per cent. If all I can contribute is £5 a month, the government will give me £5, and I will therefore be able to save £10 a month: better than nothing, for sure. But if I can save £20, I will receive £20 from the government, and contribute a total of £40 a month into an IDA: much better than £10. IDAs, thus, are inegalitarian, even though they broaden people's opportunities.

## 2.2  Failures to give individual autonomy

So far, I have criticized both the stake and IDAs for falling short of the egalitarian ideal they are meant to foster. In fact, on some occasions, Ackerman and Alstott claim that the stake will promote people's freedom; indeed, they invoke the ideals of 'freedom' and 'equality of opportunity' interchangeably. Similarly, Sherraden insists that inasmuch as their holders will have to (partly) contribute to them, IDAs will give people the opportunity to take responsibility for their own life, to make long-term plans for them and their children, and so on. (Sherraden, 1991: 201; Kelly, Gamble and Paxton, this volume: 50–6). IDAs, then, are said to help people become autonomous, in the standardly liberal sense of being able to frame, revise and pursue a multifaceted conception of the good with which they can identify over a significant period of time.

And yet, equality of opportunity is not the same as autonomy. To say that people should have more autonomy than they currently do is not to say that they should have equal opportunities. In reducing inequalities without eliminating them altogether, the stake and IDAs will make for less unfair, but not for fair, starting points; but in ensuring fairer starting points, they will thereby increase people's autonomy. Autonomy, and not equality, is the fundamental value which underpins both kinds of proposals. In that sense, arguments for the stake and for IDAs are only weakly egalitarian: they are egalitarian because they rest, if implicitly, on the view that individuals are worthy of equal concern and respect; they are weakly so, however, because they do not deliver equality of opportunity.

Notice, though, that although those proposals ultimately appeal to the value of autonomy, individuals can receive a stake or get the state to contribute to an IDA only if they intend to use their assets in certain ways. There is, in the literature, a strongly paternalistic bias in favour of 'useful' spending decisions, such as going to university, putting a down payment on a house, starting a business, and against spending decisions perceived as foolish. Ackerman and Alstott go as far as to say that high school leavers should not be entitled to receive the full stake, but only a small share of it, on the grounds that they are not educated enough, or responsible enough, to make good use of it. Insofar as highly educated people have been known to make incredibly rash financial decisions, and less educated people have been known to have good business acumen, to render the latter ineligible for a full stake sounds unduly harsh. More to the point, to give assets to individuals on the condition that they use them in particular ways introduces a bias against those who need state subsidies in order to be asset-rich; for they would lack the opportunity to implement what would be deemed irresponsible conceptions of the good, whereas those individuals lucky enough not to need those subsidies would be able to do so.

Advocates of those paternalistic strictures on eligibility for a stake or IDA could reply, as indeed Sherraden (1991: 202) does, that if public subsidies are to be used, they must be used to achieve goals which are in the public interest. This introduces quite a different rationale for IDAs, since it grounds the proposal not primarily on individual interests, but on social utility. Such rationale does not sit very well with the view – otherwise propounded by Sherraden – that welfare policies must promote individual autonomy.

## 2.3  Promoting individualism and nationalism

Before I examine the ways in which the stake and IDAs are meant to be financed, I want to express some worries about the kind of society which they seek to create. At the heart of both proposals, there is the ideal of what Rawls calls a democracy of property-owners, whereby every citizen not only enjoys civil and political rights, but also has access to private property. The stake and IDAs thus reverse the traditional understanding of the relationship between citizenship and property, whereby one could enjoy civil and political rights only if one had property.[4]

The ideal of a democracy of property-owners is a misguided goal, for the following reasons. First, an individualized stake or IDAs rooted in the institution of private property is not really conducive to the kind of ethos required by an egalitarian society. For a society to be egalitarian, it must not only be the case that people are willing to pay the amount of taxes required by equality of opportunity; it must also be the case that people, in their everyday life, as spouse, parent, economic agent, and so on, live up to the egalitarian ideal in their relationships to others. For example, a productive economic agent should not seek higher wages, thereby fostering inequality, as a condition for his working harder; a spouse should not shirk his or her obligation to share the housework (Cohen, 1997). Generally, in an egalitarian society, people should not seek only to increase the benefits that accrue to them and thus should not have an acquisitive, possessive mentality. But to give them a stake or to help them build up assets over time, and moreover to educate them into thinking of that stake as something which is theirs, for them to do with as they want, runs the risk of instilling such a mentality in them. And that is a worrisome thought for egalitarians, all the more so as people could not only end up displaying that mentality in their familial and professional relationships, but also stop supporting taxation aimed at supporting throughout their life those who are not lucky enough to be able to make good use of their resources. Note, incidentally, that this criticism applies to any welfare proposal (including the basic income proposal) which, on the one hand, aims to bring about genuine equality of opportunity and, on the other hand, confers on individuals strong property rights in income and assets which they are encouraged to regard as exclusively theirs.

Second, what underlies the stake and the IDAs, and in particular what underlies such policies insofar as they are financed by estate duties, is the view that in order to be a full member of the American or British polity, individuals must have equal opportunities, and must also pay back, upon death, what the polity has given them. On that view, there is a special, moral relationship between members of that particular community, America, or the UK, such that they have a right to the resources they need to take up some of the opportunities on offer, and a duty to provide those resources to those who need them. Thus, proposals for a stake and for IDAs are located in a body of literature where citizenship is understood not simply as a political, but also as a social ideal.[5] Nationality, thus – and this is especially true of Ackerman and Alstott's account – seems to define common membership: the fact that you and I have the same national identity and that we both live in the country of which we are nationals justifies that I be held under a moral duty to help you should you need my help.

Now, it is beyond the scope of this paper fully to examine that claim. Suffice it to say that nationality should be kept separate from issues of distributive justice. For a start, even though someone may have lived in the US for a while, she may not wish to adopt US citizenship, and may have good reasons not to do so. Besides, national identity is what holders of a given nationality think it is, and whilst many people do feel that an important part of their identity is bound up with their belonging to a national community, some do not. In any case, even if all the members of a given community think that they have special obligations to their fellow nationals, this in itself is not enough to establish that they do indeed have them.

The solution, obviously, would be to render long-term resident aliens eligible for the stake or for IDAs. Membership, then, would be defined as residing and making a life in a given community, without necessarily having an identity-based connection to it. But although that would get round the objection raised in the last paragraph, it would not get round yet another objection to community-based arguments for asset-based distribution, indeed, for any kind of demanding distribution of resources. Insofar as they rely on public funding, the stake and IDAs are expensive proposals, more obviously expensive in fact than current, income-based welfare policies. Assuming that the Americans and the British would be willing to pay higher taxes in order to fund them, it is likely that they would do so out of a strong sense of attachment to their community, to what it means to be a British, or American, citizen. And yet, if what motivates the proposal for a stake is that people should not have fewer opportunities than others on the grounds that they are born into a poor family, then the proposal itself should be extended to the world as a whole. For where we are born and grow up is as arbitrary a source of advantages or disadvantages as the family in which we are born and grow up. Clearly this implies that the US or the UK should either distribute a substantial part of their wealth to poorer countries or open their borders and allow emigrants to come in and give them the same opportunities as they do their own citizens. In linking individuals' entitlements to their membership in a given national community, one is vulnerable to the charge that not enough attention is being paid as to whether that community does indeed have rights to the totality of the wealth it has created.[6]

Advocates of the stake and of IDAs might be tempted to argue, by way of reply, that their proposals are compatible with the redistribution of resources at global level. The US and the UK, they might argue, must first fulfil their duties of justice to other countries, and then can, and must, distribute the remainder of their wealth, intra-US and -UK, in such a way that all Americans have a stake or can open government-subsidized IDAs. However, it is doubtful that the stake could be as high as $80,000, or that state subsidies for IDAs could be at the level envisaged by Sherraden. Moreover, should the fulfilment of duties to nationals of other countries make it impossible for the American and the British peoples to live by their values, namely, equality of opportunity and autonomy, an argument is needed as to which side, in that conflict, should be given pre-eminence. Again, other welfare proposals also need further argument along those lines. Thus, it is not clear at all whether the unconditional basic income would be compatible, in the ways just suggested, with the view that we have strong obligations of justice to foreigners. The point, then, is this: any proposal which regards membership as the basis for distribution – and such are the stake and IDAs – needs to account for the relationship between our obligations to fellow members and our obligations to foreigners.

## 3  Funding stakeholding

I have not said anything so far about the ways in which both proposals should be funded. Advocates of IDAs propose that businesses and charities, together with the government, contribute to such accounts, which would ease up the pressure on public resources. Sherraden (1991: 228–9), for his part, suggests not that further taxes be raised, but that current tax proceeds be reallocated to the poor, and in particular that tax benefits for the non-poor be curtailed. Similar measures have already been implemented in the UK: witness the abolition of the mortgage interest tax relief by the first New Labour government.

In general, advocates of IDAs are concerned with ensuring that individuals have a minimum amount of assets to get through important life-cycles, but they are not sensitive to inequalities consequent on the unequal transmission of assets from one generation to the next. Thus, Sherraden (1991: 223) explicitly states that account holders could at any time transfer any portion of their IDA to the IDA of their children or grandchildren: 'just as wealthy families pass along assets to their children, the IDA system would permit many non-wealthy parents and grandparents to pass along financial assets and opportunities to their offspring in the form of IDA account balances'. Clearly, though, to allow individuals to bequeath their wealth to their offspring contravenes both equality of opportunity and freedom. It is anti-egalitarian, because it leaves potential heirs vulnerable to the vagaries of their predecessors' fortune, as some parents will save for their children's benefits more than others. To be sure, insofar as children will themselves have an opportunity to get IDAs, one may think that whatever money they may lose through their parents' self-regarding consumerist attitudes or lack of foresight will not render their life less than fulfilling. Still, inequalities will arise between heirs and non-heirs. Moreover, Sherraden's suggestion constitutes a restriction on individual freedom in its implicit assumption that account holders would not be able to bequeath their IDA balance to friends or more distant relatives. Their freedom to bequeath their wealth, in short, seems implicitly to be restricted by a right others (for example their children) may have to inherit it. Insofar as equality and freedom are two of the fundamental values which motivate the proposal for IDAs, these are troublesome implications. Were Sherraden to modify his proposal accordingly, by extending the right to bequeath IDAs to non-familial relationships, he would be vulnerable to the charge, which I develop below, that inequalities would arise between heirs and non-heirs for which the latter would not be responsible.

By contrast, advocates of the stake conceive of it as a share of the wealth accumulated by our predecessors to which we all have a right and hence suggest that the government raise estate duties in order to finance it. And indeed, if the rationale for the stake is that we should not be disadvantaged by being born in a poor family, it makes sense to impose strict limits on the intergenerational transmission of wealth. Thus, Ackerman and Alstott suggest that the stake be funded through a 2 per cent tax on wealth as well as a tax on bequests. The tax on bequests, though, would be subject to a $50,000 exemption. Above that threshold, individuals would not be allowed to bequeath their wealth until they had paid their stake back. Once they had, they would be able to will sums to whomever they wish; the heirs, though, would have to pay estate duties to the value of 37 per cent to 55 per cent of the bequests. In a similar vein, Le Grand and Nissan point out that, in the UK at least, estate duties contribute to the financing of public funding only by a negligible amount, and suggest that they be raised from 6 per cent of the net value of estates to 20 per cent (Le Grand and Nissan, this volume: 36–7).

Crucially, neither of the four authors under study wish to prevent people from making considerable bequests to their spouse. As Ackerman and Alstott put it, 'the trusteeship principle limiting gifts to the next generation obviously does not apply to spouses (...) If one spouse has worked at home and reared the children in reliance of a promise of life-time support from the other, this deal is entitled to full respect by a liberal state' (Ackerman and Alstott, 1999: 93; Le Grand and Nissan, this volume).[7]

And yet, in that case, the intragenerational freedom to bequeath to one's contemporaries does not obviously justify such exemptions, and this for two reasons. First, the very reason why individuals should be given a stake for them to dispose of almost as they wish recommends that the intragenerational freedom to bequeath be restricted in the case of marital relationships. Ackerman and Alstott justify such freedom by way of an example, that of a spouse who stayed at home to bring up the children in exchange for financial support. And yet, why not hold her responsible for having forsaken remunerative activity, given that she could have made other choices? Moreover, she could have decided to use her stake to insure herself against the possibility that her husband might die before her, to set up a pension fund, to save enough money so as to buy her late husband's share of the marital home, and so on. It is arbitrary on the one hand to hold individuals accountable for failing to use their stake in a responsible way (which includes saving parts of it for rainy days), and on the other hand to allow married individuals not to do so. Incidentally, by the same token, older people who are dependent on their relatives and who survive them do not have a claim to inherit their wealth, for they too would have received a stake, and should have insured themselves against dependency on others.

Second, although intragenerational bequests do not confer on a member of the next generation an advantage which a contemporary of his does not have, they confer on married individuals advantages which their non-married contemporaries and successors do not have. This violates the individualistic premise of proposals for the stake, since the stake is justified on the grounds that people should not be adversely affected by their parents' failures, and conversely that they should not significantly benefit from their parents' success. The fact that we stand in a special relationship with certain individuals – our parents – is not so morally relevant that it should confer on us much greater material advantages. That is an attractive feature of their proposal, perhaps the most attractive. By the same token, should we not extend that claim to marital relationships, indeed, to any relationship which can confer such advantages?

At first sight, it seems that we should. Yet, equality of opportunity, which, you recall, all four authors explicitly endorse, dictates that in some cases, we should not. In what follows, I attempt to chart an egalitarian route between, on the one hand, the claim that intragenerational freedom to bequeath to spouses should not be limited, and on the other hand the intuition that inheritance should be altogether rejected.

Egalitarians, you recall, are committed to neutralizing the effects of bad brute luck on people's life. Now, brute luck plays a lesser role in marital relationships (for the kind of person I am partly depends on choices I make, and depending on the kind of person I am, I am more likely to attract partners) than in relationships between parents and children (for the latter have no control over the kind of parents they are born to) (Rakowski, 1991: 159). Although justice disallows inequalities consequent on bad brute luck, it allows inequalities consequent on choices that we make. Is there, then, a choice-based case for conferring on individuals rights to receive untaxed bequests from their spouses, even if the spouses did not have an understanding that one of them would stay at home and the other one go out and earn a living?

Notice, first, that the fact that the heir has made a choice such that he receives a bequest is not a sufficient condition for allowing him to keep the whole bequest. For an inequality would result between him and someone who sets out, successfully, to be an attractive, kind, decent, caring person and yet who does not marry, or who does but not to someone who is wealthy, or generous, enough to bequeath any money to her, or who may not know anyone who is wealthy and generous enough to bequeath any money to her.

Although making certain choices is not a sufficient condition for being entitled to extra shares of material resources one may have been bequeathed, it is a necessary condition.[8] Imagine the case of Mary, who chose not to marry people who happened to be wealthy and generous to her on the grounds that marriage is an inherently oppressive institution. She does not have a spouse to inherit from when he dies. Contrast her situation with that of someone, John, who chose to marry someone who happens to be wealthy and generous, and who bequeaths him some money. Mary would not be justified in claiming that the inequality between her and John is unjust, that John should pay taxes on the bequest and that part of the proceeds be given to her.

To recapitulate, if I choose to enter relationships and to incur the responsibilities that go with them, and if I benefit – in the form of bequests – from doing so, the resulting inequality between me and those who could have chosen to get into exactly the same kind of relationships and benefited from them but did not is not unjust. I am therefore entitled to (part of) the bequest.[9] Equality requires, thus, that all bequests be taxed so as to compensate people who could not get into the kind of marital relationships such that they would get bequests from their spouses.

I may have given the impression of belabouring my point here. Yet, everything I claimed about marital relationships applies to other relationships, such as friendships, and to the bequests one may get from parties in those relationships: egalitarians can endorse bequests in the very specific case, and only in that case, where the heir has chosen to enter into a relationship with the testator such that he receives a bequest, and where others, who did not receive a bequest, could have made that choice as well.

To be sure, there are values other than equality whose demands should be respected. Thus, there is a sense in which the value of family relationships can support the unequal transmission of wealth from the dead to their relatives through bequests. Such relationships play a very important part in people's development into flourishing adults. It is one of their important features that they involve giving presents as tokens of love and affection. In particular, family heirlooms come to have sentimental value for many people, and one can understand that they should want their relatives, for whom they care, to have them. Such argument might justify exempting people, up to a point, from paying estate duties. But it is important to be clear that such exemptions do violate the ideal of equality in the name of other values.

## 4  Conclusion

To conclude, I argued that proposals for giving a stake to each adult or for helping them to open an IDA do not bring about genuine equality of opportunity and therefore fail to achieve what they set out to do. They are, in fact, better understood as fostering individual autonomy. And yet, in recommending that constraints be imposed on the ways in which people can use their assets, advocates of stakeholding seem unwilling to grant full autonomy to those who do depend on the state for financial help. Moreover, in conceiving of private asset ownership as an attribute of citizenship, they may in fact lead recipients of the stake and holders of IDAs to acquire an acquisitive and exceedingly individualistic mentality which egalitarians, and in particular egalitarians concerned with obligations of justice to foreigners, have good reasons to resist.

However, although I have been relentlessly critical of those proposals, they constitute a welcome step away from traditional welfare policies – which indeed do not seem to work – towards a less unjust society. The points I deployed against them question the claim that they will, if implemented, bring about genuine equality of opportunity and foster genuine individual autonomy. They do not question the claim that they are the best we can hope for, given the current state of the American and British economy, and given British and American attitudes towards redistributive policies. Indeed that claim might very well be correct: in fact, I suspect that the stake and IDAs are more realistic than other welfare proposals, such as the unconditional basic income (for the latter, insofar as it does not make willingness to work a condition for receiving income, does away with centuries of work ethics). Be that as it may, it should not obscure the fact that in implementing those proposals, we would still fall short of the values they seek to realize.

## Notes

1. This paper was given, in a much shorter form, at the 2000 Annual Conference of the UK Political Studies Association. I thank the participants at the conference for a helpful discussion, as well as to Jurgen De Wispelaere, Keith Dowding and Stuart White for their written comments.
2. For accounts of the whole gamut of such proposals, see Kelly, Kelly and Gamble (1997).
3. The phrase Individual Development Accounts (IDA) was coined by Sherraden, and I shall use it throughout this paper to refer to the proposal for savings accounts. Note that, unless otherwise stated, all references in the text will be to the works listed in this paragraph.
4. Accordingly, Ackerman and Alstott argue that only American citizens who have lived in the US for a number of years should be eligible to receive the stake. For obvious reasons, they do not want to allow someone who was born in the US and got US citizenship at birth but who has always lived abroad to turn up in New York upon reaching age 21, claim his stake and leave. Nor do they want to allow a resident alien who refuses to swear allegiance to the polity to get what is, for all intents and purposes, a substantial amount of money.
5. See, for example, Marshall (1963) and Harris (1987).
6. I am arguing here that proposals for the stake and IDAs assume that our obligations to distribute resources are mostly owed to fellow nationals. Interestingly enough, Jonathan Perraton has argued that proposals for economic stakeholding in general assume incorrectly that national economies are strong and sustainable at current levels over time, and not significantly transformed by globalization. Accordingly, Perraton (1997) suggests, without, however, getting into much detail, that one should aim at implementing the stakeholding ideal at global level.

7. For a good argument in favour of stiff inheritance taxes, see Haslett (1994); for a good study of inheritance taxes in general, see Erreyghers and Vandevelde (1997).
8. For an argument to the contrary, see Scheffler (1997).
9. I say 'part of' because I may have to pay some estate duties on it so as to compensate 'unhappy loners'.

# 8
# Freedom and Democratization: Why Basic Income is to be Preferred to Basic Capital[1]

*Carole Pateman*

## 1 Basic income and basic capital

Despite the popularity of democracy in the 1990s, relatively little attention has been paid in recent academic debates to the democratic significance of a basic income. The focus is usually on such questions as social justice, relief of poverty, equality of opportunity, promotion of flexible labour markets, and individual freedom. I am not suggesting that these questions are unimportant or unrelated to democracy. Rather, this approach reflects the extent to which recent political philosophy tends to put democracy in a separate compartment, or merely takes for granted a democratic background in order to analyse social justice and other questions. Two other aspects of contemporary scholarship on stakeholding also work in the same direction. First, the insights available from three decades of feminist scholarship have been neglected, even though they bear directly on some central questions about basic income, basic capital, and democracy. Argument is often contained within some narrow parameters set by controversies about, for example, liberalism and communitarianism. Second, the theoretical framework adopted is frequently drawn from neo-classical economics.

In this chapter, more precisely, I am concerned with democratization. That is, with the creation of a more democratic society in which all citizens, women and men alike, have full standing and enjoy democratic rights and individual freedom. I shall argue that, if democratization is taken seriously, a basic income is to be preferred to basic capital (often called a stake). My idea of a 'basic income' is that a government pays a regular sum over an adult lifetime to each individual citizen. By 'basic capital' or a 'stake' I mean a one-off capital grant from a government to all citizens at, say, age 21. In both cases the payment is unconditional.[2]

Basic income and basic capital have come to be seen as two different ways of giving individuals a 'stake in society' so that they can feel that they belong and have a reason to be a responsible member of their community. For democracy to function well individuals need to be stakeholders, but if their standing and freedom as citizens are also at issue, then a stake in the form of basic capital is insufficient, and a basic income is required. Although I am going to argue for a basic income, I am not dismissing basic capital. A stake would be an advance over present arrangements in the Anglo-American countries, and, in the current political climate, may well be more easily accepted than a basic income by both the public and politicians.

Philippe Van Parijs's *Real Freedom for All* (1995) and Bruce Ackerman and Anne Alstott's *The Stakeholder Society* (1999) have become central to the debate about basic income and basic capital respectively, and I shall take these arguments as my points of reference. In many ways they are two very different books. Van Parijs presents a 'real libertarian' argument and discusses recent arguments in analytical political philosophy, while Ackerman and Alstott draw on republican political theory and write for a more general audience.

Apart from their influence, the other reason that I am concerned with *Real Freedom for All* and *The Stakeholder Society* is that in both books the aim of stakeholding is individual freedom. Ackerman and Alstott see a stake as 'making freedom's promise universal and concrete' (1999: 44), and Van Parijs is concerned with *real* individual freedom. They also agree that 'freedom' means opportunity for individuals. To frame the debate around whether basic income or a stake would best promote freedom as individual opportunity pushes aside the question of the adequacy of such a view of freedom for democratization.

Neither the idea of a basic income nor of a basic capital grant, in itself, stipulates a level at which the income or grant should be set. Ackerman and Alstott argue for a stake of $80,000, and Van Parijs argues that a basic income should be set at the highest sustainable level. My assumption is that, if a basic income is to be relevant to democratization, it should be adequate to provide what I shall call a modest but decent standard of life. This is a level sufficient to allow individuals a degree of control over their lives and to participate to the extent that they wish in the cultural, economic, social, and political life of their polity.

My argument will be that, from the perspective of democratization, a basic income should be seen as a fundamental or democratic right, like universal suffrage. This is because a basic income would help remove impediments to freedom, help citizens enjoy and exercise citizenship, and help provide the security required if citizenship is to be of equal worth to everyone. My understanding of individual freedom is as self-government or autonomy. I see this as a political form of freedom in contrast to an economic form of freedom as individual opportunity. The latter is necessary in a democracy, but is insufficient for democratization, the political process through which all citizens obtain full standing, and become first-class – democratic – citizens.

As a democratic right a basic income has the potential to assist democratization because, unlike basic capital, it can help break the long-standing link between income, marriage, employment, and citizenship. Both basic income and a stake would enlarge individual opportunities, but the opportunities provided by a basic income would be much wider. A major difference between the two forms of stakeholding is that a basic income would give citizens the freedom not to be employed. A basic income opens up two possibilities important for democratization. First, it would encourage citizens to reflect on the place of the institution of employment in a democracy; second, it has the potential to foster institutional change and uncouple standard of life and citizenship from employment.

In much discussion of basic income and basic capital the implications for women's citizenship and women's freedom is ignored. Contrary to my own view, some feminists have criticized proposals for a basic income and I discuss their criticisms below. In 1919, Bertram Pickard, who was much more aware than contemporary scholars that a state bonus (a forerunner of a basic income) was important for women, wrote that the state bonus 'must be deemed the monetary equivalent of the right to land, of the right to life and liberty' (1919: 21). My conception of the democratic significance of a basic income is in the spirit of Pickard's statement.

At first sight, it might seem that there is little to choose between basic income and basic capital as means for strengthening citizenship. Ackerman and Alstott (1999: 88, 197) state that stakeholding is 'a citizenship program', and that a stake 'serves as a mark of citizenship'. The ideal of free and equal citizenship is, they suggest, 'the master key to stakeholding' (Ackerman and Alstott, 1999: 33). Moreover, the republican tradition within which Ackerman and Alstott situate themselves emphasizes the connection between property and citizenship.

Earlier versions of republican political argument were not democratic. Only property-holders were deemed capable of exercising the rights of citizens; the propertyless were excluded from citizenship. Ackerman and Alstott universalize property-holding in the form of basic capital, but depart from republican argument by reversing the direction of the link between property and citizenship. They present a capital grant as 'creating a public foundation for private life' (1999: 186). This is a depoliticization of republican theory in which property was a private foundation for political life, for active citizenship. The sense in which Ackerman and Alstott see stakeholding as a citizenship programme is that it underwrites economic citizenship. They compare 'one citizen one vote' as the mark of political citizenship to 'one citizen one stake' as the emblem of economic citizenship. But the comparison of basic income with universal suffrage is much more apt. The standing of 'citizen' and the right to vote continue for an individual's whole adult life. Basic capital is a one-off payment at the beginning of adulthood, whereas a basic income is paid regularly throughout life. It thus provides the security necessary to participate in social and political life and to exercise citizenship; heroic efforts are not required. Universal suffrage is the emblem of equal citizenship, and a basic income is the emblem of full standing as a citizen, of citizenship that is of equal worth.

The comparison between a basic income and universal suffrage was first suggested to me by a little-noticed passage in T. H. Marshall's *Citizenship and Social Class* (1963: 116): 'to have to bargain for a living wage in a society which accepts the living wage as a social right is as absurd as to have to haggle for a vote in a society which accepts the vote as a political right'. However, there are two problems with Marshall's argument.

First, as indicated by his reference to a living wage, he linked standard of life to employment, by which he meant male employment (an issue I shall return to shortly). Second, Ackerman and Alstott's separation of citizenship into economic and political components echoes Marshall's famous categorization of social, civil, and political rights of citizens. The problem is that dividing up citizenship in such ways causes needless difficulties in thinking about democratization. Attention gets diverted into endless wrangles about which category is primary (is it economic or political citizenship?), or which rights properly can be seen as 'rights' (do social rights count?). The issue of what constitutes the democratic rights required for autonomy and full standing for all citizens is then glossed over.[3]

By a democratic right I have in mind a fundamental right in Henry Shue's (1996) sense of a right that is essential if other rights are to be enjoyed. A basic income as a democratic right can be compared to the suffrage, another fundamental right. Universal suffrage underpins an orderly change of government through free and fair elections, and so enhances citizens' security, and enables each citizen to share in collective self-government. A basic income provides the security required to maintain full standing as a citizen, and enables each citizen to exercise individual self-government. I shall first say something about security and then turn to freedom as self-government.

Ackerman and Alstott reject basic income as an illegitimate, paternalistic constraint on freedom, but Van Parijs, although presenting a libertarian argument, introduces a 'mild' paternalism. The issue of paternalism arises in connection with the question of whether payment of income to individuals in a single lump sum at one point in time (basic capital), or as a series of regular payments during their lifetime (basic income) best promotes individual freedom. The choice between the payment methods is more than a matter of administrative convenience, since, from the perspective of individual opportunity, basic income can be seen as an unjustified restriction on freedom.

The most obvious reason for preferring the regular instalments of a basic income is that a lump-sum capital grant could very easily and quickly be squandered or lost, even if individuals avoided Las Vegas or prolonged spending or drug sprees. Many responsible individuals could lose their basic capital: small businesses, for instance, have high rates of failure despite the best efforts of their owners, and stock markets crash. In Ackerman and Alstott's words a stake provides a launching pad – but an individual's trajectory could be very short indeed (1999: 215).

In his discussion of payment method, Van Parijs remarks that if the problem of individuals throwing away their stake is that the consequent poverty leads to theft, and puts at risk human dignity and worth, then income paid at regular intervals is 'the obvious choice'. Further justification is required if 'the rationale is phrased in terms of real freedom' (1995: 46). To be sure, more argument is necessary, but there is no need, as this comment suggests, sharply to separate an argument about freedom from an argument about poverty, dignity and worth, not, at least, if freedom as self-government is at issue. Dignity is not the same as freedom, but a basic income is necessary to maintain the dignity and autonomy, and to uphold the standing, of all citizens, not just those near destitution; regular payments provide the security required for the enjoyment of citizenship of equal worth.[4]

In contrast, Ackerman and Alstott see the risk of losing a stake as part of freedom. Basic capital does not offer paternalistic protection. Adults know that their actions have long-term consequences, even if many outcomes are unexpected, so they should not be prevented from deciding for themselves what to do with a lump-sum payment. Each 'competent citizen should be deemed responsible for shaping the larger contours of his existence – for better or for worse. To treat him otherwise is to treat him as an eternal child' (1999: 213). Thus, they reject the alternative suggested by Le Grand and Nissan (2000, this volume). The latter propose that their £10,000 capital stake should be administered by trustees who will scrutinize requests for payment and allow it to be paid only for a number of approved uses, such as education, starting a business, or a down payment on a home. Ackerman and Alstott see such limitations on payment of the capital sum as unacceptable 'freedom-within-boundaries' (1999: 215).

Nonetheless, Ackerman and Alstott introduce an element of paternalism into their argument in two ways. They propose that basic capital should be paid to each individual in four instalments. Individuals can then learn from any mistakes they may make at first. In answer to the problem of individuals rapidly squandering their basic capital, Ackerman and Alstott propose a combination of a capital grant with retirement pensions that are paid unconditionally to all citizens (which makes their scheme more complicated than a stake or basic income alone). This ensures that if young citizens lose their stakes they will not be destitute in their old age.

In *Real Freedom for All*, Van Parijs's real libertarianism turns out to be fairly weak and involves some significant departures from the logic of libertarianism, including the introduction of paternalism. A typical libertarian would take a position similar to that of Ackerman and Alstott. Indeed, Van Parijs duly notes that individual freedom (opportunity) would be increased if individuals received their income as a single lump-sum payment and could do with it as they wished. But he argues for basic income as follows: he assumes that individuals 'in their right minds' at any point in their lives wish to protect their freedom in later years against unwise actions when younger. Thus 'a mildly paternalistic concern for people's real freedom throughout their lives, (...) makes it sensible to hand out the basic income in the form of a (non-mortgageable) regular stream' (1995: 47).[5] This is not a very convincing argument from a libertarian standpoint, nor is it very compelling as an argument for basic income if democratization is a concern.

Ackerman and Alstott are concerned about paternalism because the opportunities opened to individuals by basic capital are opportunities to use their energies and abilities to become economically successful. This is also the view of Le Grand and Nissan (2000, this volume) who state plainly that the point of a capital grant is that it provides 'a springboard to accumulate wealth'. The problem with which Ackerman and Alstott begin is that of young individuals' unequal economic starting points. Some begin their adult journey with a handicap because of their parents' lack of economic resources. A capital stake gives each young citizen his or her fair share. It ensures that he faces a 'level playing field when he enters the marketplace as an adult', and provides resources to meet the challenges of competitive markets (1999: 22). Whether or not individuals make the most of these opportunities is up to them. As Ackerman and Alstott state, they 'are interested in opportunities, not outcomes' (1999: 24).

Equipped with their basic capital grant, young citizens, Ackerman and Alstott declare, will be able to 'inaugurate a new age of freedom' (1999: 217). However, the 'massive increase in effective freedom', and the 'promise [of] more real freedom for all', is an opportunity, no more (1999: 35, 76). A universal stake would make a big difference to the lives of many citizens, not least, as they point out, to members of minority groups and to women, but stakeholding is not a 'cradle-to-grave safety net' (1999: 119). It relies on youthful energy and enterprise, unlike a basic income; a 'basic income cushions failure; stakeholding is a launching pad for success' (1999: 215).

Paternalism looms large when freedom is seen as individual opportunity because basic income inevitably seems like a constraint on freedom. But if one begins from another conception of freedom, and from the perspective of democratization, then the problem is different. Assisting young people to make a start in their adult lives is all to the good, but basic capital is insufficient to answer the problem of how the necessary security can be furnished to enable citizens, at any time in their lives, to enjoy individual autonomy, and participate when they wish in the life of their society. The problem is not paternalism, but concerns the necessary social and political change to create a robust democracy for all citizens, whether successful or not. A basic income offers part of an answer to this problem.

Equality of opportunity is, of course, part of democracy, but individual freedom as self-government is the core requirement. To see why this is the case, it is necessary to consider very briefly why freedom is a central principle of democracy. Modern (that is, universal) democracy could not have developed without the assumption that individuals were born free, or were naturally free, and were equal to each other. It follows from the assumption of universal freedom and equality that all individuals are self-governing or autonomous – a political form of individual freedom. It also follows that the only justification for government of one individual by another (or one group by another) is agreement (consent).

If individuals are to maintain their autonomy they cannot be mere subjects who are governed, they must become citizens with rights that allow them to govern themselves collectively and individually.

In *Real Freedom*, Van Parijs rejects any necessary connection between individual freedom and democracy. On this question he follows standard libertarian doctrine, and assumes that democracy is merely incidental to freedom. He distinguishes a free society – one that can determine its own fate and exercises collective sovereignty – from a society in which the members are also individually sovereign, and considers two possible answers to the question of what constitutes individual freedom or sovereignty.

The first is that individuals have equal power in making collective decisions. Such individuals live in a 'maximally democratic society', one that 'subjects everything to collective decision making'. A 'thoroughly democratic form of collectivism' involves 'public ownership of both people and capital' (1995: 8). Not surprisingly, he rejects this nightmarish view of democracy. He also rejects a second conception of individual sovereignty, closely related to the first: that is, individual sovereignty as active participation in collective endeavours. Both these views of individual freedom are inadequate, he argues, because they posit a necessary, rather than instrumental, relationship between individual freedom and political life. They make the 'individual's relationship to (...) political life (...) a matter of definition' (1995: 17). Any connection between democracy and a maximally free society is contingent, a possible empirical condition for individual freedom.

Van Parijs identifies democracy with collective decision-making, and sets it at odds with individual freedom. But to see maximal democratic decision-making as radically collectivist is to beg a great number of questions about the meaning of 'democracy'. My references to collective self-government have nothing to do with 'collectivism' as public ownership; they refer to citizens' participation in the government of a political system. At a minimum this requires a democratic electoral procedure – 'free and fair elections' – based on universal suffrage, with its associated civil and political liberties. Individual freedom of opportunity is one of the liberties, and some citizen participation is required to keep the electoral system in operation.

Indeed, Van Parijs seems to have this conception in mind when setting out his three conditions for real freedom, that is, a society in which all the members have maximum freedom. One condition is that security in the form of a structure of rights is necessary. He says little about these rights, but his argument requires the rights necessary for formal freedom, a market economy, and the protection of private property. He occasionally refers, without elaboration, to a basic income as a right (for example, 1995: 37).

Democratic theorists have paid more attention to collective self-government than to individual self-government or autonomy. But individual freedom is not exhausted by participation in the government of the state (collective self-government). Another dimension of 'government' drops out of sight when individual freedom is interpreted as the availability of economic opportunities that individuals can pursue untrammelled by (governmental) paternalism, that is, government as the exercise of authority by one individual, or category of individuals, over another in any area of social life. Where government is unwarranted, enjoyment of self-government is denied or limited.

Individual autonomy depends not only on collective self-government and the extent of available economic opportunities, but also on the structure of institutions within which individuals interact with one another. Individual freedom as self-government requires that individuals interact within authority structures that enhance their autonomy, and that they have the standing, and are able (have the opportunities and means), to enjoy and safeguard their freedom. When the two dimensions of self-government are prised apart, questions never arise about individual freedom within familiar institutions, such as marriage. Yet feminist political theorists have criticized the curtailment of wives' self-government for three centuries, and, at least since the 1790s, have analysed the structural connection between marriage, women's livelihood and citizenship. But democratic theorists still do not give their arguments the attention they deserve, nor are they taken nearly seriously enough in the debate about basic income and basic capital.

## 2   Women and free riding

A basic income has the potential to open up avenues of institutional change necessary for democratization. For this to take place citizens must begin to consider the structural interrelationships between their institutions, and a basic income could encourage this reflection. An appreciation of the fashion in which the major social institutions of marriage, employment, and citizenship, developed together and mutually reinforced each other is absent from too many discussions of basic income and basic capital. Without such an appreciation, the democratic significance of basic income never gets onto the agenda.

As feminist scholars have been demonstrating for many years now, the social insurance system of Anglo-American countries was constructed on the assumption that wives not only were their husbands' economic dependents, but also they were lesser citizens whose benefits depended on their private status and husbands' contributions, not their own citizenship. Ackerman and Alstott acknowledge this in their proposal for unconditional retirement pensions. The addition of retirement pensions to a stake allows them to write of a transition from worker (that is, male worker) citizenship to universal economic citizenship. Their proposed unconditional payment to older citizens breaks the link, forged in the New Deal in the United States, between men's employment histories and retirement pensions. As they note, the pension would be particularly significant for older women whose benefits still largely derive from their husbands' employment.

To make this point another way, it is only paid employment that has been seen as 'work' (as the phrase 'going out to work' indicates), and as involving the tasks that are the mark of a productive citizen and contributor to society and the polity. Other contributions, notably all the work required to reproduce and maintain a healthy population, and care for the sick and infirm – the caring tasks, many of which are contributed without payment in the private household, and are undertaken by women – have been seen as irrelevant to citizenship. Despite reforms to the social insurance system, the institutional connections and beliefs about 'work', masculinity, and femininity, are still powerful social forces.

Few participants in discussions of basic income have noticed, as has Van Parijs, that free riding exists 'on a massive scale' in household interactions (1995: 143). Free riders are individuals, or a section of the population, who continually take advantage of the efforts of others with no contribution on their part. Discussions of a basic income are full of apprehension about free riding, but who are the free riders in the household?[6] Barry notes that full-time housewives can be seen as free riders (1996: 245).[7] Yet housewives are working, as feminist scholars have emphasized for a very long time, by undertaking many vital tasks in the home, not least the necessary caring work. The majority of wives are now in some form of paid employment, but their labour force participation is different from that of men. This reflects the legacy of a wage-system that enshrined the belief that husbands (men) not wives (women) are 'breadwinners'. Many more women than men work part-time, and women earn less than men. The private and public sexual division of labour, that is to say, continues to be structured so that men monopolize full-time, higher-paying, and more prestigious paid employment, and wives do a disproportionate share of unpaid work in the home. Given the structure of institutions and social beliefs, this appears as a 'rational' arrangement. The mutual reinforcement of marriage and employment explains why husbands can take advantage of the unpaid work of wives, and avoid doing their fair share of the caring work. That is why there is massive free riding in the household – by husbands.

The conditions under which the institution of employment and the Anglo-American social insurance system was constructed have now crumbled. 'Old economy' male breadwinner jobs are being swept away in global economic restructuring. New jobs have been created but many are low paid, lacking benefits, and temporary. Downsizing and economic insecurity are widespread. Views about femininity, masculinity, and marriage are changing too. We are still in the midst of these changes and the eventual outcome is uncertain, but at present we are living in circumstances in which it has become possible to rethink the connections between income and paid employment, between marriage, employment and citizenship, between the private and public division of labour, between caring work and other work, and reconsider the meaning of 'work'. This is crucial if proper account is to be taken of women's freedom, which has received rather short shrift in discussions of a basic income.

In 1792, Mary Wollstonecraft (1993) argued that rights, citizenship, and full standing for women required, among other radical changes, economic independence for both married and single women. A basic income would, for the first time, provide women with life-long (modest) economic independence and security, a major reason why it is central to democratization. Thus feminists might be expected to support the introduction of a basic income, or, more generally, stakeholding (see Parker, 1993; Alstott, 2001; McKay and Van Every, 2000).

Yet some feminists are critical of the idea of a basic income because they fear it would reinforce the existing sexual division of labour, the current pattern of free riding in the household, and women's lesser citizenship. They argue that provision of an income without having to engage in paid employment would, in light of women's position in the labour market combined with lingering beliefs about the proper tasks of women and men, give women an incentive to undertake more unpaid work in the household. Conversely, men would have a greater incentive to free ride by avoiding the necessary work of caring for others. That is to say, a basic income would reinforce existing limitations on women's freedom.[8]

Ackerman and Alstott address this issue. They argue that, in the longer run, basic capital can help diminish 'pervasive cultural vulnerabilities' (1999: 60). They reject the claim that a stake might reinforce such vulnerabilities by encouraging women to use their basic capital to subsidize their unpaid work, leaving them little better off as competitors in the market. Women's judgement, they argue, must be respected. In the short run, since it is women who are expected to combine paid employment and unpaid work in the home, basic capital will allow them to make a rational accommodation to this unfair arrangement. Over the longer term, a stake will enable 'enterprising women' to challenge tradition and 'make their own way in the world' (1999: 208).

No doubt enterprising women would improve their position if they had a capital stake – many already do – and a stake would help change women's bargaining position and view of themselves. But although cultural assumptions, views, and vulnerabilities are major obstacles to change, institutional structures are involved as well. A stake, in the long run, is much less likely than an income, which offers modest economic independence for life and makes employment truly voluntary, to change both cultural views and institutions. A basic income would also change women's standing as citizens since employment would be dethroned from its position as the only work that really counts. A basic income would not only encourage citizens to think about the implications of current arrangements, but would give men the opportunity to do their fair share of the unpaid work of caring for others.

One crucial difference between a stake and a basic income is that the new opportunities made available by a basic income (set at the requisite level) would not be confined to the competitive market. On the one hand, a basic income acts as a subsidy that allows individuals to take low-paid jobs. On the other, it gives citizens the freedom not to be employed and uncouples standard of life from the institution of employment. Both basic capital and basic income would enable individuals to make the kinds of choices discussed by Ackerman and Alstott in their 'profiles in freedom' (1999: ch. 4). Stakeholding would make it possible for anyone (at any point in their life, not merely while they are young, if they had a basic income) to go back to school, or to retrain to move to a new occupation, or to open a business.

But a basic income would do more than this. If it allowed citizens to live at a modest but decent standard, they could 'take time off', for example, to do voluntary work, develop their political capacities and skills, learn to surf, to write or paint, devote themselves to family life – or undertake caring work – or just have a period of self-reassessment or contemplation. By loosening the tie between marriage, income, and employment, a basic income can assist, in a way that basic capital for young people cannot, in removing impediments to freedom. It would allow individuals more easily to refuse to enter or to leave relationships that violate individual self-government, or that involve unsafe, unhealthy, or demeaning conditions.

The freedom to take a break from, or not to engage in, paid employment is a freedom that runs counter to the direction of recent public policy and much political rhetoric. Some commentators even claim that the capacities and skills necessary for citizenship can be developed only through employment. A widespread assumption underlying the reforms based on 'workfare' is that, ideally, the whole adult population should be in paid employment – including the mothers of young children, which is a major historical shift. Whether, in light of current technological change and productivity increases, such a policy of universal employment is feasible is an open question, especially if it is employment at a living wage ('full employment' in the past referred to male employment). The effect of such policies and rhetoric is to draw even tighter the long-standing link between employment and citizenship, at the very time when change makes possible a reassessment of the connection.

It is also worth noting that a reinforcement of male free riding is a likely outcome of universal employment. Advocates of workfare tend to remain silent about how the necessary caring work would be undertaken if all adults were employed. Either the tacit assumption seems to be that employment patterns would remain sexually differentiated, and women would continue to do most of the unpaid caring work. Or it is assumed that care would be provided through the market. But there seems little evidence that all citizens would have sufficient means to be able to purchase the necessary services, or that care of sufficient quality and quantity would be profitable enough to be made available.

To move the discussion of basic income forward, two changes are needed. First, democratization and women's freedom must be brought into the argument. Proposals for stakeholding are about social change, and the direction of social and political change depends, among other things, on the reasons why it is advocated and the claims made about what it is expected to achieve. If the beneficial consequences for women are not a prominent part of the debate, and if the reasons for supporting a basic income do not emphasize its democratic potential, then the outcome is unlikely to strengthen democracy or women's freedom. So it is vital for a case to be made in terms of democratization, which, if it is not to reproduce the long history of 'democracy' as a masculine preserve, necessarily includes women's standing and freedom.

Ackerman and Alstott argue that a stake encourages individuals, in a way that a basic income cannot, to reflect upon what they want to do with their lives, and appraise their situation. 'Civic reflection' and attention to 'the fate of the nation' become possible when economic anxieties are lifted (1999: 185). A 'purer form of patriotism' will arise out of the 'simple gratitude to the nation' that citizens will feel as they think about their capital grant and the debt that they owe to their country for the economic citizenship that comes with basic capital (1999: 186, also 43–4). Patriotism and gratitude, however, have only a tenuous connection to individual freedom.

Provision of a one-off capital grant will no doubt encourage individuals to consider what courses of action are open to them, and might even foster reflection on the debt they owe to their country. But it seems implausible that it would help open up reflection on the political implications of the structural connections between marriage, employment, and citizenship. A one-off payment, argued for in terms of economic citizenship and economic success, does not provide a context that gives encouragement to think about broader connections between social institutions and democratization. In contrast, a basic income, which provided a modest standard of living independently of employment, would offer an incentive for citizens to think in wider terms about the institutions within which they live. It has the potential to assist in an institutional and cultural democratic transformation.

It is impossible to predict what the outcome of a stake or a basic income might be. All human activities have unintended and unforeseen consequences. The fears of feminist critics of a basic income could be borne out, and the possibility is certainly increased if feminist scholars and feminist insights, together with democratization, remain outside the debates about a basic income.

The second requirement is that theoretical arguments about basic income acknowledge the relationship between individuals' freedom and the structure of institutions. Many unnecessary problems arise when political theorists borrow from neo-classical economic theory. An abstractly individualistic theoretical framework is imported that works against an appreciation of the democratizing potential of basic income. Van Parijs's conception of freedom illustrates how the separation of individuals from institutions robs real freedom of the limits required for a plausible account of basic income.

I referred earlier to Van Parijs's (1995) three conditions for real freedom. The first was the security of a structure of rights, and the second is that 'each person has the greatest possible opportunity to do whatever she might want to do' (Van Parijs, 1995: 25).[9] This is maximum freedom or real freedom for all (subject only to the limitations of security of rights and self-ownership).[10] He states that he decided against a definition of freedom in terms of what individuals actually want to do because focusing on 'might want' avoids the problem of want manipulation.[11] He argues that really to be free means not just that the formal right exists to do whatever individuals might want to do, but that they have the means to do so (another claim drawn from anti-libertarian sources). A basic income provides the requisite means. Whether or not Van Parijs's claim that a basic income should be set at the highest sustainable level involves a bigger or smaller amount than my assumption of a sum sufficient to sustain a modest but decent standard of life is an empirical question. However, I doubt that a level sufficient to underwrite his real freedom is possible, since real freedom has no limits.

Van Parijs states that real freedom is not merely the freedom to consume but to be able to choose among different ways of life. A real libertarian is not concerned with maintaining a living standard or obtaining what he wants. There must be opportunities to do what one might want to do. Van Parijs gives two brief examples: if a person lives in a commune, the assumption is 'innocuously enough' that they might, one day, want to live alone; if you live in the country, you might want to live in the city (1995: 38). But I might want to build and live in a replica of the White House in the Malibu hills, I might want to ride to an orbiting space station, I might want to ... What I might want to do at some stage of my life is unlimited.

Van Parijs's argument rests on concepts, drawn from economic theory, such as preference satisfaction, rents, opportunity costs, and endowments. Despite Van Parijs's caveat about consumption, his 'individual' closely resembles the consumer of neo-classical economics. This individual has desires that know no limits, since what he might want to do is determined by his subjective preferences (measured through market prices), and individuals can have preferences or tastes for anything whatsoever.[12] Van Parijs's 'individuals' are, in effect, mere vessels for preferences, severed from social relationships.

Consider his analysis of free riding in the household. He recognizes that it occurs on a large scale, but he reduces the problem to a comparison of two sets of preferences or tastes. Free riding, Van Parijs states, occurs when benefits enjoyed by both partners in a household are produced by only one of them, the partner who happens to care most about the particular benefit. His example is that the partner who most strongly prefers tidiness will make sure that the home is tidy. But 'tidiness' is part of the more general work of housekeeping, and there is abundant empirical evidence that shows that it is the female partner who is most likely to do the housework, including tidying up. The empirical data do not show this pattern just by chance – female partners do not by some quirk happen to prefer tidiness more strongly than their male partners. Rather, as feminist scholarship has demonstrated at length, this persistent pattern of behaviour is the result of the interlocking structure of two institutions, marriage and employment, and social beliefs about what it means to be a wife or husband.

The institution of marriage has vanished in Van Parijs's analysis of free riding in the household and there are merely two individuals, indistinguishable except for their different tastes for tidy surroundings. Thus he can recognize that free riding exists, but not that it is a problem about men (husbands) and caring work. He has nothing to say about the structure of relations between the sexes and a whole area of debate is, therefore, removed from discussion of basic income.

Yet, in the end, either individuals and institutions have to be brought back together, or some other connection between them must be postulated. The connection that Van Parijs (1995: 230) makes in his closing pages is through 'solidaristic patriotism'. He argues that the 'political feasibility' of justice is, in part, a matter of the design of institutions that 'approximate one-man-one-vote [*sic*] democracy on a world scale' (1995: 228–9). Solidaristic patriotism is needed to foster a commitment to a conception of justice and 'pride in the collective project in which [individuals] are (...) involved' (Van Parijs, 1995: 230). He even toys with the idea of compulsory public service to maintain social cohesion. This is hardly a move one would expect from a libertarian, but it is indicative of the problems generated by the abstractly individualist approach of economic theory. These familiar problems have been extensively explored by theorists such as Hegel, Durkheim, and Parsons. Yet political theory deriving from the concepts and assumptions of economic theory is written as if their arguments did not exist, and as if Hobbes had not given us his great lesson in the political consequences of atomistic individualism in *Leviathan*.

Van Parijs states that compulsory public service is the indirect and instrumental way that real libertarians can restrict freedom and take account of some 'anti-individualist' concerns of communitarians (1995: 231). But basic capital and basic income are about the enlargement of individual freedom, not compulsion; the resort to compulsion is an artefact of a theoretical starting point. And why should communitarians be the reference point, especially if the concern is individual freedom (see also Ackerman and Alstott, 1999: 43–4, 186)? Have other contributors to political theory nothing to say of relevance to individual freedom?

## 3 Basic income as a citizenship right

I now want to return to the comparison between universal suffrage and a basic income, which raises a problem that I have not seen discussed. Universal suffrage means that the vote is no longer a privilege but a democratic right. Thus, virtually everyone must be able easily to meet qualifications for enfranchisement; hence the importance of age, or in the case of candidates for naturalization, length of residence, and being of sound mind.[13] Similarly, if a basic income is to be a democratic right, all citizens must be able to qualify: there can be no conditions.

Apprehension about free riding has led to many proposals for conditions for the payment of a basic income, such as Atkinson's (1996) 'participation income' (see Anderson, 2001; Galston, 2001; Phelps, 2001). Both Ackerman and Alstott and Van Parijs introduce conditions. The former restrict full stakeholding to individuals who have a high school diploma, and make loss of part of basic capital a penalty for certain crimes. Van Parijs suggests that under certain conditions, usually found in poor countries, a work test is appropriate. Ackerman and Alstott could respond that their criteria resemble those for the suffrage: virtually everyone could meet them. Van Parijs believes the relevant circumstances are unlikely to obtain in rich countries such as the United States or Britain.

Once conditions are introduced, however generously interpreted, a basic income becomes a privilege not a right. The problem then arises of the status of those who fail to, or refuse to, meet the conditions. Are they to become second-class citizens? This problem has been glossed over in current debates, but once democratization is at the centre of argument the question of conditional citizenship becomes harder to avoid. It is unconditional – democratic – citizenship that is at the heart of the case for both basic income and basic capital. Ackerman and Alstott argue that, in the end, the justification of a stake 'rests on each American's claim to respect as a free and equal citizen' (1999: 209). Both basic capital and basic income have symbolic as well as material significance by helping to remove the temptation for some citizens to see others as less worthy of respect, and so as lesser citizens, because of their lack of economic resources.

They also argue that individuals (and their success) depend on a complex web of cooperation by others, and that stakeholding recognizes this social fact. Here Ackerman and Alstott are drawing on the tradition of argument that all citizens have a right to a fair share in the collective patrimony because the wealth and resources of a society are built by the cooperative endeavours of preceding and present generations. In the twenty-first century surely it is time that all citizens in a democracy should enjoy a share of the patrimony in the form of the security and freedom of a guaranteed basic income.

## Notes

1. I have been interested in basic income for some years, but have only now begun to write about it. I wish to thank Manchester University for a Hallsworth Fellowship that gave me three months to read in 1997, and especially David Purdy for sharing his manuscript and for our conversations. Thanks also to Jurgen de Wispelaere, and participants at two seminars at the Research School of Social Sciences, ANU in the fall of 2000.
2. For ease of exposition I shall refer to 'citizens', leaving open the question of permanent residents. I shall also leave children aside, together with some other issues that are outside the scope of this chapter.
3. On Marshall, see also Pateman (1996). The problems are exacerbated by the existence of two UN Covenants, one dealing with civil and political rights, and the other with economic, social and cultural rights. Moreover, as feminist legal scholars have pointed out, standard interpretations of 'human rights' have endlessly reproduced the separation between public (political) and private, a separation that also characterizes most discussions of a basic income.
4. For an argument that destitution in the form of homelessness is a denial of individual freedom, see Waldron (1993c).
5. Van Parijs and Ackerman and Alstott treat the question of method of payment as a problem about personal identity, in the sense of whether one is the same person at 60 as at 20. If the self is a series of discrete entities over time, then the later self cannot blame the earlier for youthful folly. The problem of personal identity is interesting, but of little concern in discussions of a stake and a basic income, which are about citizenship and social and political change, not individual identity. The latter issue assumes a central place in individualist theoretical frameworks (extreme individualism in Van Parijs's case).
6. I make some general comments on the free-rider objection in Pateman (2001).
7. McKay and Van Every (2000: 281) remark that critics of the free-rider objection argue in 'masculinist terms which ignore the implicit relegation of family carers to this category'.
8. Like Robeyns (2001) I have frequently encountered this objection when I have talked about a basic income, but less often seen it in academic discussions (see also the comments in Walter, 1989: 123–5).
9. The third condition is self-ownership, which I will not pursue in this chapter. Van Parijs (1995: 9) states that the idea of self-ownership cannot be attacked on grounds of freedom. For such a criticism see Pateman (2002).

10. Strictly, real freedom involves leximin opportunity, but this is not relevant to my argument. Leximin means that the person with least opportunities has no fewer opportunities than does the person with least opportunities under any other arrangement. If there is such an alternative feasible arrangement, the calculation is made for the person with the second-least opportunities.

11. He also extends real freedom beyond coercion to include obstacles that have not been produced by anyone: 'Even stating that I am not free to travel faster than light is only slightly odd, if at all' (1995: 23). For some other comments on his conception of freedom see Barry (1996: 250–5).

12. The problem then arises of why, if tastes vary, income should not vary also. In discussing undominated diversity, Van Parijs rescues his assumption that a basic income will be paid at a uniform level by introducing the restriction that preferences must be genuine, and available to and understood by others. However, this presupposes the network of social relationships that is absent from his examples, which highlight such bizarre cases as individuals who prefer to be blind rather than sighted, crippled rather than able bodied.

13. The debacle in Florida in the 2000 Presidential election drew attention to the 14 states that continue to strip former felons of the franchise for life (around one and a half million people).

# 9
# Assessing the Unconditional Stake[1]

*Robert van der Veen*

## 1  Introduction

In this volume, the idea of granting each citizen the right to an equal and unconditional share in the wealth of society is subsumed under the rubric of stakeholding. The idea presupposes that individuals, as citizens of a (national) state, have claims of distributive justice which go far beyond the bottom-line requirement that for a society to be called a just one, all members must be able to secure at least a minimally decent living, that is, must have a material 'stake' in social cooperation.[2] Unconditional stakeholding also entertains more ambitious pro-grammes of redistribution than those commonly embodied in the institutions of the status quo – the welfare state, for the time being. For it aims at granting individuals economic independence as a matter of citizen status, whereas welfare state redistribution is conditional upon economic contingencies of need and dependence.

Unconditional stakeholding comes in two contrasting forms: basic income and basic capital. Each has its own origins. I will not discuss these here, except to mention that proposals for basic income and basic capital seem to have had no historical connections, until quite recently.[3] So it may be more accurate to say that there are two separate ideas here, which favour granting equal shares with no strings attached, and which one can try to assess in the common framework of stakeholding. But note that the term seems to be most appropriate for defending basic cap-ital endowments. As far as I can see, the large literature on basic income of the last three decades has never used the metaphor of stakeholding to describe the normative and policy issues with which it is concerned. Somehow, a 'stake' is more easily associated with possessing a capital stock rather than an income stream. This association is not necessary, of course, and so the framework of comparison that I have in mind is meant to be entirely neutral with respect to the form of the unconditional stake.

The framework is provided by two of the most elaborate defences of basic income and basic capital: Van Parijs (1995) and Ackerman and Alstott (1999). Both share a liberal egalitarian perspective on distributive justice. Both pay close attention to sources of fair taxation for funding unconditional stakes, given how personal endowments (native talent, inherited wealth, job assets and social capital) interact to affect lifetime earning power in a market economy. Finally, both claim that the unconditional stake is the most fair and efficient way of promoting equality of opportunity (or 'real freedom') in a liberal state, in particular compared to policies that subsidize work of low productivity, and selectively compensate for involuntary unemployment or disability. While I support this last claim, it is a controversial one, involving several unsettled issues which I have tried to address elsewhere.[4] Here I want to focus on the further question of what is the most attractive way of working out the idea of the unconditional stake. Since the proposal of basic capital has re-emerged only quite recently, and partly in opposition to basic income, it will be necessary to pay close attention to the arguments of Ackerman and Alstott in the following comparisons.

Basic income and basic capital may be contrasted on three main points: *convertibility, welfare state reform* and *cultural content of freedom*. Despite appearances to the contrary, I argue that the two versions of the unconditional stake are largely compatible on the first two of these points. Where they really diverge is on the third point. Basic capital envisages a 'culture of property ownership'. Basic income hopes to engender a 'culture of disposable time'. Perhaps these two cultures – neither of which actually exist to any significant extent, I hasten to add – could be reconciled to some extent. Both, after all, arise from the ideal of a free society which generalizes the privilege of being a 'person of independent means' to each citizen. But each has a sufficiently different orientation on the content of this ideal to explain why basic capital and basic income have been regarded as distinct alternatives of unconditional stakeholding.

The outline of my argument is as follows. Considering convertibility first, any stream of regular income payments during a given period can be transformed into an equivalent stock of capital and vice versa, given the rate of interest. To put the contrast sharply, basic capital permits the conversion of a stock into an annual stream, while basic income prohibits the conversion of the annual stream into a stock. At issue here are different views on reasonable precaution against irresponsible behaviour. On the liberal conception of opportunity egalitarianism, it is a matter of principle that individuals are responsible for their lifetime decisions in earning, spending, saving, and investing, once they can count on their fair share. Basic capital seems to take this all the way. It holds that the capacity for responsible action over long periods of time is robust enough to rule that persons who waste or gamble away their fair share have no claims on the state to be bailed out when they fall into need. Basic income strongly rejects this 'starting gate' conception of responsible action. It holds that people have good reason for pre-committing themselves to spreading their fair share evenly across time, so that they will be protected from predictable failures to take care of their future interests.

But judging from the stakeholding proposal of Ackerman and Alstott, this contrast is misleadingly overdrawn. As I show in the next two sections, the convertibility issue actually loses much of its significance. The main reasons emerge from a comparison between the stances of basic income and basic capital concerning the second point of difference, on how best to reform the welfare state. There are several ways of introducing a substantial basic income. But certainly in Europe, where the idea originated as a definite proposal of social policy, basic income builds on the foundations of a universalistic minimum income guarantee. It might be thought that those who endorse the basic capital form of the unconditional stake will want to limit the safety nets of the welfare state to an absolute minimum. After all, if people are capable of responsible managing of capital stakes, they can be left to their own devices, and the welfare state becomes largely redundant. But despite rhetoric about the harsh lot awaiting 'stakeblowers', this is not what Ackerman and Alstott argue for. Quite unexpectedly, their view on unconditional stakeholding turns out to require a highly inclusive set of state provisions for guaranteeing a minimum income, and mostly at a 'decent' level of subsistence, not a bare poverty line. Details aside, these provisions are remarkably similar to the ones which are commonly envisaged as the starting point of the basic income programme. As a consequence, the dispute about making available Ackerman and Alstott's basic capital of $80,000 during early adulthood, or alternatively dispensing it in annual instalments, is considerably restricted in scope. Indeed that dispute is limited to an unconditional stake of a size less than the amount of equivalent capital tied up in welfare state provisions over the entire life of stakeholding citizens, including a universal citizens' pension.

In section 4, I present some rough calculations to illustrate this claim. Under these conditions, then, people would seem to be sufficiently protected against their own possible short-sightedness to make the unconditional stake fully convertible, with either basic capital or basic income as the 'default' setting. Which of these two settings should be preferred depends on further considerations, to which I turn in the last two sections. The calculations just mentioned are based on the key variables of Ackerman and Alstott's stakeholding proposal, notably the capital size, the real rate of interest, and the indicative figure for a decent subsistence income. The importance of the third point of contrast between basic capital and basic income is now shown by calculating the size of the capital that would convert into a subsistence annuity during working age, at the same real rate of interest. That capital is almost three times as large as Ackerman and Alstott's stakeholder endowment of $80,000. What this reveals, as I argue in section 5, is that the basic income programme is committed to distribute an unconditional stake of this magnitude over the lifetime of each citizen. For its goal is to liberate all individuals from the subsistence constraint, on a timescale which is dictated only by the limitations of economic sustainability. By contrast, the programme envisaged by Ackerman and Alstott does not seem geared to raising the basic capital of successive stakeholders along a similar trajectory. In section 6, I will speculate on how this can be explained by the two cultures of stakeholding mentioned above.

## 2   Streams into stocks?

In their comment on alternative forms of stakeholding, Ackerman and Alstott polemically remark that basic income is said to be 'better because we are more likely to prevent people from "wasting" their stake if we pay it out in dribs and drabs over time' (1999: 214). One reason why they resist this is that consuming an $80,000 stake in relatively small annual portions may actually be seen as something of a waste (1999: 215). What the state can do is try to create social conditions in which the stake is likely to be managed responsibly. But Ackerman and Alstott feel no need for legal paternalism across the board. For they think that few stakeholders would prefer drawing a small annuity during most of their lives anyway, because the stake can be put to far better uses at an age when most are not in a position to take up a serious project of long-term investment (1999: 119). Given how unequally wealth is distributed among persons, and across age groups, especially in the United States, this last point is a powerful one.

So the permissiveness of the basic capital position presents a challenge to basic income. It is fair to say that so far, most supporters of basic income have not been all that concerned about the issue of convertibility. They see that income as an emancipatory alternative to welfare, rather than as a sum of wealth which happens to be allocated periodically. But among thoughtful contemporary defenders, who do recognize that the unconditional stake can take these two forms, there is extreme reluctance to allow streams to be turned into stocks. A fairly strong paternalist rationale is given in *Real Freedom for All*. For Van Parijs, the key reason for prohibiting the convertibility of basic income rests on 'a universal desire on people's part, when "in their right minds", to protect their freedom at older ages against the weakness of their will at younger ages and to do so pretty homogeneously throughout their lifetimes' (1995: 47). Meeting this desire requires that basic income be restricted to a 'non-mortgageable' regular income stream, which guarantees 'fresh starts' in each (monthly or annual) period.[5] That there is such a universal wish to protect future interests 'homogeneously' may well be doubted. But even if true, it is a decisive consideration only if people also universally believe that the potential gains of being able to invest their 'mortgaged' basic income are outweighed by the potentially bad consequences of 'wasting' it at relatively early ages. This is precisely what Ackerman and Alstott want to deny, as we have just seen.

I conclude that the empirical argument in favour of prohibiting convertibility is rather weak as it stands, even though it does provide grounds for some restrictions. Meanwhile in a recent restatement, Van Parijs suggests that the gap between a regular basic income and a one-off capital endowment might be somewhat reduced. If one could borrow against one's future income stream on the understanding that not all of the stream can be seized by creditors, when payback conditions are not met by someone who wasted the loan, then the market will restrict full convertibility.[6] The converse would be to stipulate that a capital endowment can be put at risk only after its owner has reserved a certain fraction of it to cover against becoming destitute later in life. That looks like a reasonable way to specify limits of convertibility. As we shall see, Ackerman and Alstott's stakeholder proposal amply satisfies this more modest precautionary motive. First of all, the $80,000 which is credited to the account of every stakeholder at age 18 can only be accessed conditional upon completion of high school. If it is not used for tuition in a college, then it becomes available at age 21 in four regular annual instalments, adding the accumulated interest. But one could still suppose at this stage of the story that under a financially equivalent basic income proposal, the corresponding income stream would be equal to the annuity that someone with an average life expectancy of, say, 80 years could buy at 18. That would indeed be too small a sum to constitute a credible basic income.

But reading on, secondly, Ackerman and Alstott's precautionary measures extend far beyond making the stake available in four instalments. As becomes clear in Part II of their book, the unconditional stake could be quite a lot larger than $80,000, if there were no pressing need to take account of young people's inability to properly envisage their own interests beyond retirement (1999: 134–5). Ackerman and Alstott therefore propose to replace the worker-related pensions under the existing laws of Social Security by a universal and tax-financed citizens' pension, on the grounds that this is a warranted and justifiable 'expansion' of the individual's stake in a liberal society (1999: 140–9). The expression of an 'expanded stake' is somewhat misleading here. It is better to say that stakeholding, as Ackerman and Alstott conceive of it, requires a (largely) unconditional stake on reaching adulthood, and an earmarked part which is legally tied up to prevent people from suffering the consequences of their myopia. Just like Van Parijs, therefore, Ackerman and Alstott accept strongly paternalistic reasons of institutional design after all, even though these reasons focus on a more limited failure on the part of the young to form a realistic image of what their existence beyond working age involves, rather than positing a general incapacity of people to appropriately weigh their future interests at any two points in time.

The implication is that stakeholding is by no means a pure basic capital proposal. What Ackerman and Alstott propose instead is granting rights to a *comprehensive stake*, which consists of the $80,000 capital at age 18, and the income stream dispensed under the citizens' pension. While I will follow their terminology in calling the pension an 'expanded stake', the logic of the matter is that it is a 'conditional' stake, which limits the freely disposable capital at adulthood to being equal to $80,000 plus the (average) present value of the pension rights.

This shows that the disagreement on convertibility between Van Parijs and Ackerman and Alstott is far less marked than it seemed to be initially, despite their different views on the capacity for responsible action over time. The issue is narrowed down to whether people can be relied upon to take proper account of their future interests during their working lives, before retirement. Now for Ackerman and Alstott, the very point of stakeholding is that most young adults can indeed be trusted to do so, and especially if they are given the equal opportunity to take up a long-term perspective, by investing a substantial sum of capital. By contrast, Van Parijs has to maintain that everybody, not merely the young, would want to be protected against grave failures originating from weakness of will in this shorter time perspective as well, since he stipulates that the universal desire to so protect oneself holds 'pretty homogeneously' from present to future. As I said above, this is an implausibly strong view. But nonetheless, such failures can of course occur, and some social provisions are surely required to deal with the consequences of 'blowing one's stake'. So it is of interest to see whether Ackerman and Alstott's account of expanded stakeholding might include such provisions. To a surprising extent it does, as will be shown next.

## 3   Expanded stakeholding and the welfare state

I now discuss the second area of contention between basic income and basic capital: their respective attitudes to welfare state reform. More precisely, what is at issue here is how the two competing proposals respond to a central concern of the welfare state: guaranteeing income security at some decent subsistence level. Roughly, the strategy of basic income consists in streamlining a diversity of arrangements for securing minimum incomes, and then gradually replacing these arrangements by a single unconditional subsistence dispensation. On the face of it, a principled supporter of basic capital should be critical of that strategy. For it necessarily involves considerably strengthening the welfare state's core business, before the further step of moving beyond the conditionalities of welfare benefits is taken. The strategy makes good sense when stakeholding is a matter of streams. For even though the principle of guaranteeing a minimum income in response to a diversity of social contingencies has become central to the welfare state after the Second World War, it is certainly not an institutional reality in all welfare states.

But just for this reason, the basic income strategy goes against the stock conception of stakeholding. Indeed, as Ackerman and Alstott tell us, 'Our goal is to transcend the welfare state mentality, which sets conditions on the receipt of "aid". In a stakeholding society, stakes are a matter of right, not a handout' (1999: 9). Taken by itself, this statement might reflect a wish to replace means- and work-tested income rights by a general right to unconditional citizens' income. But that is not what Ackerman and Alstott mean to say at all. That they have the stock conception firmly in mind is shown when they add: 'The diversity of individuals' life choices (and the predictable failure of some) is no excuse for depriving each American of the wherewithal to attempt her own pursuit of happiness' (1999: 9). Clearly, granting each American this 'wherewithal' is meant to do away with the need for keeping in place any provisions of 'aid' that precede the citizens' pension. Or so it seems. In fact, it is not like this at all. As I will now show, Ackerman and Alstott's view of welfare state reform under expanded stakeholding is very similar to the basic income strategy, even though they do not advertise this.[7]

To explain the similarity, I first describe how basic income might transform the welfare state, especially in the north-west European context. Three stages of a stylized programme can be distinguished. In the first, the goal is to build upon existing elements of state benefit, seeking to make these part of an integrated system organized around a uniform minimum guarantee for households over the life-cycle, with a major portion of the finance residing under the regime of general taxation. The next stage aims at getting rid of means testing in the arrangements of old age and childhood. This second stage establishes universal access to those benefits conditional only on citizenship, and replaces old-age 'insurance premiums' as well as earmarked childcare contributions by income tax. Effectively, this turns the pension into a basic income at the guaranteed minimum level of single persons. It also involves fixing individual childcare allowances at some fraction of household subsistence income. Different proposals disagree on the size of this fraction.

The third and final stage of the basic income programme is the decisive one. Its aim is to eliminate the multiple conditionalities (of means, work, and willingness to seek employment) in the arrangements of social protection located in-between childhood and retirement. The method is to proceed gradually from below, through progressive replacement of conditional benefits by unconditional income grants. These grants start at a level well below subsistence (*partial* basic income), and steadily move upwards to finally cover the individual's subsistence level entirely (*full* basic income). Typically this operation is carried through by means of a negative income tax, with the basic income as a refundable tax credit, which can be paid out in advance instalments in order to avoid the insecurity involved in setting off tax against credit at the end of the year. As long as basic incomes remain partial, the conditional benefits of working life – mainly work-tested social security and means-tested general assistance – must remain available to selectively top up the income of eligible individuals.

The basic income programme presupposes that the welfare state actually aspires to secure the subsistence needs of all citizens to a large extent – this is the basis on which it proposes to integrate functionally different arrangements into one universalistic scheme. Note also that the relevant subsistence norm of the programme is that of the individual, who may (but need not) be living in a single-person household. Since the subsistence norm for a (administratively certified) couple is often substantially below that of two single persons, a significant tax cost is attached to individualizing subsistence entitlements, even before these become fully unconditional. It is important that this cost be internalized in the final stage, when basic income's most controversial aspects of removing the tests of work and willingness to work are addressed in the final stage. Thus it may be wise to bring the non-household tested benefits of collective worker insurance under the universal regime of the subsistence guarantee, while at the same time introducing a modest partial basic income. For instance, compulsory employee insurance of unemployment and disability risks can be split up into two parts. The first part is financed by general taxation, and it specifically covers these risks, including those of the self-employed, up to the social minimum level (minus the partial basic income). The second part of social insurance continues to serve its original function, and remains financed by workers' and employers' contributions. It can be operated under rules allowing more freedom of choice to insure against different levels of above-subsistence income loss.[8]

This sketch is not meant to be representative of all basic income proposals. It is only intended to facilitate comparison with stakeholding, as envisaged by Ackerman and Alstott. Now as already mentioned, one important element of the basic income programme is taken care of by the idea of an 'expanded stake': the citizens' pension. Given the motivation of protecting young stakeholders against the future consequences of their short-sightedness, the citizens' pension could conceivably be means tested. However, Ackerman and Alstott strongly argue that the unconditional payment of a 'dignity-preserving' minimum income of $670 a month will serve to avoid both problems of moral hazard, as well as the stigmatizing effect of means testing (1999: 137–8). As they are ready to admit, then, 'our citizens' pension is, in effect, a basic income under another name' (1999: 214).

Next, what about child allowances? Ackerman and Alstott do not consider this to be a central topic of their book. Nonetheless, they squarely support the idea. As they say, compensating caregivers for their crucial work makes good sense, given the concerns of the liberal state with equal opportunity (1999: 175), and given their view that insufficient childcare is an important source of unequal opportunity suffered by adults from families with low parental income and wealth (1999: 26). For these reasons, the universalistic child allowance arrangements of the basic income programme are an integral part of Ackerman and Alstott's 'expanded stake', just as the citizens' pension is. Indeed, if Ackerman and Alstott are right about the importance of childcare, young stake-holders (especially from poor backgrounds) should be willing to invest backwards a part of their capital stake, just as they want to invest forward part of it in order to secure a dignified citizens' pension.

With these elements of expanded stakeholding in place, the major contrast with the basic income programme concerns the arrangements of social protection during working life. To be sure, there are differences here, given Ackerman and Alstott's principled position that the liberal state should not be in the business of forcing stakeholders to insure against short-term risks (1999: 136). Moreover, one should keep in mind the fundamental rule of unconditional stakeholdership: 'If you plan ahead and act sensibly you may win big. But if you mess up, you live with the consequences' (1999: 215). But again, these principles turn out to be modified by reasonable considerations. First, Ackerman and Alstott endorse the state's role in enforcing collective social insurance against the risks of unemployment and disability, on the familiar ground that it efficiently substitutes for the insurance that most citizens would want to buy. Second, despite their strong conception of personal responsibility, Ackerman and Alstott admit that the state has an obliga-tion to supplement institutions of compassion in civil society, such as churches, and that it must accept a modest back-up role of helping people in trouble. They do specify that 'the level of assistance to stake-blowers will seem low in comparison, say, to the levels prevailing in European welfare states' (1999: 196).

As to the first consideration, notice that the costs and benefits of com-pulsory social insurance could be regarded as being outside the purview of the stakeholder concept. The reason is that social insurance originates from an efficiency motive rather than being an instrument for achieving equality of opportunity. Indeed, Ackerman and Alstott do take this view, when they remark that unemployment insurance might be designed to cover the specific risks of wageworkers, not homemakers, and have pre-mium contributions that match coverage (1999: 140). Nonetheless, it is well known that social insurance serves different functions. For one thing, it clearly protects households, not merely workers, from falling below subsistence. Moreover, it often insures against disability risks outside of the workplace. And it often equalizes ratios of premiums and coverage across sectors, thus achieving solidarity between workers in occupations with different risk profiles. It may therefore make sense to disentangle these multiple purposes of social insurance in the way proposed above, by incorporating coverage of unemployment and disability risks up to subsistence level under a general tax-financed scheme, and giving the principle of insurance more leeway in covering against risks of income loss beyond that level.

There is little in Ackerman and Alstott's account which would lead them to deny that to some extent (which admittedly varies across welfare states), compulsory social insurance serves the redistributive purpose of general social protection. Therefore, whether or not one goes along with the two-tier conception mentioned above, at least some part of US Social Security can sensibly be subsumed under the category of 'expanded stakeholding', together with universal childcare and old-age support. I am not sure whether Ackerman and Alstott would agree with this perhaps somewhat European interpretation. But it is not an implausible one, if stakeholding is not an ideal exclusively reserved for Americans.[9]

What can be said, secondly, about the reticence of Ackerman and Alstott to accepting a law of (means-, work- and asset-tested) general assistance? Since this really is the quintessential form of a 'welfare state handout', their aim is to minimize its role in stakeholder society, as we have seen. But whatever the level and duration of benefits under an appropriate back-up scheme may actually be, the scheme is part of the expanded stake as well. On the logic of Ackerman and Alstott's own account, general assistance serves to protect individuals against the consequences of irresponsibly losing the financial independence offered by the stake, just like the citizens' pension does. What is different of course is the social attribution of blameworthiness in each case. As we have seen, Ackerman and Alstott choose to dispense the citizens' pension unconditionally, while it could in principle be means tested. By contrast, the right to the back-up supplement seems to be designed to bring out the culpability of the stakeblower. But such a backward-looking instruction raises problems. Administrators will have to exercise discretion in dealing with very diverse histories of stakeblowing in order to fine-tune a level of assistance commensurate to the degree of hardship and irresponsibility. This resuscitates the old distinction between the deserving and undeserving poor. So it seems that in Ackerman and Alstott's view, a (hopefully small) pocket of Victorian welfare must remain in place, for the purpose of reminding citizens of the fundamental principle of basic capital stakeholding.

I am not sure this is the best way of minimizing the back-up role of general assistance. But whatever the case may be, enough has been said above to show that expanded stakeholding is largely compatible with the reconstruction of welfare state arrangements envisaged by the basic income programme. Turning back to the convertibility issue, one can now see that Ackerman and Alstott's conception does in fact recommend provisions over and beyond the citizens' pension. If it is agreed that those provisions serve to protect against the downside of losing the stake, then citizens under a basic income regime should be allowed to convert their streams into equivalent stocks to a far greater extent than its proponents are currently prepared to grant. Note however that this conclusion has been reached only by recognizing that the capital endowment on which Ackerman and Alstott focus their attention actually comprises a relatively small part of the fair share involved in the overall project of stakeholding.

## 4   The present value of stakeholding

To make this last point more vividly, I return to the notion of comprehensive stakeholder value introduced in section 2. How large would the unconditional stake offered to young Americans be, had Ackerman and Alstott gone all the way along the basic capital path, ignoring their own arguments of tying up some of the capital for the reasons listed above? If what liberal society were to owe its citizens in the name of equal opportunity would be a truly unconditional stake, then we are looking at a capital sum equal to the original endowment of $80,000 and the present value of the whole of the expanded stake. Consider first the present value, at age 18, of the citizens' pension. I here assume the real interest rate of 2 per cent which Ackerman and Alstott take as their reference for such calculations, and an average duration of the pension of 15 years (from age 65 to 80). I also take as given the monthly level of $670 which Ackerman and Alstott cite as the dignity-preserving subsistence income (1999: 153). Considered as an annuity, the citizens' pension could then be bought for $103,380, at age 65. At age 18, this sum would be worth $40,701. That is to say, the capital to be set aside at age 18 for buying a pension at age 65 when death is expected at 80, is almost $41,000.[10]

This sum is only one part of the expanded stake's present value. As I argued, the stakeholding proposal should also arrange for the payment of child allowances, as well as for some social security and general assistance, to be financed from general taxation. To illustrate, I take child allowance to be at one quarter of subsistence income ($167.50 a month) per child. And very crudely, suppose that the average person's take-up of the benefits during working life is equivalent to three consecutive years of subsistence, which are cashed in from age 41 to 43. These two components of the expanded stake are convertible into capital sums of $43,043 and $14,032 respectively, at the age of stakeholding.[11] So with the citizens' pension included, the average present value of the expanded stake adds up to $99,665. Rounding off to one hundred thousand (real) dollars, the expanded stake amounts to 1.25 of the unconditional stake of $80,000. The comprehensive stake is therefore about $180,000 on average, or 2.25 times the unconditional stake.

The point of this calculation is not only to bring out the extent to which a sensible basic capital rests on welfare state foundations. It also enables one to see how unconditional stakeholding cashes out in the alternative basic income form. Supposing that the provisions of the expanded stake are in place, one must then calculate the equivalent basic income dispensed annually to stakeholders. This involves converting into a 47-year annuity. Ackerman and Alstott's proposed $80,000-worth of basic capital at age 18, as well as the part of conditional benefits that would be automatically replaced by basic income, again assuming that on average, these conditional benefits amount to three years' worth of subsistence income from age 41 to 43. The resulting basic income annuity is equivalent to a capital of $85,139, and yields annual income of $2811. Within the parameters of Ackerman and Alstott's proposal, as interpreted above, the equivalent income stream is clearly a partial basic income. Given a subsistence income of $8040 per year (12 times $670) this partial basic income comes to 35 per cent of subsistence, payable from adulthood to retirement age, after which people receive the citizens' pension.[12] It is not very hard to see that the basic income programme will require a larger annuity at the end of the line.

## 5 Upping the stake

This points us to the third point of contrast between the basic income and basic capital: their respective views on the content of individual freedom. To get a proper perspective on this key issue I must first address a dynamic problem of the basic income programme. The problem is raised by the observation that the level of basic income which matches a basic capital of the size envisaged by Ackerman and Alstott (about $85,000, as shown above) will be perceived as inadequate. Clearly, the corresponding partial basic income annuity (of about $2800) just marks off an arbitrary moment of transition in the programme's third stage of replacing conditional subsistence benefits by a full basic income. This obviously assumes that a full basic income is actually within the limits of economic sustainability.

How are we to understand this important assumption? First, there is much uncertainty about the level of basic income that can durably be sustained at any given moment, in the economic sense of being compatible with the behaviour of the agents responsible for contributing the taxes to finance it.[13] Since a full basic income is defined by reference to the single person's subsistence requirement, the additional tax cost of introducing it immediately will be very high, as we have seen. It may well be infeasible to impose such a rise in the tax burden at once. In almost all countries where basic income is seriously discussed, economists therefore agree that sustaining a full basic income requires a transition period of partial basic income, to be measured in decades rather than years.[14] So the major economic assumption of the programme must be interpreted as saying that the maximum feasible level at which a partial basic income can be pitched is capable of rising over time, following its introduction, in such a way that it will match the ruling norm of subsistence income at the end of the transition period.

But secondly, in order to make any sort of educated guess about how long the transition would take, it should be clear how the norm of subsistence itself is evolving over time. In part, that is an issue of democratic choice. It involves normative questions of how to index the subsistence income. For example, should the level of subsistence income remain constant in real terms, as in our examples above, or should it be linked to the growth of per capita real income? The basic income programme will certainly be more ambitious on the second than on the first of these political decisions. I believe that something like the ambitious aim is implicitly posed by the programme. For in the history of welfare states, at least of most European ones, per capita income, average wages, and basic need-covering income requirements have indeed grown roughly at the same long-term average real rates. To claim that the political norm of sufficiency should be kept fixed in a growing economy, when a basic income programme is set under way, is to accept a steadily decreasing real share of transfer income entitlements, even though the unconditional portion of that share would be rising.[15] It is not clear whether this can be justified on opportunity egalitarian grounds, if the more ambitious aim is actually feasible.[16]

These considerations make one aware that the basic income programme poses dynamic requirements which need not necessarily be shared by a programme of basic capital stakeholding. To bring this out, just suppose that a full basic income is ultimately attainable when the subsistence income is (at least) indexed to inflation. Assuming again that the provisions of Ackerman and Alstott's expanded stake are in place, ask what the unconditional stake corresponding to the full basic income would have to be. Even ignoring the possible growth trend of subsistence income, that stake is huge in comparison to the one proposed by Ackerman and Alstott. At 2 per cent real interest, the capital necessary to buy an (inflation-proof) annuity of $8040 for 47 years, from age 18 to age 65, is $243,504. After subtracting the average sum which stakeholders have to reserve in return for conditional benefits during working age, estimated above at $14,704, the unconditional stake would be $228,000, that is 2.86 times the original $80,000 on average. Intuitively, it seems fanciful to propose anything like this. But if it is fanciful, then that means that the guiding aim of the basic income programme cannot be simply translated into the aim of raising the corresponding capital values.

## 6   Two cultures of stakeholding

At least one thing is clear. Ackerman and Alstott have not considered the issue of upping the stake to such a massive extent. Perhaps this is because they are mainly concerned about the political feasibility of the stakeholder proposal. From that point of view, it would surely be unwise to announce a redistributive goal that exhausts the limits of what might be economically feasible.[17] Yet to me, their story mainly suggests that the size of the stake is comfortably adequate for its purposes, though perhaps not ideally so. For as they say, the 'stake should be big enough to provide each citizen with a cushion against market shocks and to enable her to take a long-term perspective as she determines the most sensible ways of investing in herself, her family, her career, and her community' (1999: 58). And, taking the first of these investment prospects as a standard, 'eighty thousand dollars is enough to pay for four years of tuition at the average private college in the United States' (1999: 58). One might want to quarrel about this adequacy judgement, but the message is reasonably clear. Whether the stake is $80,000 or $100,000 at the point of introduction, there seems to be no question of regarding it as merely a 'partial basic capital', which would need to be raised over time in order to match anything like the equivalent of the basic income programme.

I am not claiming here that Ackerman and Alstott are necessarily opposed to endowing young stakeholders with increasing amounts of starting capital, if this could be safely funded. Indeed, to the extent that they are committed to the kind of liberal egalitarianism that Van Parijs spells out most explicitly, they would have to endorse the principle of maximizing the opportunities of the worst off. And if it is true that the fairest and most effective single policy instrument of pursuing that project is the unconditional stake – a general claim which Ackerman and Alstott share with Van Parijs as well – then they should advocate policies aiming at the highest sustainable basic capital, regardless of whether it is politically wise to say so all the time.

But whatever the abstract logic of the liberal egalitarian case may be, it does not appear that Ackerman and Alstott are committed to it in the same way as Van Parijs, who does indeed insist that the goal of real freedom for all requires the highest sustainable basic income. Why would this be? I can only speculate. But I think it is because the reasons for keeping on raising the capital stake are much less compelling than the reasons for raising basic income up to the level of subsistence. To put it in marginal terms, it seems that over a certain range (say between 40 per cent and 100 per cent of the full basic income capital equivalent calculated above), the perceived value of increasing the unconditional stake by an additional $1000 is significantly higher when the desired form of stakeholding is basic income than when it is basic capital. I suggest that the explanation of this must be sought in a 'cultural' difference between the notions of freedom on which the two kinds of proposal tend to focus. As has been well documented by the research of John Cunliffe and Guido Erreyghers (2003) into precursors of the stakeholding idea, basic income is fundamentally oriented to mastering the subsistence constraint, whereas basic capital stresses the liberating effects of independent property ownership.[18]

This contrast is by no means absolute. Yet it clarifies a lot of the tension existing between the two versions of the stakeholding ideal. That tension is occasionally exemplified by Ackerman and Alstott. After a critical but soft-hearted discussion of how basic income imposes paternalistic restrictions, they suddenly conclude with the barbed one-liner: 'The basic income cushions failure; stakeholding is a launching pad for success' (1999: 215). This suggests that in comparison with basic income, the culture of basic capital not only embraces a more optimistic view on the capacity for personal responsibility, but also a decidedly more *productivist* notion of personal independence. You are responsible for messing up, but if you play it right, you may 'win big'. This appeals to the American dream of emancipation through entrepreneurship. But it is also, as Ackerman and Alstott stipulate, part of a larger political objective 'to revitalize a very old republican tradition that links property and citizenship into an indissoluble whole' (1999: 11). Initiated into the long-term responsibilities of property ownership by classes named 'How to Manage Your Stake', the young are prepared for the time of entry into the marketplace – the place where, they are told, the stakes of the game are high. And as this 'cultural dynamic of stakeholding' takes root, the institutions of basic capital create and reinforce an orientation to take advantage of opportunities for earning money rather than cashing in on opportunities to consume or take up free time, time, that is, spent outside the marketplace. As young stakeholders learn to prove their independence in the market, they are held to become more capable of civic reflection in the political realm as well. And in turn this is reinforced by the recognition that basic capital provides an egalitarian foundation for public life. Thus, 'broadening the property base enhances the stability and quality of political life of the republic' (1999: 185).

As Ackerman and Alstott emphasize, consumption and 'leisure-' intensive uses of the capital stake are not officially discouraged, let alone forbidden. But it is difficult to avoid the conclusion that such uses are non-standard items in the *repertoire* of basic capital. There are many ways of blowing your stake besides losing it at the baccarat table, or spending it on surfboards and trips to Hawaii. Frittering it away in small amounts on a slightly better car or a nicer vacation is another. And according to Ackerman and Alstott, it is one that the basic income form of the stake definitely encourages (1999: 214–15). There is another reason why the worth of any of these unproductive behaviours cannot be regarded as being on the same moral footing with wealth accumulation. For as Ackerman and Alstott insist, stakeholders are under an obligation of fairness to bear death duties that amount to the repayment of the original stake, with interest.[19] If honouring such an obligation of 'liberal trusteeship' is an operative norm in the culture of basic capital, that culture must foster decidedly acquisitive attitudes. And if the capital stake were to become equal to the present value of a subsistence annuity as time went on, instead of remaining at the relatively modest sum Ackerman and Alstott have in mind, capital accumulation would have to become a major preoccupation in the life of stakeholders. An individual estate would then have to exceed 700,000 real dollars, upon death at 80. Perhaps this, too, explains why Ackerman and Alstott do not contemplate raising initial endowment to such an extent.

From the basic income perspective, a regular annual stake opens a host of very different prospects. By contrast, these prospects become increasingly real as the level of the stake becomes adequate to meet basic needs. Freedom from the subsistence constraint naturally fosters a culture of spending time outside the market domain, for the sake of productive activities in households and localities, as well as 'pure leisure'. So it is not surprising that the basic income movement envisages a cultural dynamic of stakeholding which upgrades domestic care and voluntary community services, and aims to establish dense networks of socially beneficial practices that do not depend on financial incentives. While that culture in its early grassroots forms may certainly have been stuck in single-minded opposition to the ethos of industry and personal wealth, its more recent forms stress the advantages of moving freely between remunerated and non-remunerated activities over the life-cycle, for both men and women.

This holds out the promise of a swifter convergence of gender roles than the culture of basic capital can offer. The culture of basic income, in any case, is far more interested in expanding the realm of personal relationships into the political arena. But it is also more interested in the actual content of paid work. Of course, the more one is liberated from the subsistence constraint, the easier it will become to take the time to invest in marketable skills or think seriously about starting up a promising business venture. But this also creates demands for more rewarding ways of earning a living. Such demands become less illusory as the level of basic income rises toward subsistence, because the exit option gives the workers increased bargaining power to influence the conditions of their contracts. Thus, real possibilities exist for improving the quality of low-productivity jobs. And there will be many of these, because basic income also has an indirect wage-subsidizing effect. So when stakeholding is a matter of regular income streams, it is natural to look at improving the labour market from below, in a way that basic capital is far more insensitive to. For all of these reasons, the culture of basic income hopes to create a market game in which the financial stakes are reduced in return for increased time-autonomy and quality of life.

In sum, the two cultures just sketched have diverging views on the content of individual freedom offered by stakeholding. Even though basic capital and basic income can be cast in the common framework of opportunity egalitarianism, as exemplified by the works I have focused on in this chapter, these divergences seem to be significant enough to understand why the two versions of stakeholding are still quite separate.

## Notes

1. Amsterdam School for Social Science Research, University of Amsterdam. I am grateful for the opportunity to write this chapter as a Visiting Fellow to the Social and Political Theory Program of the Research School of Social Sciences, Australian National University, and to the Netherlands Organization of Scientific Research (NWO) for funding part of the research.

2. Waldron (1993: 264–7).
3. For historical overviews of basic income see Van Trier (1996) and Van Parijs (1992a). Cunliffe and Erreyghers (2003) show that in nineteenth-century Belgium, liberally inspired basic income and basic capital proposals similar to those of Van Parijs (1995) and Ackerman and Alstott (1999), were put forward independently by Charlier and Huet. Strangely, despite their proximity in time and place, these two precursors of unconditional stakeholding do not seem to have been aware of each other's work.
4. Van der Veen (1998, 2002).
5. Van Parijs (1995: 47, and 248, n. 30)
6. Van Parijs (2001: 3).
7. Ackerman and Alstott are wary of stressing this aspect. They are concerned that the greater complexity of expanded stakeholding will distract attention from the simplicity and virtue of the unconditional stake, and its funding from a flat tax on wealth. They also believe that the welfare reforms of expanded stakeholding can be undertaken only after the unconditional stake has been established (1999: 16–17).
8. A strikingly coherent policy document following the logic of the basic income programme in many of these details was published by a governmental advisory commission in the Netherlands (WRR, 1985). Note that it did not venture to propose a full basic income, though this was clearly perceived as being the ultimate consequence by many critics in the ensuing debate. See Groot and van der Veen (2000) for an overview.
9. My view that subsistence coverage of Social Security can be made part of expanded stakeholding is supported by the fact that Ackerman and Alstott consider replacing the payroll funding of the whole of Social Security (and Medicare) by a general 'privilege tax', not just the citizens' pension (1999: 159, 227–8). This way of funding implies that unemployment pay, for example, is not regarded as pure insurance, but rather as an element of expanded stakeholding. See also (1999: 177).
10. The calculation uses the annuity formula, according to which an annual income stream of \$1 to be received at the end of each year for t years can be purchased today at a capital cost of \$ $[1 - (1 + r)^{-t}]/r$, where the annual rate of interest is r. At t = 15, r = 0.02, and annual subsistence income of $12 \times \$670 = \$8,040$, the pension annuity at age 65 costs $\$8.040[1 - (1.02)^{-15}]/0.02 = \$103,308$. Discounting back 47 years to age 18 at compound interest of 2 per cent, this sum is divided by $(1.02)^{47}$, yielding \$40,763 as the present value of the citizens' pension.
11. Child allowance: At the stakeholder's birth, buying an 18-year annuity of one fourth of annual subsistence income (\$8.040/4 = \$2.010) requires capital of $\$2.010[1 - (1.02)^{-18}]/0.02 = \$30,134$. Were that capital invested instead to become available at age 18, it would be compounded by a factor of $(1.02)^{18}$, to \$43,038. Working age conditional benefits: at age 41, a three-year annuity of \$8040 requires \$23,186. Discounted back 23 years, the capital value of that sum is \$14,704 at age 18.
12. What partly replaces the cost of paying out three years of subsistence is a three-year annuity of \$1, bought at age 41, and multiplied by the level of basic income (B) we are seeking to derive. Denoting the present value of this annuity at age 18 by 'X', add BX to the basic capital of \$80,000. The 47-year

annuity which this augmented capital buys at age 18 now gives us the level of basic income. Thus B is solved from: $B = [80,000 + BX]/[(1 - (1.02)^{-47})/0.02]$ ; $X = [(1 - (1.02)^{-3})/(0.02)(1.02)^{23}]$. B amounts to \$2,811 per year, or $2,811/8,040 = 0.35$ of subsistence income. I stress that these calculations are based upon the 2 per cent rate of real interest that AA take as the right figure for this kind of exercise, because AA do not always observe this rule. For example, when stating the annuity equivalent to the \$80,000 at age 18 as (at least) \$4,000, they must be using a *nominal* rate of interest of 5 per cent (211, 212). At that rate, the 47-year annuity which a stake of \$80,000 can buy (excluding the refinement of adding BX) is \$4,449. This is somewhat misleading, because that annual amount depreciates at a rate of 3 per cent inflation per year.

13. The uncertainty arises because it is not clear how factor owners will actually respond to increased rates of tax on their market returns, once the different institutional set-up of basic income is in place. See Atkinson (1995: ch. 7), for an overview of the difficulties in determining the relationship between taxation, benefits, and work incentives under a basic income system.

14. A notable exception is Ireland, where a politically influential paper claims that a full basic income could be introduced within three years, at a flat rate tax of about 50 per cent (Clark and Healy, 1997).

15. To take another example from the Netherlands, a long-term study conducted by the governmental Central Planning Bureau favoured a 'Balanced Growth Scenario', which has a partial basic income rising to full basic income within 25 years, with subsistence income indexed only to inflation. See Centraal Planbureau (1992: section 3.3). The main point of this scenario was to show how a leaner welfare state might contribute to improved competitiveness of the Dutch economy. Obviously, that is not exactly how supporters of basic income stakeholding would want to motivate their programme.

16. How strong that assumption is can be seen by its consequences. If subsistence is indexed to per capita income, then sustainability of a full basic income implies that the ratio of partial basic income to per capita income must rise. The final result may be characterized as a state of 'weak abundance'. But if these same conditions of sustainability were to indefinitely hold thereafter, then it would be possible to move beyond full basic income to a notional limit state of 'strong abundance', in which basic income finally absorbs the whole of per capita income. The consequences of such an extended transition were set out in van der Veen and Van Parijs (1986: 635–55; revised as Van Parijs, 1989: ch. 8; van der Veen, 1991: ch. 4). The two concepts of abundance are presented formally in Van Parijs (1995: 86–7).

17. Note that Ackerman and Alstott do say 'we would be advocating an even higher stake were it not for the need to hold resources in reserve in order to fund serious efforts to improve opportunities for those at the bottom' (1999: 201). Such resources must be targeted at the rural and inner city poor, for example. This reminds us that stakeholding (including its expanded provisions) is of course not the only instrument of opportunity equalization. But basic income proponents realize that as well, and yet it does not prevent them from wanting to raise partial basic incomes over time. So this reason for limiting the capital stake cannot be the one that explains the dynamic contrast between the two views.

18. Cunliffe and Erreyghers (2003: section 4).
19. This repayment obligation is a controversial feature. According to Cunliffe and Erreyghers, basic capital schemes must rely upon a payback condition to replenish the stakeholding fund. I am not sure this is necessarily the case, if only because Ackerman and Alstott point out that there must be a sustainable way of funding (they propose a wealth tax of 2 per cent on a broadly defined base exempting the first $80,000) before payback from the first cohort of stakeholders can be collected. But in any case, it seems that a scheme of repayment *with interest* cannot be the only way of financing a basic capital.

# 10
## Radical Liberalism
*Bruce Ackerman*[1]

## 1 Introduction

Is the Left brain-dead? Or does it only seem that way? I take the more hopeful view, though I hardly wish to deny the obvious: plutocracy is on the rise in the West, and the Left has no serious programme for confronting it. Nationalization isn't credible, and nothing has taken its place. The rich will always be with us, but is it really right for 1 per cent of Americans to own almost 40 per cent of disposable assets?[2] And as this volume suggests, the Brits aren't all that far behind the curve (this volume: chs 2, 3). What *is* to be done?

The silence is deafening, but perhaps it owes more to an awkward moment of intellectual transition. Over the past generation, the Marxist Left has declined in vitality, but there has been a countervailing rise on the Liberal Left.[3] John Rawls and Jurgen Habermas and Ronald Dworkin and Brian Barry and Michael Walzer and Amartya Sen and Peter Singer and Benjamin Barber and Martha Nussbaum and many more have transformed the liberal tradition. For most of the last century, liberalism has been the intellectual preserve of cautious complexifiers like Isaiah Berlin or Michael Oakeshott or extravagant free-marketeers like Friedrich Hayek or Robert Nozick. But the past generation has seen the rebirth of the radical reformist spirit of Bentham and Mill – if not their nineteenth-century utilitarianism. The question is whether this renascent Philosophical Radicalism has something practical to say about plutocracy and its problems.

Plutocracy takes many forms, and it is a Marxist mistake to suppose that there is one Big Answer. *The Stakeholder Society* (1999) confronts the most obvious part of the problem: the fact that the rich have so much more money than the rest of us. But there are many other parts that demand attention: the increasing power of big money in politics, for example. Unless we confront this problem head-on, *The Stakeholder Society*'s response to the economic part doesn't have much of a future – leftist parties will drift ever-rightwards to gain the massive funding required for modern electoral campaigning.

I have nothing but praise for Tony Blair's promise to provide a small capital grant to the next generation of Britons. But a few thousand pounds in Baby Bonds is pretty small change compared to $80,000 *now*.[4] Unless and until New Labour figures out a new way to finance its political future, it will predictably avoid any proposal that involves redistributing wealth on anything like this scale. So if you are persuaded that something like *The Stakeholder Society* is a good idea, place an order for my latest book, *Voting with Dollars* (Ackerman and Ayres, 2002), which confronts the problem of money in politics in a similar spirit.

Several contributors note that *The Stakeholder Society* is written in a style that aims to engage the interest of a broader public in a renewed assault on plutocracy. This ambition raises questions of substance, not only style. As my list of leading liberal lights suggests, the intellectual scene is full of foundational debates on the methods of political philosophy, and not merely its more particular conclusions. Though the Rawlsian paradigm has a definite salience, there is much more going on – and only a fool would predict the shape of the intellectual landscape in a decade or two.

I took this ferment into account when framing a practical proposal like stakeholding. It seemed unwise to tie my argument too closely to the doctrines of any particular philosophical writer – not only because the general public would find erudite detours tedious, but because it would present a misleading picture of the intellectual scene. There is no such thing as liberal orthodoxy at present. Rather than rooting practical proposals in particular theoretical frameworks, it is more important to suggest how they are more-or-less compatible with the variety of philosophical liberalisms presently on the table for discussion.

I continue to think my decision was a wise one, but it came at a price. The theoretical debate continues for a reason. There is a lot at stake both philosophically and practically – as is suggested by the critiques offered by a democratic feminist like Carole Pateman, a strong egalitarian like Cécile Fabre and a pro-property contractarian like Gijs Van Donselaar. Their critical task would have been easier if I had followed the example of Philippe van Parijs' fine book (1995), and self-consciously rooted my practical proposal in a more systematic effort in liberal political theory. It's not as if I haven't written one. My work on *Social Justice in the Liberal*

*State* (1980) was the principal preoccupation of my life throughout the 1970s – ah, sweet youth! Though a quarter of a century has passed, I remain committed to the book's general approach and most of its more particular conclusions. *The Stakeholder Society* is best seen as a practical follow-up – giving real-world shape to one, but only one, of the conclusions reached in the course of my philosophical thought experiments.

For those who missed it the first time around, my earlier work rejected both utilitarianism and contractarianism and presented a version of liberalism based on mutually respectful dialogue. Since modern men and women profoundly disagree about the good life, they will only succeed in shouting at one another if they use the public forum as a way of vindicating their particular ideals for living. If they hope for mutually respectful dialogue, they must self-consciously impose two basic constraints on their public conversation. I define these constraints by the *Neutrality Principle*: when entering the public sphere, no participant should expect the state to endorse her ideal of the good life as superior to her rivals' or to declare her intrinsically superior to her fellow citizens. These Neutrality constraints serve as the hallmark of a liberal political culture. They define the limits of legitimate public justifications that the state may adopt while it sets about resolving the fundamental problems of social justice.

I will use this chapter to elaborate upon the links between this philosophical enterprise and the more practical recommendations in *The Stakeholder Society* – at least where this helps me respond to my critics' concerns. Given the limitations of space, I won't waste time repeating elaborate philosophical arguments. I will simply help myself to the conclusions reached in the *Liberal State*. Readers interested in more sustained arguments know where to look.

## 2  Free lunches?

Stakeholding is an unconditional grant – each young adult gets a large chunk of capital with which she can shape her life, and it is up to her to decide what to do with it. Unconditionality seems to offend a widespread moral intuition. From early on, we are taught that we should work for what we get. And yet stakeholding seems to suggest that there *is* such a thing as a free lunch after all: $80,000 can buy a lifetime of lunches, if that's what you use it for! Stuart White tries to work up the philosophical status of this intuition in his interesting papers.

White's principal target isn't stakeholding, but Van Parijs's proposal for a basic income – each month, each adult gets $X from the state without doing anything for it. White's choice of target is significant. As a matter of cultural diagnostics, basic income runs afoul of conventional morality more blatantly than stakeholding. In the public mind, the receipt of a basic income check every month is readily associated with the receipt of a monthly pay cheque – and you don't get your pay cheque without working for it! Why should you get your basic income cheque without any reciprocating act toward the community?

Van Parijs gives many answers, but it is a philosopher's mistake to think that only arguments count. His proposal goes against the grain of the workaday culture, and that is an unfortunate, though not an insuperable, obstacle for politicians who might want to implement it. Even the term 'basic income' conjures up an unfortunate analogy with 'working income', triggering adverse intuitions deeply rooted in conventional morality.

In contrast, stakeholding suggests analogies of a different kind. Consider the lucky upper-class person who reaches maturity to learn that she has received an inheritance of £50,000 from a maternal grandfather she hardly knows. Do we ask whether she has done anything to deserve it? Do we require her to give something back to the community as a condition for her receiving it? No. So why should anybody raise such questions when *everybody* gets what the rich young lady or gentleman currently receives? This point serves to deflect the conventional intuition about free lunches. Apparently, there *is* a context in which people often get something for nothing. And that context is inheritance.

Stakeholding is a morally superior alternative to private inheritance. In one way or another, each generation must pass on its assets to the next. Our present system places far too much weight on morally arbitrary factors – how well your parents and grandparents did in the marketplace, how many children and grandchildren they happen to have had, how quickly they die, and so forth. None of this has anything to do with the recipient's moral qualities or dignity as a human being. Worse yet, the entire system is becoming increasingly dysfunctional as average life-expectancies increase. As the new century dawns, private inheritance is turning into a mechanism through which sixty year olds receive large sums from ninety year olds. Even young people from the upper classes watch their parents get large sums at a time when it is *they* who need the capital to make life-shaping decisions. If these young adults are lucky, their parents will do the right thing and pass a chunk onto them; but if their parents choose to hoard all the wealth until they die, tough luck. Even a prince of the realm might have a problem if his parents were sufficiently stupid and stingy.

Contrast this arbitrary mess with stakeholding. Neither your grandparents nor your parents built this country single-handed. The nation's wealth is the product of the blood and tears of countless citizens. In contrast to all this sacrifice and saving, the rising generation has done precisely zero to create the nation's wealth. Given this fact it is only fair for the national patrimony to be transferred to citizens on the basis of their common citizenship, not their particular bloodlines. With stakeholding, everybody gets an equal share of the national inheritance, not a favoured few; and they get it at the right time – early adulthood, when getting it can be of real help in shaping the entire course of their adult lives.

Within this framework, intuitions about 'free lunches' lose their grip. You can't blame stakeholders for failing to work for their stakes – they couldn't possibly have done so unless they were born to an earlier generation. The distinctive intellectual challenge is to work out a fair way of distributing assets to citizens who will get lots of assets even though they *don't* deserve them. And if this is the challenge, stakeholding looks a lot better than the existing elitist system based on blood-lines and a well-timed death in the family.

From this perspective, two aspects of the British policy debate strike me as noteworthy. First, the very idea of a 'Baby Bond' is absolutely brilliant: it graphically portrays precisely the right point – that stakeholding is a morally superior form of inheritance. All babies look more or less alike – so cute, so innocent. At the threshold of life, none can be blamed or credited with their parents' financial success or lack of it. Yet all are Britons, and each is entitled to a share of the patrimony. A picture is worth a thousand words, and it was a masterstroke of Blair's to introduce stakeholding in this way. Once it is established in law, it will be time enough to increase the value of the stake, making it a truly significant birthright of citizenship.

The second advance involves funding. Julian Le Grand and David Nissan suggest that the inheritance tax be used as a dedicated source of funding, and they are entirely right – because stakeholding is a morally superior version of private inheritance, it only makes sense to dedicate these taxes to the programme. They should also be increased substantially beyond current British levels. Some private inheritance should be tolerated on consequentialist grounds. Like all taxes, those on inheritance change the leisure–labour trade-off – discouraging some work, encouraging some splurging in old age, and the like. But in contrast to most other taxes, the primary activity involved – giving your kids a head start over their competitors, even when they don't deserve it – isn't particularly worthy of public support.

It is unfortunate, then, that the current thinking from the Prime Minister's office – as reflected in the paper by Kelly, Gamble, and

Paxton – doesn't incorporate this aspect of Le Grand and Nissan. It is true, of course, that President Bush is such a partisan of plutocracy that he is vigorously campaigning for the repeal of all 'death taxes'. But I had supposed that New Labour was different – and that, by linking Baby Bonds to inheritance taxes, it would be symbolizing its determination to halt the dangerous drift to plutocracy that is undermining the public commitment to social justice throughout the West.[5]

Gijs van Donselaar disagrees. On his view, the inheritance tax is little better than 'a tax on love' (this volume: 107). But most parents manage to show their love without showering their kids with wads of cash on their deathbeds. And it is an open empirical question whether the prospect of large bequests encourages more love or more hate amongst plutocratic families – doctoral candidates in sociology take note! In any event, big bequests represent misplaced acts of love – resembling a loving parent's decision to smooth his child's path to admission at Yale by giving the university ten million dollars or making large campaign contributions to gain a dimwit daughter's employment at the White House. In all these cases, loving parents will undoubtedly press for improper advantages for their children. But it is the mark of a just society that these pressures are resisted and that ongoing efforts are made to ensure a level playing field for the next generation.

Interestingly, van Donselaar agrees that rich kids don't deserve their bequests, but attacks Stakeholder's effort to increase fairness: '[N]o one deserves his (lack of) talents either (...) Why is it so important – in the name of equal citizenship – to share external resources while not so important to share talents?' (this volume: 105). Van Donselaar speculates as to my answer, but he would have done better to reread the chapter from the *Liberal State* that he cites in another context.[6] Rather than failing to 'think through these conceptual complexities' (this volume: 107), my earlier book devotes many pages to confronting them.

Recall that the *Liberal State* analyses problems of distributive justice in general, intergenerational justice in particular, by considering how a political community would talk about them in a public conversation constrained by Neutrality – the state will not endorse the claim of any participant that she, or her ideals of the good life, are inherently superior to her fellow citizens'. These conversational constraints cut differently so far as the distribution of money and genes is concerned. By considering these differences, it won't be hard to come up with a straightforward answer to van Donselaar's charge of inconsistency.

Liberal conversationalists have no trouble determining that a young woman who inherits a million pounds is better off than a contemporary who gets nothing. First, since money can purchase almost anything, she can use the money to achieve almost any ideal of the good she affirms. Second, if she wishes to be an ascetic, she can simply give the money away to her favourite charity, and be no worse off for the bequest. Hence it is no problem figuring out what equal citizenship demands in the case of money – each young adult should be granted the prima facie right[7] to an equal amount as he begins his life as an adult.

Things get trickier when the conversation turns to the justice of genetic inheritance. The *Liberal State* explores this matter through a thought-experiment that many thought fanciful when the book came out in 1980, but which looks a bit less futuristic nowadays. I posit the existence of a Master Geneticist who, after studying the relevant DNA maps, can provide perfect information about the genetic capacities of each citizen: A has the genetic wherewithal to be a maths whiz, but has trouble connecting with human beings; B will barely master the multiplication table, but has a great intuitive understanding of others' emotions; and so forth. Armed with this (perfectly accurate) information, suppose that B complains that his genetic inheritance puts him in an unfair position vis-à-vis A – it is his considered opinion that maths is the greatest thing there is, and that empathy is greatly overrated. What is more, he insists that A's genetic advantage is unjust and that A-types should pay over some money compensation to the B-types as a consequence. In other words, suppose that A asks the question that van Donselaar says I haven't thought about.

Now B may or may not be right about his underlying valuation of maths versus empathy – this is a question upon which people may reasonably disagree. But that is just the problem so far as the liberal state is concerned. Bound by the principle of Neutrality, no government official can ever award B compensation on the grounds that his maths-poor/empathy-rich genes make him worse off than A; and vice versa. In the eyes of the liberal state, the genetic equipment provided to A is no worse than that provided to B, and neither has a legitimate complaint of injustice.

The upshot is that van Donselaar is wrong in saying that there is something inconsistent about left liberals insisting on equal financial stakes but refusing to countenance widespread redistribution on the basis of the fact that different people have different talents. To the contrary, my position derives from much more fundamental ideals of political legitimacy – in particular, the principle that all claims about justice should be tested through public conversation constrained by Neutrality.

Dialogic theories of liberalism are themselves controversial, and the *Liberal State* has received its share of criticism during the quarter century since it has seen the light. But van Donselaar doesn't describe my views, much less dispute them. He simply 'speculates' that I refuse to endorse widespread 'talent-pooling' for the same reasons he does! In van Donselaar's view, David Gauthier has the right theory on the subject. Gauthier abhors 'parasitism' – a condition under which A is better off than she would have been in the absence of B, while B is worse off than he would have been in the absence of A. Since all forms of talent pooling involve parasitism, van Donselaar commends Gauthier to my attention in an effort to help me out of my non-existent difficulty.

I reject Gauthier's principle on principle. Consider the plight of C, a profoundly disabled person who is blind and can't walk. Suppose that he too asks for a special subsidy to help him out of his situation. The *Liberal State* argues that he can expect a very different answer from people like A and B. In C's case, liberal conversationalists won't be obliged to engage in a public ranking of the relative worth of particular virtues, like empathy or mathematical ability. C's genetic situation is so dire that it makes it harder for him to achieve *any* of the different life-plans pursued by citizens of a modern society. Given this fact, the liberal state can give him special relief without violating Neutrality: 'Since you are at a disadvantage in pursuing any ideal, others will outcompete you if we ask you to pay the cost of wheelchairs and Braille-readers out of the $80,000 stake you receive on an equal basis with all your fellow citizens. Instead, these and similar expenses will come out of a special compensation fund. Only in this way can we re-establish a level playing field between you and fellow-citizens who were luckier in the genetic lottery.'

I consider the Cs of this world to be victims of 'genetic domination', but in Gauthier's terms they are simply 'parasites'. They would be worse off without their more talented citizens, while the latter would be better off – at least financially – if the dominated didn't exist. So in Gauthier's (and van Donselaar's) view, C can claim no right of assistance, though charitable folk may choose to be kind. In contrast, victims of the genetic lottery are perfectly entitled to vindicate their claims within the dialogue of justice that lies at the core of my *Liberal State*. Just as the children of poor parents shouldn't be victimized by their elders' market misfortunes, victims of genetic domination shouldn't be victimized by their bad genetic luck. van Donselaar's claims notwithstanding, *The Stakeholder Society* is part of a much broader approach to inheritance that includes genes as well as material assets.

My rejection of 'anti-parasitism' as a principle points to an even deeper issue regarding the place of the market in liberal political philosophy. For thinkers like Gauthier and van Donselaar, the market is foundational – if A doesn't have anything that B wants, then he shouldn't be able to coerce a transfer; if he succeeds in coercion, then he is a parasite. Although I am a friend of market exchange, it is not the be-all and end-all of my philosophy. The *Liberal State* puts the market in its place by locating it within the larger framework of liberal culture, defined by a public dialogue worthy of free and equal citizens. Despite his disabilities, C can still fully participate in this ongoing dialogue of citizenship. Just because he can't do well in market trades doesn't diminish his standing as a rational being who can stand before his fellow citizens and tell them: 'I, no less than you, have aims in life which I hope to achieve before I die. Why then do you deny me the right to inherit resources – both genetic and material – that are no worse than those available to you?' I myself don't think that there is a good answer to this question. Do you?

To put our ultimate disagreement in a single line, van Donselaar's philosophy is based on market exchange and mine is based on political dialogue. If you are in doubt about the way to go, this chapter is much too short to try to help you out. Only one thing is clear: even if you come out for a market-based theory of liberal justice, the case for stakeholding is surprisingly robust. This is the first affirmative lesson of van Donselaar's paper, which derives a kind of stakeholding from market-based premises. The bad news is that his stake comes with too many strings attached – grantees can't spend their money on anything they like, as contemplated by the Blair plan; they can't even buy a house with it, as contemplated by the Le Grand–Nissan proposal. They can only use it for 'productive' investments.

I am not persuaded by the case for this severe limitation, even granting van Donselaar's premises. As is usual in such exercises, he makes his argument through a 'state of nature' parable. His story involves two people, Lazy and Crazy, and four plots of land on a newly discovered desert island. Lazy is such a happy-go-lucky guy that one plot will serve his purposes of sunbathing, fruit picking and the like. But Crazy is Mr Protestant Ethic, eager to transform all the plots at his disposal into cornucopias of production. In van Donselaar's view, Lazy should not be allowed to stake his claim to two plots, as he would in *The Stakeholder Society*, and then sell his second plot to Crazy at a mutually agreed price. This transaction would enable Lazy to appropriate some of Crazy's productivity, and thereby violate Gauthier's anti-parasite principle. For van Donselaar, this suggests that a strong productivity clause should attach to any stakeholding grant.

But this conclusion depends on very contingent features of the desert island parable. Suppose, for example, that Lazy remains addicted to sunbathing, but that both of his plots contain wonderful beaches. Rather than contenting himself with one plot, Lazy wants to retain both so that he can add zest to his sunbathing by alternating beaches on a daily basis. With this small change, van Donselaar's example unravels. Lazy is no longer exploiting Crazy when he insists on taking the second plot, since he wants to put it to an affirmative use. Even accepting Gauthier's principle about parasitism, Lazy is no longer violating it when he insists that Crazy pay for his second plot. For under this description of the island, Lazy is actually losing something when he sells – he is giving up the chance to sunbathe on a second beach. Note that Lazy is no less Lazy in this alternative story – he is simply Lazy more extravagantly. Van Donselaar's emphasis on productivity isn't analytically robust, but an arbitrary artefact of the very particular state-of-nature story that he chooses to tell. Why should we choose his version of the 'state of nature' story instead of this nearly identical alternative?[8]

I could make similar points about his other desert island scenarios, but it is more important to challenge a more fundamental premise: his basic story begins with Lazy and Crazy as fully formed adults, but a satisfactory analysis should begin at a much earlier stage in their development. From the moment van Donselaar's eponymous heroes emerged from the womb, they confronted a lengthy period of socialization – perhaps they learned to speak French, not English; worship Allah, not Jehovah; behave this way, not that. They became Lazy and Crazy only through a complex interaction with their educational environment – and this engagement must itself be interrogated from the perspective of legitimacy and justice. What kind of education do the young have a right to expect at the hands of their elders?

Van Donselaar glances at the philosophy of education, but characteristically, only at its economic dimensions. The *Liberal State* takes a more fundamental approach. Skills' training for the marketplace is important, but it is even more important to provide the young with a truly liberal education, introducing them to the broad horizon of moral ideals affirmed by a pluralist modern society. Within the framework of liberal theory, an acceptable education can't satisfy itself with the dogmatic assertion of some moral truths affirmed by some members of the political community. Instead, liberal education gives students tools for the critical assessment of the ideals for living that are open to them as adults in a free society. At the end of the day, particular students may well decide to reaffirm the tried-and-true values taught by their parents. But this reaffirmation won't be the product of brainwashing, but a considered assessment made after an appreciation of the alternative ideals affirmed by others living out their lives in a diverse political community.

Given these principles of liberal education, van Donselaar's emphasis on 'productivity' has a distinctly dogmatic ring. Consider, for example, that the school system is introducing a group of fifteen year olds to the values affirmed throughout the ages by philosophical and religious ascetics – who retreat from the distractions of the world to cultivate their spirituality. van Donselaar has only one word to describe such people: they are Lazy, and if he had his way, the students would be told: 'You are free to follow these ascetics in your adult life, but be warned, you will lose your stake if you do! The $80,000 is reserved for citizens who have better things to do with their money than to buy a shack in the desert and live as parasites for the rest of their lives!'

My objection to this is not merely consequentialist – though it *is* likely that van Donselaar's version of the stake will interact with the educational system to produce less spiritual, more money-grubbing, types than we would have otherwise. My principal objection is to a system of education that allows teachers to wield an economic club in favour of commercialized ideals and against spiritual ones (Ackerman, 1980: ch. 5).

It is hard to say whether van Donselaar would continue to demand that stakeholding be linked to productivity once he reflected more broadly on its educational implications. At present, his analysis is artificially truncated by 'state of nature' stories that fail to confront the fact that real-world men and women don't arrive on desert islands as fully formed adults, in the manner of Botticelli's *Venus*. They reach it instead through a process of education whose character is profoundly affected by a stakeholding programme that conditions access to resources on the basis of market productivity.

Van Donselaar attempts the most fundamental critique of unconditional stakeholding in this volume. Some of his doubts are shared, however, by Julian Le Grand and David Nissan – central contributors to the intellectual movement that has encouraged New Labour to put a high priority on capital grants. In contrast to van Donselaar, their limitations are entirely prudential in nature. Rather than allowing eighteen year olds to blow their stakes on joy-rides, they would require them to convince trustees that they will make good use of their money by investing in education, or a business, or a home. I oppose this in principle: so long as he has been provided with a half-decent education, each citizen should be treated as a free and equal citizen, and given the chance to take responsibility for his own life by shaping his own future with his own money. The very ritual of grovelling before a 'trustee' is objectionable. It is also a recipe for a bureaucratic nightmare.[9]

Perhaps for this reason, the Blair government seems to be taking my view of this matter. The programme described by Kelly, Gamble, and Paxton doesn't contain any constraints on the freedom of stakeholders. Indeed, it even refuses to take some precautions proposed in *The Stakeholder Society*, and that I continue to find sensible. For one thing, the Blair government seems to be planning to allow eighteen year olds to cash in their Baby Bonds and this seems to me too early in life to receive a one-time capital grant. Unless the money is needed for university education, I think it should be distributed to young adults in their early twenties, after they have gained more practical experience. Despite the paternalism involved, I also think that special restrictions are appropriate in the case of school drop-outs, who might otherwise find themselves too easily bilked by fast-talking con men. Perhaps the trusteeship proposed by Le Grand and Nissan may make sense in this limited class of cases. But the large majority of young adults in their twenties can handle such decisions perfectly well, thank you.

## 3   The view from the Left?

The *Liberal State* imagines a society in which each generation provides generously for the victims of genetic domination, establishes a serious system of liberal education for all, and regulates the transmission of material wealth primarily through a system of citizen stakeholding, not private inheritance.

Once young adults claim their stakes, the liberal state ensures them a legal framework that enables collaboration on mutually acceptable terms – both in competitive markets and in civil society associations. Each citizen is free to make any offers she likes in economic and social life, but she can't force others to accept. Within the span of a single lifetime, the free exchange of offers and acceptances will generate very significant inequalities. Some people will become rich but utterly fail to establish satisfying social relationships, and some will have fulfilling social lives but economic success eludes their grasp. Many will attain middling achievements across the board, while still others will be spectacularly successful or unsuccessful in realizing their projects for living.

The liberal state will cushion the worst blows with appropriate safety nets, but broadly speaking, it will hold individuals responsible for their own fates. So long as each citizen starts from fair starting points, it is up to him or her, and not the political community, to determine the nature of the good life, and the best way of pursuing it. The principal role of the state is to prevent the rich from entrenching their financial superiority into the social structure by passing their advantages on to their children.

This is my vision of social justice in a liberal state, and Cécile Fabre finds it insufficiently egalitarian. I can accommodate some of her objections, but some very real differences remain. The path of accommodation begins with an obvious fact: we currently live in a plutocratic world far removed from my ideal, let alone Fabre's. Since the rich constantly seek to entrench their children into power, there will always be a need for progressive politics aiming to check this ongoing push to plutocracy. We will never reach the end of history. This means that liberals not only need an adequate account of their fundamental ideals, but also require a distinctive 'theory of the second best'. This more practical discipline considers the perplexities of designing policies that will effectively move society in the right – or should I say, left – direction.[10]

I can accommodate some, but not all, of Fabre's more specific complaints about stakeholding within this 'second best' rubric. For example, she rightly points out that 'it is not always a matter of choice that I want to go to university', and asks whether the existence of such unchosen desires might lead the egalitarian to 'modify the [stakeholding] proposal, and instead of giving the same sum to everybody, to give them a sum which is tailored to the cost of what is unchosen in their conception of the good' (this volume: 116).

I agree that lots of poor children don't ever seriously consider higher education, and that this is a very real problem, rooted in a pervasive failure to provide them with anything resembling a liberal education.[11] But I wouldn't try to solve this problem by compensating children for their bad educations with a bigger financial stake – as Fabre's formula would suggest. I would go to the heart of the matter by spending more money on the quality of liberal education – and thereby enable more poor kids to recognize that university is within the practical range of existential possibility.

Perhaps Fabre disagrees – but if so, we are disagreeing about a point in second-best theory, dealing with the best means of moving society in the direction of ideals to which both of us subscribe. Some of her other complaints suggest a more profound disagreement: 'I may not always be responsible for the fact that my conception of the good is beyond my financial means, or uses up most of them. Suppose that Paul loves photography, which is an expensive hobby, and that Fred loves fishing which is ( ... ) cheap' (this volume: 116). Fabre wants to give Paul a bigger stake to compensate him for his extra photography costs.

This is not the sort of disparity that can be fairly attributed to a failure of liberal education; on the contrary, a successful system will character-istically generate a citizenry that is chock full of such disagreements. Although photography-buffs might sympathize with Paul's frustration, he can't expect the liberal state to increase his citizen-stake on the ground that photography is especially worthy of state support – such a rationale is a plain offence to the Neutrality principle. Though Fred's fishing might be cheap, this hardly means that he doesn't have other good uses for his entire stake. If he wants to give Paul the gift of a fancy camera, that's OK with the liberal state. But it's equally OK if Fred finds something better to do with his money. If Paul is only willing to pursue his hobby by taking some of Fred's stake, then he must learn to sacrifice his 'love' for photography at the altar of equal citizenship.

Since Fabre disagrees, I can no longer hope to accommodate our dis-pute at the level of second-best theory. We are disagreeing about the very meaning of the concept of egalitarianism. This is a dispute, if you like, in 'ideal theory'.[12] The distinction between ideal and second-best theory offers a fruitful perspective for analysing all of Fabre's many examples – narrowing some seeming disagreements on important mat-ters of policy. But when all is said in an accommodating spirit, there is no gainsaying her rejection of the liberal aspirations of a stakeholder society: 'For a society to be egalitarian, it must not only be the case that people are willing to pay the amount of taxes required by equality of opportunity; it must also be the case that people, in their everyday life... live up to the egalitarian ideal in their relationships to others' (this volume: 121).

Here is where an unbridgeable divide opens. Citizens of the ideal *Liberal State* are free to organize their lives *any way they want, with whomever they want, on any terms that are mutually agreeable*.[13] They don't achieve political unity by adopting a uniform pattern of everyday life – egalitarian or otherwise. They achieve it through a distinctive form of political dialogue, carefully constructed to respect their right to live very different lives.

Consider, for example, Fabre's dismissive treatment of workers who insist on getting more pay for working harder. She condemns such benighted souls for 'fostering inequality' and finds their presence incompatible with a truly just society. I couldn't disagree more. The political community doesn't have the legitimate authority to determine how much, or whether, I work. That's up to me to decide in the light of offers that others make for my services. In selecting amongst competing offers, my ideals will be put to a practical test – but in a world of equal starting points, citizens aren't under any grinding economic compulsion to ignore their ideals so that they can put bread on the table. For example, strong egalitarians who share Cécile Fabre's views are provided with effective options within the framework of *The Stakeholder Society*. Upon receipt of their citizen-stakes, they are perfectly free to contribute their $80,000 to a kibbutz that aspires to a life of perfect equality for its members. But they don't have the right to force everybody else into a kibbutz so that they too may enjoy the joys of everyday equality.

My objection – and it is not a small one – is to Fabre's effort to subordinate wide-ranging freedom of association to one-size-fits-all equality. The *Liberal State* offers a more satisfactory value synthesis. It respects each citizen's claim to *equality* by guaranteeing her an equal stake and a first-class liberal education (together with special compensation for serious genetic handicaps). It respects *freedom* by enabling each citizen to use her initial endowment in the way that seems best, thereby enabling her to confront the great question – what is the meaning of life? – and live out her individual answer in the way that makes the most sense to her. This value synthesis, in turn, sets a basic problem for liberal politics – to sustain the liberal synthesis over time by preventing the freedom of one generation to destroy the equality of the next.

Although this understanding of equal freedom sets me apart from Cécile Fabre, it allows for a deeper rapprochement with Carole Pateman. We both reject the classical Marxist emphasis on paid work as the key to social status and social justice. But we also reject the classical night-watchman state of laissez-faire theory. Our affirmative programme is similar. We see the state providing an education for women that enables them to challenge sex-stereotypes, and encourages them to consider the full range of life-options available in a pluralist society. We also believe that equal citizenship has an economic component: women, no less than men, have a fundamental right to an unconditional cash grant that gives real meaning to their claims for self-determination. And we link this economic demand to a larger vision of political life.

It is here where we diverge, though not by as much as may appear. One of my big points for stakeholding is its impact on political identity. As each young adult comes forward to receive her $80,000 grant, she will come to appreciate that liberalism is a lot more than an apologia for the rich and powerful to do what they like. And as citizens use their stake to take charge of their lives, they will reflect on the nature of the political responsibilities that it entails. Some cynics will undoubtedly take their $80,000 and scoff at the foolish taxpayers who have provided an endless string of free lunches. But many will reciprocate with a sense of loyalty to the liberal regime that made stakeholding a reality.

Once this reciprocating dynamic of commitment takes hold, millions of stakeholders will be quietly searching for suitable occasions upon which they can give back something to the political community. It is impossible to predict how this new citizen energy will work itself out over time. But it will serve as a crucially important resource for political life, pushing it in the direction of democratic self-rule. Stakeholding will come to seem the beginning, not the end, of an ongoing political effort to advance the principles of equal freedom.

Pateman recognizes all this, and urges feminists to support stakeholding as a significant improvement over the status quo. Nevertheless, she thinks that a basic income programme will serve her purposes even better. A serious comparison between stakeholding and basic income is a complex multi-faceted affair. Since Anne Alstott and I have undertaken it elsewhere (Ackerman and Alstott, 2003), I shall focus upon a key proviso that Pateman attaches to her argument. She only approves a programme that guarantees citizens a 'modest but decent' standard of living. Unfortunately, she doesn't tell us what this is, or why she thinks Britain or other Western nations can afford it. Nevertheless, it is certain that her preferred alternative is far more expensive than stakeholding. Although $80,000 sounds like a lot of money, it implies an annual lifetime payment in the range of $4000 – and surely this isn't nearly enough to satisfy Pateman's demand for a 'modest but decent' minimum in a country like Britain? To add to the fiscal crunch, the costs of stakeholding phase in gradually, as each cohort rises to maturity, but Pateman's basic income will start funding a 'modest but decent' life for all citizens at the very same moment.

This leaves one large question open for Pateman: How does she evaluate an $80,000 stake when compared to an *inadequate* basic income? If this is the question, I urge her to give stakeholding a second chance. Within the terms of her argument, an inadequate basic income won't allow its recipients to cut their links with the world of paid work, and may well operate as a subsidy for low-skilled, low-paid employment. In contrast, the owner of an $80,000 stake has much more real freedom to modulate her engagement with paid labour. To be sure, she can't escape the workplace for her entire life, but this isn't an option with an inadequate basic income either. On the contrary, under the competing programme, a period of unpaid unemployment condemns the recipient to a desperate hand-to-mouth existence. In contrast, a stakeholder may actually live at a 'modest but decent' standard for an extended period, and engage in a variety of non-profit activities that will, according to Pateman, 'provide a context that gives encouragement to think about broader connections between social institutions and democratization' (this volume: 21).

Operating within real-world constraints, Carole Pateman may well find that stakeholding does a much better job of generating the thoughtful reflection on institutional alternatives that she emphasizes. Of course, a lot will depend upon the precise grant levels she believes are appropriate, given existing economic realities. Such a judgement requires a lot of fiscal and econometric analysis, but it also demands the comprehensive policy framework suggested by Robert van der Veen's chapter. As he makes clear, Alstott and I have never supposed that stakeholding should serve as the be-all and end-all of liberal social policy. Instead, we have tried to locate our initiative within a larger system of citizenship grants that extend from the cradle to the grave. Such a framework makes it clear that liberal states throughout the West are spending far more than $80,000 on each citizen throughout the course of his lifetime. Stakeholding seeks to revise the standard pattern of benefits distributed over this life cycle. Speaking broadly, we presently divide each citizen's life into three parts: youthful vulnerability, adult maturity, and elderly decline, and provide different sorts of grants for each period. During youthful vulnerability, the state intervenes with heavy subsidies in the form of education, health care, and child allowances. But once the citizen arrives at 'maturity', subsidies become more selective, pouring in once again only during the phase of elderly decline.

Stakeholding suggests the need for greater sophistication in our understanding of the rise to maturity. At present, the crucial moment of transition comes at the end of formal education: while you're in school, you're still a child; but once you've left, welcome to the adult world. But school leaving is a very bad marker of the transition, since people leave at very different ages. As a consequence, the current marker 'maturity' legitimates a system of educational subsidy that massively benefits the people who don't need it. We pour huge subsidies into those 'immature' students going to university, while ignoring the needs of millions of 'mature' young workers who leave school at an earlier age. As a consequence, university students start off their working lives with huge sums of human capital, while school-leavers of the same age don't receive anything comparable in terms of 'old-fashioned capital'. Stakeholding corrects this imbalance, and thereby allows ordinary people to confront the challenges of maturity with something resembling the economic self-confidence of their university-bound contemporaries. It establishes a new definition of social maturity, recognizing that *all* young adults enter a crucial stage of self-definition in their late teens and early twenties.

This life-cycle perspective helps refine Van der Veen's speculations about the cultural impact of stakeholding. Like Pateman, he underestimates the extent to which stakeholders will use their capital to achieve a more flexible relationship to paid work, and therefore discounts the extent to which stakeholding opens up new cultural spaces for non-market activities. But he is right to suggest that stakeholding has a special value for young adults aiming to shape their lives as a whole in more productive directions. Van der Veen seems to be damning this aspect of the initiative with faint praise, suggesting a relationship to 'the American dream of emancipation through entrepreneurship' (this volume: 159). But from my talks with young adults in lots of places, I think that I am diagnosing a more universal phenomenon. Once we put the class of university graduates to one side, most people in their early twenties are living lives of quiet desperation. The world tells them to put aside their childish dreams and settle down decisively into one rut or another. And they have little choice but to agree, because they have no capital of their own.

But with stakeholding, there would be a new freedom to experiment with their abilities and interests, to invest in new skills and to explore alternative forms of living. Some of this churning will take classic entrepreneurial forms. Much more will be personally enriching, providing the experiential basis for a lifetime's development as a human being. Beyond any particular activity, stakeholding will be carrying a distinctive message for young adults: do not resign yourselves too quickly to a bitter acceptance of life in a particular pigeonhole; you can and should be an active participant in shaping the contours of your life. Don't count yourself out too soon!

Many of my readers, thinking perhaps of their own children, will worry about how some adults will blow their stake in the course of abusing their new-found gift of freedom. But most of my readers are themselves quite wealthy, and fear – perhaps rightly – that their pampered children don't know the value of money, and can't be trusted with $80,000. They should consider, however, that most of their children would be spending most of their stake on higher education.[14] The principal beneficiaries of stakeholding will be other people's kids – kids who graduate from third-rate schools to confront third-rate jobs without ever getting half a chance to find out whether there was more to life. Living under straitened circumstances throughout their young lives, these people will have a very clear sense of the value of money. Some will undoubtedly blow their stakes, but many more will recognize that they have been given a precious chance to build a life that is both more secure and more rewarding.

## 4   Radical liberalism?

Every movement deserves a name, but modern liberalism has been deprived of its obvious title. 'Neo-liberalism' functions today as little more than an epithet, condemning liberals as hide-bound reactionaries offering up warmed-over versions of nineteenth-century laissez-faire.

But the current vitality of liberal philosophy tells a different story. Stakeholding and basic income may be among the first practical proposals to emerge from this on-going effort to rethink the liberal tradition. They won't be the last, and we will soon enough be awash with policy debates that reflect and refine the philosophical debates of the last generation. A decade hence, radical liberalism will be a force in the world of policy-wonkdom. But will it be a force in the World?

## Notes

1. I am, as always, grateful to Anne Alstott, but on this occasion, we thought it best for me to serve as sole author, since the chapter draws so heavily on my earlier work in political philosophy.
2. See Ackerman and Alstott (1999: 99, top 1 per cent owned 38.5 per cent in 1995). This percentage is only a rough approximation, containing serious overestimates and underestimates. It is an underestimate, since it is based on Federal Reserve data that can't possibly report the enormous sums that the rich have squirrelled away in Swiss bank accounts and similar places. It is an overstatement, since it focuses on disposable wealth, and doesn't take into account the wealth that is locked into Social Security's promise of government pensions for future retired and disabled persons. Since these payments will be much more egalitarian, taking them into account significantly reduces the share of the top 1 per cent – but there are many vexed technical issues in calculating by how much. I suspect that the second factor outweighs the first, and that the top 1 per cent probably owns somewhat less than 40 per cent of *all* assets, but that's just a guess.
3. Consider the trajectories of the three leading 'analytic Marxists' of the last generation: Jon Elster's recent work has nothing to do with Marxism, and Jerry Cohen now spends his time sparring with the likes of Rawls and Nozick. Compare the early *Karl Marx's Theory of History: A Defense* (1978) with the later *If You're An Egalitarian, How Come You're So Rich?* (2000). Only John Roemer (1994, 2001) continues to make important contributions to the tradition. Jurgen Habermas's transformation into a Left Liberal is also a significant sign of the times. With the departure of so many serious thinkers, the vacuum is being filled by books that are utterly lacking in empirical substance and analytic rigor (for example, Hardt and Antonio Negri, 2000).

4. No economist has yet analysed British data to determine how large a stake can be raised by a significant tax on wealth of the kind proposed by *Stakeholder*. By the way, Alstott and I have updated our analysis since the book's publication. On the basis of 1998 data, we find that we can finance an $80,000 stake while allowing all taxpayers to exempt their first $230,000 from our proposed wealth tax. This means that a married couple starts paying only if their assets total $460,000 – a sum that only the top 15 per cent of American households possess. The Dow Jones in 1998 was roughly at the level it is at the time of this writing: Christmas, 2002.

5. *The Stakeholder Society* accepted the system of inheritance taxation in the United States, as it existed at the time of the book's publication. But in future work, Anne Alstott and I hope to integrate some more innovative ideas about inheritance taxation into our overall proposal.

6. See his citation, at p. 3, to the *Liberal State*'s discussion of the principle of undominated genetic diversity. The arguments presented in this chapter derive from the chapter cited by van Donselaar.

7. Prima facie, to take into account a Rawls-like proviso for inequalities in starting points that improves the position of the worst off (Ackerman, 1980: 257–61).

8. Arbitrary characterizations of the decisive thought-experiment is a characteristic difficulty suffered by much state-of-nature modelling (Ackerman, 1980: 336–42).

9. Anne Alstott and I expand on this point in a related essay (Ackerman and Alstott, 2003).

10. Part 3 of the *Liberal State* devotes itself with the elaboration of 'second best' theory, and related perplexities.

11. Fabre doesn't mention the more important practical case involving the miseducation of masses of poor children, but focuses on the case of the relatively pampered few who are pushed by their parents into university even though they would themselves prefer to do something else (this volume: 116). No matter: the point made in the text applies to both.

12. It isn't absolutely clear whether Fabre does hold a competing ideal in the millions of real-world cases like that of Fred and Paul. Early in her text, she suggests that she only means to tailor the size of stakes to take into account preferences that are 'not a matter of choice' (this volume: 116). But if the choice between fishing and photography isn't 'a matter of choice', what is?

13. In real-world settings, this ideal of transactional flexibility must be modified by laws combating racism and other forms of discrimination, as well as laws controlling monopolistic behaviour (Ackerman, 1980: chs 4, 8).

14. It is a complex, and inevitably controversial, task to integrate stakeholding with methods of financing higher education. For some reflections on the problem in the American context, see Ackerman and Alstott (1999: 51–6).

# Bibliography

Ackerman, B. (1980) *Social Justice in a Liberal State*. New Haven: Yale University Press.

Ackerman, B. and A. Alstott (1999) *The Stakeholder Society*. New Haven: Yale University Press.

Ackerman, B. and A. Alstott (2003) 'Why Stakeholding?', in Erik Olin Wright (ed.) *Rethinking Distribution*. London: Verso.

Ackerman, B. and I. Ayres (2002) *Voting with Dollars: A New Paradigm for Campaign Finance*. New Haven: Yale University Press.

Agulnik, P. and J. Le Grand (1998) 'Tax relief and partnership pensions', *Fiscal Studies* 19 (4), pp. 403–28.

Almond, G. and S. Verba (1963) *The Civic Culture: Political Attitudes and Democracy in Five Nations*. Princeton, NJ: Princeton University Press.

Alstott, A. (2001) 'Good for Women', in P. Van Parijs, J. Cohen and J. Rogers (eds) *What's Wrong with a Free Lunch?* Boston: Beacon Press.

Anderson, E. (2001) 'Optional Freedoms', in P. Van Parijs, J. Cohen and J. Rogers (eds) *What's Wrong with a Free Lunch?* Boston: Beacon Press.

Arneson, R. (1989) 'Equality and equal opportunity for welfare', *Philosophical Studies* 56, pp. 77–93.

Arneson, R. (1990) 'Liberalism, distributive subjectivism, and equal opportunity for welfare', *Philosophy and Public Affairs* 19, pp. 158–94.

Atkinson, A. B. (1972) *Unequal Shares. Wealth in Britain*. London: Allen Lane.

Atkinson, A. B. (1995) *Public Economics in Action. The Basic Income/Flat Tax Proposal*. Oxford: Clarendon Press.

Atkinson, A. B. (1996) 'The case for a participation income', *Political Quarterly* 67, pp. 67–70.

Baldwin, P. (1990) *The Politics of Social Solidarity. Class Bases of the European Welfare State 1875–1975*. Cambridge: Cambridge University Press.

Baldwin, P. (1995) *Beyond the Safety Net*. Canberra: Department of Social Security.

Banks, J. and S. Tanner (1999) *Household Saving in the UK*. London: Institute for Fiscal Studies.

Barry, B. (1996) 'Real freedom and basic income', *The Journal of Political Philosophy* 4, pp. 242–76, reprinted in A. Reeves and A. Williams (eds) (2002) *Real Libertarianism Reassessed*. London: Macmillan – now Palgrave Macmillan.

Barry, B. (1997) 'The Attractions of Basic Income', in J. Franklin (ed.), *Equality*. London: IPPR.

Barry, B. (2001) 'UBI and the Work Ethic', in P. Van Parijs, J. Cohen and J. Rogers (eds) *What's Wrong with a Free Lunch?* Boston: Beacon Press.

Beeferman, L. and S. Venner (2001) *Promising State Asset Development Policies. Promoting Economic Well-Being Among Low-Income Households*. Waltham, MA: Asset Development Institute, Center on Hunger and Poverty, Brandeis University.

Beveridge, W. (1942) *Social Insurance and Allied Services*. London: HMSO.

Block, F., R.A. Cloward, B. Ehrenreich and F.F. Piven (1987) *The Mean Season: the Attack on the Welfare State*. New York: Pantheon.

Bowles, S. and H. Gintis (1998) *Recasting Egalitarianism*. London: Verso.

Bowles, S. and H. Gintis (1999) 'Is egalitarianism passé? Homo reciprocans and the future of egalitarian politics', *Boston Review* 23, pp. 4–10.

Brittan, S. (1983) *The Role and Limits of Government: Essays in Political Economy*. Minneapolis: University of Minnesota Press.

Budd, A., P. Levine and P. Smith (1988) 'Unemployment, vacancies and the long-term unemployed', *Economic Journal* 98, pp. 1071–91.

Bynner, J. and W. Paxton (2001) *The Asset-Effect*. London: IPPR.

Castles, F. G. (1985) *The Working Class and the Welfare State*. Sydney: Allen & Unwin.

Castles, F. G. (1997) 'The institutional design of the Australian welfare state', *International Social Security Review* 50, pp. 25–42.

Centraal Planbureau (1992) *Nederland in Drievoud*. The Hague: SdU Press.

Chapman, B., P. N. Junankar and C. Kapuscinski (1992) 'Projections of long-term unemployment', *Australian Bulletin of Labor* 18 (3), pp. 195–207.

Clark, C. M. A. and J. Healy (1997) *Pathways to a Basic Income*. Dublin: CORI Justice Commission.

Clarke, T. and J. Taylor (1999) 'Income inequality: A tale of two cycles', *Fiscal Studies* 20 (4), pp. 387–409.

Cohen, G. A. (1978) *Karl Marx's Theory of History: A Defense*. Cambridge, MA: Harvard University Press.

Cohen, G. A. (1989) 'On the currency of egalitarian justice', *Ethics* 99 (4), pp. 916–44.

Cohen, G. A. (1997a) 'On the site of distributive justice', *Philosophy and Public Affairs* 26 (1), pp. 3–30.

Cohen, G. A. (1997b) 'Back to Socialist Basics: Appendix on Money and Liberty', in J. Franklin (ed.) *Equality*. London: IPPR.

Cohen, G. A. (2000) *If You're an Egalitarian, How Come You're So Rich?* Cambridge, MA: Harvard University Press.

Cohen, J. (2003) 'For a Democratic Society', in S. Freeman (ed.) *The Cambridge Companion to Rawls*. Cambridge: Cambridge University Press.

Crosland, A. (1956) *The Future of Socialism*. London: Cape.

Crouch, C., D. Finegold and M. Sako (1999) *Are Skills the Answer? The Political Economy of Skill Creation in Advanced Industrial Countries*. Oxford: Oxford University Press.

Cunliffe, J. and G. Erreyghers (2003) '"Basic income? Basic capital!" Origins and issues of a debate', *Journal of Political Philosophy*, 11, pp. 89–110.

Cunliffe, J., G. Erreyghers and W. Van Trier (2002) 'Basic Income: Pedigree and Problems', in A. Reeves and A. Williams (eds) *Real Libertarianism Reassessed*. London: Macmillan – now Palgrave Macmillan.

Den Hartogh, Govert (1995) 'Het basisinkomen als grondrecht', in Robert J. van der Veen and Dick Pels (eds) *Het basisinkomen: Sluitstuk van de verzorgingsstaat?* Amsterdam, Van Gennep, pp. 124–56.

De Wispelaere, J. (2000) 'Sharing job resources: ethical reflections on the justification of basic income', *Analyse & Kritik* 22 (2), pp. 237–56.

De Wispelaere, J. and L. Stirton (2003) 'The Administration of Universal Tax Credits', paper prepared for the 53rd UK Political Studies Association conference, University of Leicester.

Dworkin, R. (1981) 'What is equality? Part 2: Equality of resources', *Philosophy and Public Affairs* 10 (4), pp. 283–345, reprinted in R. Dworkin (2000) *Sovereign Virtue*. Cambridge, MA: Harvard University Press.

Edwards, L. (2000) *Testing Public Opinion on Asset-based Welfare*. London: IPPR.

Elster, J. (1986) 'Comment on Van der Veen and Van Parijs', *Theory and Society* 15, pp. 709–21.

Erreyghers, G. and T. Vandevelde (eds) (1997) *Is Inheritance Legitimate?* Heidelberg: Springer Verlag.

Fabian Society (2000) *Paying for Progress: A New Politics of Tax for Public Spending*. London: Fabian Society.

Field, F. (1996) *How to Pay for the Future: Building a Stakeholders' Welfare*. London: Institute of Community Studies.

Fitzpatrick, T. (1999) *Freedom and Security. An Introduction to the Basic Income Debate*. London: Macmillan – now Palgrave Macmillan.

Fogel, R. W. (2000) *The Fourth Great Awakening and the Future of Egalitarianism*. Chicago: University of Chicago Press.

Freeman, R. (1999) *The New Inequality: Creating Solutions for Poor America*. Boston: Beacon Press.

Friedman, R. and M. Sherraden (2001) 'Asset-Based Policy in the United States', paper presented at the International Assets Seminar, Center for Social Development/IPPR, London.

Gallie, D. (2002) 'The Quality of Working Life in Welfare Strategy', in G. Esping-Andersen (ed.) *Why We Need a New Welfare State*. Oxford: Oxford University Press.

Galston, W. A. (2001) 'What About Reciprocity?, in P. Van Parijs, J. Cohen and J. Rogers (eds) *What's Wrong with a Free Lunch?* Boston: Beacon Press.

Gauthier, D. (1986) *Morals by Agreement*. Oxford: Oxford Clarendon Press.

Goodin, R. E. (2000) 'Crumbling pillars: social security futures', *Political Quarterly* 71, pp. 144–50.

Goodin, R. E. (2001a) 'Democratic wealth, democratic welfare. Is flux enough?' *New Political Economy* 6, pp. 67–79.

Goodin, R. E. (2001b) 'Something for nothing?' in P. Van Parijs, J. Cohen and J. Rogers (eds) *What's Wrong with a Free Lunch?* Boston: Beacon Press.

Goodin, R. E. (2002) 'Structures of mutual obligation', *Journal of Social Policy* 3 (4), pp. 579–96.

Goodin, R. E., J. Le Grand, et al. (1987) *Not Only the Poor. The Middle Classes and the Welfare State*. London: Allen & Unwin.

Green, D. (1993) *Reinventing Civil Society. The Rediscovery of Welfare without Politics*. London: Institute of Economic Affairs.

Groot, L., *Basic Income and Unemployment* (PhD thesis, Netherlands School for Economic and Social Research, University of Utrecht, 1999).

Groot, L. and R. van der Veen (2000) 'Clues and Leads in the Debate on Basic Income in the Netherlands', in R. van der Veen and L. Groot (eds) *Basic Income on the Agenda*. Amsterdam: Amsterdam University Press.

Halstead, T. and M. Lind (2001) *The Radical Center: The Future of American Politics*. New York: Doubleday.

Hancock, K. (1979) 'The first half-century of Australian wage policy', *Journal of Industrial Relations* 21, pp. 129–60.

Hardt, M. and A. Negri (2000) *Empire*. Cambridge, MA: Harvard University Press.

Harris, D. (1987) *Justifying State Welfare*. Oxford: Blackwell.

Haslett, D. (1994) *Capitalism with Morality*. Oxford: Clarendon Press.

Haveman, R. (1988) *Starting Even. An Equal Opportunity Program to Combat the Nation's New Poverty*. New York: Simon and Schuster.

Hills, J., J. Le Grand and D. Piachaud (eds) (2002) *Understanding Social Exclusion*. Oxford: Oxford University Press.

HM Treasury (2001a) *Saving and Assets for All*. London: HM Treasury.

HM Treasury (2001b) *Delivering Saving and Assets*. London: HM Treasury.

Holtham, Gerald (1999) 'Ownership and Social Democracy', in A. Gamble and T. Wright (eds) *The New Social Democracy*. Oxford: Blackwell.

Hutton, W. (1994) *The State We're In*. London: Jonathan Cape.

Inland Revenue (1998) *Inland Revenue Statistics 1998*. London: HMSO.

Inland Revenue (2001) *Inland Revenue Statistics 2001*. London: HMSO.

Jones, C. (1990) 'Hong Kong, Singapore and Taiwan. Oikonomic welfare states', *Government & Opposition* 25, pp. 446–62.

Kay, J. (1996) *The Economics of Business*. Oxford: Oxford University Press.

Kelly, G., D. Kelly and A. Gamble (eds) (1997) *Stakeholder Capitalism*. London: Macmillan – now Palgrave Macmillan.

Kelly, G. and R. Lissauer (2000) *Ownership for All*. London: IPPR.

King, D. and M. Wickham-Jones (1999) 'From Clinton to Blair: The Democratic (Party) origins of welfare to work', *Political Quarterly* 70, pp. 62–74.

Kohli, M., M. Rein, A. M. Guillemard and H. van Gunsteren (eds) (1991) *Time for Retirement. Comparative Studies of Early Exit from the Labor Force*. Cambridge: Cambridge University Press.

Krouse, R. and M. McPherson (1988) 'Capitalism, "property-owning democracy" and the welfare state', in A. Gutmann (ed.) *Democracy and the Welfare State*. Princeton, NJ: Princeton University Press.

Kuttner, R. (1998) 'Rampant bull', *The American Prospect* 39, pp. 30–6.

Lake, C. (2001) *Equality and Responsibility*. Oxford: Oxford University Press.

Leadbeater, C. and G. Mulgan (1996) *Mistakeholding: Whatever Happened to Labour's Big Idea?* London: Demos.

Le Grand, J. (1982) *The Strategy of Equality*. London: Allen & Unwin.

Le Grand, J. (1989) 'Markets, Welfare and Equality', in J. Le Grand and S. Estrin (eds) *Market Socialism*. Oxford: Oxford University Press.

Le Grand, J. and S. Estrin (eds) (1989) *Market Socialism*. Oxford: Oxford University Press.

Marshall, T. H. (1963) 'Citizenship and Social Class', in *Sociology at the Crossroads and Other Essays*. London: Heinemann.

McKay, A. and J. Van Every (2000) 'Gender, family, and income maintenance. A feminist case for citizens basic income', *Social Politics* 7, pp. 266–84.

Mead, L. (1992) *The New Politics of Poverty*. New York: Basic Books.

Meade, J. (1964) *Efficiency, Equality and the Ownership of Property*. London: Allen & Unwin.

Meade, J. (1989) *Agathatopia: The Economics of Partnership*. Aberdeen: University of Aberdeen.

Meadows, P. (1996) *Work Out – or Work In? Contributions to the Debate on the Future of Work*. York: Joseph Rowntree Foundation.

Mill, J. S. (1985) *On Liberty*. Harmondsworth: Penguin.

Miller, D. (2000) *Principles of Social Justice*. Cambridge, MA: Harvard University Press.

Moene, K. O. and M. Wallerstein (1995) 'How social democracy worked: labor-market institutions', *Politics & Society* 23, pp. 185–212.

Murphy, L. and T. Nagel (2002) *The Myth of Ownership. Taxes and Justice*. New York: Oxford University Press.

Nissan, D. and J. Le Grand (2000) *A Capital Idea: Start-Up Grants for Young People*. London: Fabian Society.

Nozick, R. (1974) *Anarchy, State and Utopia*. Oxford: Blackwell.

Okun, A. (1975) *Equality and Efficiency: The Big Trade-off*. Washington D.C.: Brookings Institution.

Oppenheim, C. (1998) 'Welfare to Work: Taxes and Benefits', in J. McCormick and C. Oppenheim (eds) *Welfare in Working Order*. London: IPPR.

Paine, T. (1987) 'Agrarian Justice', in M. Foot and I. Kramnick (eds) *The Thomas Paine Reader*. Harmondsworth: Penguin.

Parker, H. (1993) *A Citizen's Income and Women*, BIRG Discussion Paper No. 2. London: Citizens' Income Study Centre.

Pateman, C. (1996) 'Democratization and Citizenship in the 1990s: The Legacy of T. H. Marshal', *The Vilhelm Aubert Memorial Lecture*. Oslo: Institute for Social Research and Department of Sociology, University of Oslo.

Pateman, C. (2001) 'The Equivalent of the Right to Life, Land, and Liberty? Democracy and the Idea of a Basic Income', *mimeo*.

Pateman, C. (2002) 'Self-ownership and property in the person. Democratization and a tale of two concepts', *Journal of Political Philosophy* 10, pp. 20–53.

Pateman, C. (2003) 'Democratizing citizenship: some advantages of a basic income', in Erik Olin Wright (ed.) *Rethinking Redistribution*. London: Verso.

Paxton, W. (2001) 'Assets: A Third Pillar of Welfare', in S. Regan (ed.) *Assets and Progressive Welfare*. London: IPPR.

Paxton, W. (2002) *Wealth Distribution – the Evidence*. London: IPPR.

Paxton, W. and S. Regan (2001) 'Progressing asset-based policies in the UK', paper prepared for International Assets Seminar, Center for Social Development/ Institute for Public Policy Research, London, January 2001.

Perraton, J. (1997) 'The Global Economy', in G. Kelly, D. Kelly and A. Gamble (eds) *Stakeholder Capitalism*. London: Macmillan – now Palgrave Macmillan.

Perri 6 (1999) *Preventive Government*. London: Demos.

Perun, P. (1999) *Matching Private Savings with Federal Dollars: USA Accounts and Other Subsidies for Saving*, The Retirement Project No. 8, Washington: the Urban Institute.

Pettit, P. (1997) *Republicanism. A Theory of Freedom and Government*. Oxford: Oxford University Press.

Pettit, P. (1999) 'Republican Freedom and Contestatory Democratization', in I. Shapiro and C. Hacker-Cordón (eds) *Democracy's Value*. Cambridge: Cambridge University Press.

Phelps, E. S. (2001) 'Subsidize Wages', in P. Van Parijs, J. Cohen and J. Rogers (eds) *What's Wrong with a Free Lunch?* Boston: Beacon Press.

Pickard, B. (1919) *A Reasonable Revolution*. London: Allen & Unwin.

Pierson, P. (eds) (2001) *The New Politics of the Welfare State*. New York: Oxford University Press.

Prabhakar, R. (2003) *Stakeholding and New Labour*. London: Macmillan – now Palgrave Macmillan.

Rakowski, E. (1991) *Equal Justice*. Oxford: Clarendon Press.

Rawls, J. (1974) 'Reply to Alexander and Musgrave', *Quarterly Journal of Economics* 88, pp. 633–55.

Rawls, J. (1993) *Political Liberalism*. New York: Columbia University Press.

Rawls, J. (1999) *A Theory of Justice*. revd edn. Cambridge, MA: Harvard University Press.

Rawls, J. (2001) *Justice as Fairness: A Restatement*. Cambridge, MA: Harvard University Press.

Regan, S. (2001a) 'Asset-based Welfare: Options and Policy Design Questions', in S. Regan (ed.) *Asset-based Welfare – The International Experience*. London: Institute for Public Policy Research.

Regan, S. (ed.) (2001b) *Asset-based Welfare – The International Experience*. London: Institute for Public Policy Research.

Ripstein, A. (1999) *Equality, Responsibility and the Law*. Cambridge: Cambridge University Press.

Robertson, J. (1996) 'Towards a new social compact. Citizen's income and radical tax reform', *Political Quarterly* 67, pp. 54–8.

Robeyns, I. (2000) 'Hush Money or Emancipation Fee? A Gender Analysis of Basic Income', in Van der Veen, R. J. and L. Groot (eds) *Basic Income on the Agenda*. Amsterdam: Amsterdam University Press.

Robeyns, I. (2001) 'Will a basic income do justice to women?', *Analyse & Kritik* 23 (1), pp. 88–105.

Roemer, J. (1994) *A Future for Socialism*. Cambridge, MA: Harvard University Press.

Roemer, J. (1998) 'The Limits of Private-Property-based Egalitarianism', in S. Bowles and H. Gintis (eds) *Recasting Egalitarianism: New Rules for Communities, States and Markets*. London: Verso.

Roemer, J. (2001) *Political Competition*. Cambridge, MA: Harvard University Press.

Rogers, J. and W. Streeck (1994) 'Productive Solidarities: Economic Strategy and Left Politics', in D. Miliband (ed.) *Reinventing the Left*. Oxford: Polity Press.

Rosanvallon, P. (2000) *The New Social Question: Rethinking the Welfare State*, trans. B. Harshaw. Princeton, NJ: Princeton University Press.

Rousseau, J.-J. (1984) *A Discourse on Inequality*, trans. M. Cranston. Harmondsworth: Penguin.

Rousseau, J.-J. (1994) 'Discourse on Political Economy', in *The Social Contract*, trans. C. Betts. Oxford: Oxford University Press.

Sandford, C. (1971) *Taxing Personal Wealth*. London: Allen & Unwin.

Scheffler, S. (1997) 'Relationships and Responsibilities', *Philosophy and Public Affairs* 26 (3), pp. 189–208.

Sen, A. (1982) 'Rights and Agency', *Philosophy and Public Affairs* 11 (1), pp. 3–39.

Sherraden, M. (1991) *Assets and the Poor: A New American Welfare Policy*. New York: ME Sharpe.

Sherraden, M., D. Page-Adams and L. Johnson (1999) *Downpayments on the American Dream Policy Demonstration. A National Demonstration of Individual Development Accounts*. St Louis: Center for Social Development.

Shue, H. (1996) *Basic Rights: Subsistence, Affluence and U. S. Foreign Policy*. 2nd edn. Princeton, NJ: Princeton University Press.

Simon, W. (1991) 'Social-republican property', *UCLA Law Review* 38, pp. 1335–413.

Skidelsky, R. (2000) 'A Stake in the Heart', *Times Literary Supplement*. January 21, p. 8.

Skinner, Q. (1998) *Liberty Before Liberalism*. Cambridge: Cambridge University Press.

Skocpol, T. (1997) 'A Partnership with American Families', in S. Greenberg and T. Skocpol (eds) *The New Majority: Toward a Popular Progressive Politics*. New Haven: Yale University Press.

Snower, Dennis J. (1993) 'The future of the welfare state', *Economic Journal* 103, pp. 700–17.

Standing, G. (1999) *Global Labour Flexibility: Seeking Distributive Justice*. London: Macmillan – now Palgrave Macmillan.

Standing, G. (2002) *Beyond the New Paternalism: Basic Security as Equality*. London: Verso.

Steiner, H. (1992) 'Three Just Taxes', in P. Van Parijs (ed.) *Arguing for Basic Income*. London: Verso.

Steiner, H. (1994) *An Essay on Rights*. Oxford: Blackwell.

Titmuss, R. (2001) *Welfare and Wellbeing: Richard Titmuss's Contribution to Social Policy*, ed by P. Alcock, H. Glennerster, A. Oakely and A. Sinfield. Bristol: Policy Press.

Tocqueville, A. de (1966) *Democracy in America*, trans. G. Lawrence, ed by J. P. Mayer and M. Lerner. New York: Harper & Row.

Unger, R. and C. West (1998) *The Future of American Progressivism: An Initiative for Political and Economic Reform*. Boston: Beacon Press.

Vallentyne, P. (1997) 'Self-ownership and equality: Brute luck, gifts, universal dominance, and leximin', *Ethics* 107, pp. 321–43.

Vallentyne, P. and H. Steiner (eds) (2000) *Left Libertarianism and its Critics: The Contemporary Debate*. Basingstoke: Palgrave – now Palgrave Macmillan.

Vandenbroucke, F. (2000) *Responsibility, Well-Being, Information, and the Design of Distributive Policies*. Discussion Paper 00.03, Center for Economic Studies, Department of Economics, Katholieke Universitiet Leuven.

Van der Veen, R. J. (1997) 'Real freedom and basic income: Comment on Brian Barry', *Journal of Political Philosophy* 5, pp. 274–86, reprinted in A. Reeves and A. Williams (eds) (2002) *Real Libertarianism Reassessed*. London: Macmillan – now Palgrave Macmillan.

Van der Veen, R. J. (1998) 'Real freedom versus reciprocity: competing views on the justice of unconditional basic income', *Political Studies* 46, pp. 140–63.

Van der Veen, R. J. (2002) 'Basic income versus wage subsidies: Competing instruments in an optimal tax model with a maximin objective', *mimeo*.

Van der Veen, R. J. and L. Groot (eds) (2000) *Basic Income on the Agenda: Policy Objectives and Political Chances*. Amsterdam: Amsterdam University Press.

Van der Veen, R. J. and P. Van Parijs (1987) 'A capitalist road to communism', *Theory and Society* 15 (5), pp. 635–55, reprinted in R. J. van der Veen (1991) *Between Exploitation and Communism*. Groningen: Wolters Noordhoff and P. Van Parijs (1989) *Marxism Recycled*. Cambridge: Cambridge University Press.

Van Donselaar, G. (1997) *The Benefit of Another's Pains: Parasitism, Scarcity, Basic Income*. Amsterdam: University of Amsterdam.

Van Parijs, P. (1991) 'Why surfers should be fed: The liberal case for an unconditional basic income', *Philosophy and Public Affairs* 20, pp. 101–31.

Van Parijs, P. (1992a) 'Competing Justifications of Basic Income', in P. Van Parijs (ed.) *Arguing for Basic Income*. London: Verso.

Van Parijs, P. (1992b) 'The Second Marriage of Justice and Efficiency', in P. Van Parijs (ed.) *Arguing for Basic Income*. London: Verso.

Van Parijs, P. (ed.) (1992c) *Arguing for Basic Income. Ethical Foundations for a Radical Reform*. London: Verso.

Van Parijs, P. (1995) *Real Freedom for All: What (If Anything) Can Justify Capitalism?* Oxford: Clarendon Press.

Van Parijs, P. (1999) 'Contestatory Democracy versus Real Freedom for All,' in I. Shapiro and C. Hacker-Cordón (eds) *Democracy's Value*. Cambridge: Cambridge University Press.

Van Parijs, P. (2001) 'A Basic Income for All', in P. Van Parijs, J. Cohen and J. Rogers (eds) *What's Wrong with a Free Lunch?* Boston: Beacon Press.

Van Parijs, P., J. Cohen and J. Rogers (eds) (2001) *What's Wrong with a Free Lunch?* Boston: Beacon Press.

Van Trier, W. (1996) *Everyone A King*. Antwerp: UFSIA.

Varian, H. (1985) 'Dworkin on equality of resources', *Economics and Philosophy* 1 (1), pp. 110–25.

Wakefield, M. and C. Emmerson (2001) *Asset-based Welfare – Well Fair?* London: IFS.

Waldron, J. (1993a) *Liberal Rights: Collected Papers 1981–1991*. Cambridge: Cambridge University Press.

Waldron, J. (1993b) 'John Rawls and the Social Minimum', in *Liberal Rights*. Cambridge: Cambridge University Press.

Waldron, J. (1993c) 'Homelessness and the Issue of Freedom', in *Liberal Rights*. Cambridge: Cambridge University Press.

Walter, T. (1989) *Basic Income: Freedom from Poverty, Freedom to Work*. London: Marion Boyers.

Western, B. and K. Beckett (1999) 'How unregulated is the U.S. labor market? The penal system as a labor market institution', *American Journal of Sociology* 104, pp. 1030–60.

White, M. (1991) *Against Unemployment*. London: Policy Studies Institute.

White, S. (1997) 'Liberal equality, exploitation and the case for an unconditional basic income', *Political Studies* 45, pp. 312–26.

White, S. (2000a) 'Social rights and the social contract: political theory and the new welfare politics', *British Journal of Political Science* 30, pp. 507–32.

White, S. (2000b) 'Rediscovering Republican Political Economy', *Imprints* 4 (3), pp. 213–34.

White, S. (2002) 'Fair Reciprocity and Basic Income', in A. Reeves and A. Williams (eds) *Real Libertarianism Reassessed*. London: Macmillan – now Palgrave Macmillan.

White, S. (2003a) *The Civic Minimum: On the Rights and Obligations of Economic Citizenship*. Oxford: Oxford University Press.

White, S. (2003b) 'The Citizen's Stake and Paternalism', in Erik Olin Wright (ed.) *Redesigning Redistribution*. London: Verso.

Widerquist, K. (1999) 'Reciprocity and the guaranteed income', *Politics & Society* 27 (3), pp. 387–402.

Wigley, S. (2002) 'Basic Income and the Means to Self-Govern', paper prepared for the 9th Bi-annual Congress of the Basic Income European Network, International Labour Office Geneva.

Wollstonecraft, M. (1993) 'A Vindication of the Rights of Woman', in *Political Writings*, ed J. Todd. Toronto, Ontario: University of Toronto Press.

World Bank (2001) *World Development Report 2000/2001: Attacking Poverty*. New York: Oxford University Press.

WRR (Wetenschappelijke Raad voor het Regeringsbeleid [Netherlands Scientific Council for Government Policy]) (1985) *Safeguarding Social Security*. The Hague: WRR.

# Index